Managing Customers Profitably

Lynette Ryals

A John Wiley and Sons, Ltd, Publication

Other Wiley Editorial Offices

John Wiley & Sons Inc., 111 River Street, Hoboken, NJ 07030, USA

Jossey-Bass, 989 Market Street, San Francisco, CA 94103-1741, USA

Wiley-VCH Verlag GmbH, Boschstr. 12, D-69469 Weinheim, Germany

John Wiley & Sons Australia Ltd, 42 McDougall Street, Milton, Queensland 4064, Australia

John Wiley & Sons (Asia) Pte Ltd, 2 Clementi Loop #02-01, Jin Xing Distripark, Singapore 129809

John Wiley & Sons Canada Ltd, 6045 Freemont Blvd., Mississauga, Ontario, L5R 4J3 Canada

Wiley also publishes its books in a variety of electronic formats. Some content that appears in print may
not be available in electronic books.

Library of Congress Cataloging in Publication Data

Ryals, Lynette.
   Managing customers profitably / Lynette Ryals.
     p. cm.
   Includes bibliographical references and index.
   ISBN 978-0-470-06063-6 (cloth)
   1. Customer relations—Management.   I. Title.
   HF5415.5.R93 2008
   658.8′12—dc22
                  2008038652

British Library Cataloguing in Publication Data

A catalogue record for this book is available from the British Library

ISBN 978-0-470-06063-6   (H/B)

Typeset in 10/12pt Garamond by Integra Software Services Pvt. Ltd, Pondicherry, India
Printed and bound in Great Britain by CPI Antony Rowe, Chippenham, Wiltshire

Contents

Contents

Foreword

Neil Rackham

Salespeople have earned themselves a notorious reputation for their ignorance of all things financial. Years ago, when I was working in Xerox, I was at an awards dinner sitting with some of the corporation's most successful salespeople. The dinner speaker told an old jest about a car dealership whose slogan was, 'We lose on every car we sell, but we make it up in volume'. One of the top performers sitting next to me frowned. 'What's wrong with that?' he asked, genuinely puzzled. Admittedly, this was some time ago and few top salespeople today could prosper with such spectacular ignorance. But, in lesser ways, the phobia for finance is still alive and well across the world's sales forces.

Why is this? Why, for example, would a perfectly useful training course called *Finance for Salespeople* be the least popular and worst attended out of a dozen sales related offerings at a large training centre? Why is it, when I meet with my fellow assessors to compare notes on candidates we have interviewed for sales management jobs, that time and again we rate an otherwise promising applicant as 'weak' on basic numeracy and financial knowledge? What causes a flurry of twitching Blackberries in the audience at sales conferences whenever the CFO comes on stage? I could go on, but the point is clear. Salespeople throughout history have shown a distinct aversion to finance.

Some argue that the cause is hard-wired. Sales DNA, they believe, is different from financial DNA. Those with a predisposition for people and relationships are less likely to have an aptitude for figures. Personally, I find this argument unconvincing. I suspect that it is a stereotype which, over time, has become a self-fulfilling prophesy. This has happened before. In the 1950s it was widely assumed that only extroverts could succeed in selling. The prevailing stereotype of the salesperson was that of an outgoing 'life of the party' individual who was cheerfully loud and relentlessly sociable. The introverted 'quiet types' were counselled away from careers in sales and guided towards more suitable occupations. And this was done for an apparently sound reason. Studies at the time showed that more than 80% of salespeople scored above average for extroversion on personality tests, so that these tests were often used as a selection tool. In consequence the stereotype became self-fulfilling. We now know, of course, that this was a false dichotomy. Introverts can be just as successful as extroverts in sales roles. But few people would have believed that in 1950.

Today we may be emerging from the legacy of a similar stereotype. We have been conditioned to see financial ability and sales ability almost as opposites. There is enough anecdotal evidence all around us to confirm that at one time this may have been a legitimate belief. But that is no longer tenable today. An increasing number of people are both financially savvy and skilled in the sales arena. The argument that sales DNA is somehow different just does not hold up. The author of this book is a living case study. Lynette Ryals has been a fund manager in the City and a stockbroker. She is a Registered Representative of the London Stock Exchange and, to date, the only woman in the UK who has passed the Fellowship examinations of the Society of Investment Professionals. Her financial qualifications are impeccable. Her sales credentials are equally impressive. As Professor of Strategic Sales and Account Management at Cranfield she has produced a stream of useful and practical publications on high-level selling. She is testimony that there is no reason why selling and financial abilities should be at opposite poles. Which brings us back to the original question: why are most salespeople so unsophisticated when it comes to financial concepts and models?

Lest I seem to be unduly hard on the sales profession, I should hasten to add that finance can be equally unsophisticated when it comes to sales. I recall working with a Division of a global company based in the States. The company had gone through a spate of mergers and, as so often happened, the number crunchers were in the ascendancy. There were finance people everywhere. The Division President, himself an accountant, had decided to shake up the sales function and appointed one of his trusted finance team as the new head of sales. The new broom, driven by a thirst for numbers, began to introduce productivity metrics, including cost per call. He was horrified to find that the average b2b sales call was costing the company upwards of $900. He decided that this was outrageously high and set about reducing cost per call. To start, he demanded more calls per day from his salespeople. This enabled him, as he put it, 'to dramatically increase efficiency'. Next, he began to fret about the length of calls. 'Why does it take an hour or more to meet with a customer?' he asked. 'If we could cut each meeting to no more than 30 minutes, we could make even more calls.' Anyone with an understanding of consultative selling will be able to predict what happened:

- calls per day increased;
- the average dollar size of each sale fell;
- overall sales revenue declined;
- profitability fell spectacularly;
- top salespeople left;
- the new broom was soon replaced.

The folklore of sales is rich in cautionary tales like this one. Last year I was working with the management team of one of the largest service companies in Britain. They were planning to introduce new sales metrics and were attracted to the idea of increasing sales efficiency. I took them through this case study as an example of how not to do it. Afterwards the Head of Finance confessed that, until the meeting, he had assumed that if you made more calls, you would get more sales, without impacting profitability. In many companies, both sides of the great divide between sales and finance have much to learn.

Within the world of sales, there is another gap. At one extreme there are the sophisticated players such as GE or IBM. These corporations have been developing advanced strategies and sales tools to allow them to optimize the profitability of their customer relationships. Many of the frameworks explained in this book would be familiar to their key account salespeople. At the other extreme there is the average smaller company that is still in the thinking stage about whether to measure and reward their sales force based on the profitability of the business they generate, rather than purely on revenue. These companies, who are in the majority, still pay salespeople on sales volume and, as a result, have been losing ground. Business customers have become adept at preying on unsophisticated sales forces. One industrial buyer told me, 'I always ask salespeople if they are rewarded for volume or for profitability. If the answer is "volume", then I can usually get an extra 5% discount.'

The reality is that yesterday's simplistic view that a sales force can generate profitable revenue just from generating sales volume has never been tenable in high-end selling and is rapidly becoming untenable for sales as a whole. Customer profitability has rightly become the mantra. But what is a profitable customer? As Lynette Ryals shows, this is not quite so straightforward a question as it sounds. What is the difference between the relational value of a customer and the financial value? How does this affect customer profitability? What role does customer retention play? Why is lifetime value so important a concept? How can you use tools such as CRM to improve customer profitability? You will find these, and many other important questions, answered clearly and concisely in *Managing Customers Profitably*.

I have been searching for a book like this for a long time. So many of the salespeople I work with – and their managers – realize that the days of selling harder are gone and that future winners must strive to sell ever smarter. But this realization is of little use unless there is somewhere to go for practical how-to-do-it help. Until now, solid help has been almost impossible for individual sales practitioners to find. Armed with the models and advice in this book, salespeople should now be well placed to outsell their competition. People who can put aside traditional ways of thinking and adopt instead the rational frameworks laid out here will greatly benefit themselves and their companies. In a world where the cost of pursuing a sales opportunity is often well into six figures, failure to understand customer profitability can be fatal. *Managing Customers Profitably* contains all you need to know to compete with the best and the brightest. Professor Ryals has done an outstanding job of bringing together the finest of cutting-edge thinking and has done so with a rare clarity. This book makes an important contribution. It deserves recognition as a milestone among sales books.

Neil Rackham, author of the best-selling titles
Major Account Sales Strategy and *SPIN Selling* and Visiting Professor
at Cranfield School of Management and at Portsmouth Business School.

Acknowledgements

This book is based on what I have learned from my research, teaching, and consultancy over the past years. There are many companies and individuals whose contribution I would like to acknowledge, some of whom I can name and many others I cannot. All of you have contributed, thank you!

Some of my Cranfield colleagues deserve a special mention. It was Professor Simon Knox who first suggested that I should focus on customer profitability analysis during the early weeks of my Ph.D. Other colleagues who have been especially helpful in explaining particular techniques, suggesting new approaches, and correcting my mistakes include Dr Ruth Bender, Dr Sue Holt, Dr Andrew Humphries, Dr Stan Maklan, Professor Malcolm McDonald, Keith Parker, Alan Smart, and Diana Woodburn.

I have taught and consulted on these issues with a large number of companies and individuals, and I have greatly appreciated their contribution to the development of the techniques in this book. Two of them deserve specific mention. Chris Howe, Divisional Business Director for Addleshaw Goddard, the major legal practice, provided patient explanations of customer profitability analysis in professional service firms. Neil Rackham gave his support and encouragement. Thanks also to the editorial team at Wiley. The mistakes that remain are, of course, my own.

Finally, I would like to mention my family, especially my father, Roy Ryals. My interest in business and ease with numbers were inherited from him and have proved remarkably useful in my research.

Professor Lynette Ryals
Cranfield School of Management
November 2008

Introduction

Marketing teams and sales forces are under pressure to justify their spending and, in some cases, even to justify their very existence. More and more companies are making deep cuts in their sales force and looking to outsource sales and marketing activities. This is a fact of 21st century business life.

One major reason why we have got ourselves into this predicament is that, for too long, we have treated marketing and sales activities as an art, not as a science. Marketing and sales people simply have to get more professional about the way in which they conduct business.

A key element of this increasing business-like approach is that salespeople need to recognize that not all customers are good customers, and not all opportunities make good sales deals. We need to become a lot more discriminating about the customers we acquire and how much we spend on them.

This book is designed to equip marketing and sales managers with the tools they need in this new world. It gives you all the analysis, tools, and techniques that you need to manage customers profitably.

The book has three sections:

- Section One: How to value customers.
- Section Two: How to manage a customer portfolio.
- Section Three: How to make strategic decisions to maximize the value of your customers.

The first section provides detailed instructions on how to value customers using customer profitability analysis (historic value) and customer lifetime value/customer equity (forecast value). The uses and limitations of each tool are described. This section also looks at how to determine the relational value of a customer (such as the value of advocacy). This first section is both detailed and practical; it gives you all the information you need to figure out the value of your customer relationships.

Section Two looks at what you should do with the knowledge that some customers are more valuable than others. This section shows you how to develop a view about your customer portfolio, how to segment your market, and how to manage your customers to ensure that you maximize their value. In this section, a powerful combination of strategic ideas and applied tools enables you to make profit-maximizing decisions about which customers to serve and how much service you should provide.

Section Three focuses in on three strategies that can make – or break – the marketing and sales numbers. Implementation is famously the graveyard of strategy, and this section looks at how marketing and sales managers can and should apply the new thinking to their customer base. At the end of this section, you will be able to identify which customers you want to acquire and retain, what your pricing and discounting strategies should be, and how to develop powerful breakthrough value propositions that make your firm unique in the minds of the customer.

The overall theme of this book is that customers are not intrinsically profitable. It is the actions of sales and marketing managers that affect the value that the firm gets from its customers. Reading this book will enable you to understand how to value customers and how to manage your relationships with them profitably.

Section One

How to value your customers

The first section of this book examines different methods of valuing customers and provides detailed step-by-step guidelines on how and where to find the information you need.

Chapter 1 sets out the latest thinking on valuing and managing customers, describing the problem of customer churn, the use of customer profitability analysis, and what we mean by the term 'relationship marketing'. It raises some vital questions about the proportion of sales and marketing spend that is directed to customer retention versus customer acquisition, and offers a diagnostic and some chapter questions and answers to get you thinking about the issues.

In Chapter 2, we examine some of the applications of historic customer profitability analysis, including questions about the level of granularity that your analysis should use (a diagnostic is provided), and how to identify customer dependency or 'skew' in the portfolio. Chapter 3 then sets out specific methods and worksheets for calculating customer-by-customer profitability analysis, including a breakdown of customer costs. Chapter 4 details an alternative method of calculating customer profitability analysis where there is a large portfolio of customers using a 'top down' approach based on decision tree analysis.

Chapters 5 and 6 move on to the application and calculation of customer-by-customer lifetime value, showing how to forecast customer revenues and costs and how to apply discounting techniques to express these future values in terms of today's money. Chapter 7 demonstrates the alternative, top-down approach to calculating the customer equity (the total lifetime value) of a large number of customers, using revenue and cost drivers.

Finally, Chapter 8 looks at the difficult question of the relational value that customers may bring, showing you how to determine the four sources of relational value (reference, referral, learning, and innovation) and how to use this information to improve your management of customer relationships, for example in identifying key accounts.

When you have read this section, you will be able to:

- understand the difference between historic (customer profitability analysis) and forecast (customer lifetime value, customer equity) methods of valuing customers, and appreciate the strengths and limitations of each;
- identify the customer dependency within your portfolio, and appreciate issues of customer churn and payback;
- calculate customer profitability, customer lifetime value, and customer equity;
- determine the relational value of customers;
- identify which customers are key accounts, based on their financial and relational value.

1

Latest thinking on valuing and managing customers

What's in this chapter

- Two-minute chapter summary
- How customer management is changing
- Relationship marketing
- Marketing is a science, not an art
- How to value customer relationships
- Where to find out more

Key concepts discussed in this chapter

Customer churn	Rate at which customers are lost each year (therefore, the inverse of customer retention). Can be expressed as a percentage of the average number of customers in the year, so a customer churn of 50% means that the company loses one in two customers.
Customer profitability	The profitability of a one-year relationship with a customer, which is driven by: • revenues (which goods or services the customer purchased; prices, quantities, and discounts); • cost to make the goods or deliver the services; • costs to serve (marketing, sales, customer service, administration); • customer-specific overheads (dedicated packaging, warehousing, logistics, on-site customer teams, etc.).

Relationship marketing	An approach to marketing and sales that looks to balance customer acquisition and customer retention. Relationship marketing places more emphasis on customer retention than traditional approaches. Based on the notion that retained customers tend to be more profitable (although the profitability will depend on how the relationship is managed). In relationship marketing, the overall relationship with the customer is considered to be more important than the individual products or services that the customer buys.
The true value of a customer	Comprises both financial and relational value. Customers have value because of the money they generate for companies, but they may also have value because of their profile, brand, willingness to recommend the supplier, etc. This is the relational value. The financial and relational value of customers is not always positive. It can be negative (cost the company money). Some customers might be unprofitable; others might spread bad news or malicious rumours about the company and damage its reputation.

Key tools explained in this chapter

- Sales and costs trend diagnostic (Table 1.1): This simple tool looks at the four key elements of customer profitability (revenues, direct costs, costs to serve, and customer-specific overhead costs) and the rate and direction of change in each cost element. The diagnostic indicates whether customer profitability is rising or falling, and suggests actions to improve the situation.

Two-minute chapter summary

Whether business-to-business or business-to-consumer, and whether manufacturing or services, there has been a shift over the past 10 years to relationship marketing (building longer-term relationships with customers). This is because acquiring customers is relatively expensive, and retained customers are generally more profitable.

However, companies need to be careful that lavish loyalty programmes aimed at retaining customers do not make the costs of customer retention higher than the additional returns. As companies move to a relational way of managing their customers, they need to deal with important questions about how much they spend on looking after their customers.

The costs of looking after customers fall into three categories: the direct costs of providing goods or services; the costs to serve (marketing, sales, customer service, and admin); and customer-specific overheads (where relevant).

This new focus on the costs and returns to customer relationships means that companies are demanding that their marketing and sales functions are accountable and measurable. Therefore, marketing is no longer considered an art. Measurement is aided by the development of new data tools such as customer relationship management (CRM) systems that enable a company to see the whole of its relationship with a customer. This is a challenge to the traditional 'silo' structure and mentality of many organizations.

The big new idea that has arisen from all these developments is the notion of customer relationships as assets in which the organization invests. In some ways, we can think of customer assets as being a portfolio, analogous to a portfolio of products or brands, although customers can join or leave the portfolio of their own volition (that is, they can start or cease buying) in ways that brands cannot.

Two streams of thought have emerged about how to value customer assets. The first stream focuses on the financial value of customer assets and looks at financial measures of value such as customer profitability analysis, customer lifetime value, or customer equity. The second broad approach notes that customers have relational value in the sense that they can make recommendations, attract other customers through their high profile, provide information, or help with new product development. Both these approaches are useful and the true value of a customer is in fact the financial *plus* the relational value.

How customer management is changing

Over the past 10 years or so, a major change has taken place in the way that companies think about customer management (sales, marketing, and customer services). This change has come about because of a shift from product-based to relationship-based marketing. In the relationship marketing world, companies believe that value comes from their relationships with their customers, rather than from the products that they push out into the market.

The relationship marketing concept has spread like wildfire and most marketing and sales people are now aware of the notion that happy customers are (generally) loyal customers, and loyal customers are (generally) more profitable. There are

> Happy customers are (generally) loyal customers, and loyal customers are (generally) more profitable.

important limits to these ideas, which we will explore in later chapters, but the overall point is correct.

We see the evidence of relationship marketing all around us, whether it is the supermarket loyalty card, a multi-retailer loyalty scheme such as the UK's Nectar card (Figure 1.1), or a business-to-business customer retention scheme.

Figure 1.1 Nectar loyalty card (reproduced by permission of Loyalty Management Group Ltd)
Source: www.Nectar.com

Each time the Nectar card is used, points are added to the card holder's account. These points can be redeemed in high street stores, to obtain a range of goods from the online catalogue, for travel or eating out, or even donated to charity. There is also a business version of the card (http://www.Nectar.com/rewards/generalSearchHome.nectar).

Relationship marketing

Relationship marketing focuses on customers and long-term relationship building rather than on products (Christopher, Payne and Ballantyne, 2002). The idea that relationships are more important than products has been expressed another way – when was the last time one of your products paid an invoice?

Focusing on customer relationships rather than products has a profound impact on the way that companies think and behave. The traditional organizational view that closing a series of product or service sales is the route to success tends to result in relatively aggressive sales approaches. In this transactional view, the focus is on customer acquisition rather than retention because, in a product-centred world, it doesn't really matter who the sale is made to. What is important is making the sale. Firms that pursue this strategy can achieve rapid growth through making a series of individual sales to numerous customers. However, there is a downside. This can lead to a reduced emphasis on after-sales service, customers who feel pressurized or unhappy, and higher customer losses ('churn').

The phenomenon of customer 'churn' means that the sales team is always racing to replace customers who leave, rather like having to keep pouring water into a leaky bucket to replace what is lost. Relationship marketing aims to fix the leak by plugging the hole in the bucket (reducing customer churn). Focusing purely on customer

> Customer 'churn' means that the sales team is always racing to replace customers who leave. Relationship marketing aims to fix the leak by reducing customer churn.

acquisition might be an appropriate strategy for a start-up firm that needs to accumulate a critical mass of customers quickly, but it is now widely recognized as less efficient in mature markets. Customer churn is a problem, for example, for mobile phone network providers in both the US and UK. In the early days, these businesses focused on fast growth and customer acquisition. Customer loss levels were high. Recognition of the need to reduce customer churn by providers such as Orange has led to a need for solutions aimed at reducing customer defections (Figure 1.2).

In the relationship marketing world, organizations such as Orange aim to develop a better balance between customer acquisition and customer retention. By contrast with the product-based view, for relationship marketers it *does* matter who the next sale is to, because relationship marketers want to develop long-term relationships with their customers. The customer experience is also important, because relationship marketers want their customers to come back, time and time again.

This shift from a product focus to a relationship focus affects the entire way that a firm interacts with its customers. As the organization shifts to a customer focus, the sales function learns to behave in a relational, not a purely transactional way.

> The shift from a product focus to a relationship focus affects the entire way that a firm interacts with its customers.

The marketing function begins to include relationship-building activities for customers, such as loyalty cards. Customer service (pre-, during, and after-sale) is recognized as increasingly important. As the relational focus increases, the organization learns to think about its overall relationship with the customer as a whole, rather than the

Orange Business Services selects CHIL solution
154 words
19 January 2007
DMEurope
English

Orange Business Services in the UK has successfully deployed CHIL's new Tariff Review Service Solution, enabling them to analyse each of its customer's usage patterns online and recommend the most suitable Orange Business Services tariff plan for them. The deployment is expected to lead to higher customer satisfaction, lower call centre costs, and a reduction in customer churn.

Where Have All the Customers Gone? Latest Diamond Whitepaper Offers Prescription for 'Curing Customer Churn'; Consulting Firm Finds that Careful Diagnosis Can Eliminate Root Causes of Customer Defections
1143 words
15 January 2007
15:00
PR Newswire (U.S.)
English
Taken from PR Newswire (U.S)
Used by permission of Diamond Management & Technology Consultants Inc.

CHICAGO, Jan. 15 /PR Newswire/ – There's nothing more disheartening to a marketer than spending millions to attract new customers, only to miss out on long-term, profitable relationships because something, somewhere, somehow went wrong.

But instead of pointing fingers, Diamond Management & Technology Consultants, Inc. (Nasdaq: DTPI), recommends that companies precisely pinpoint the problems that need fixing. Using a combination of careful call monitoring, detailed process analysis, primary research, and data analytics to identify the root causes of customer churn can eliminate the 'blame game' and get the organization pulling in the same direction.

Customer churn is commonly measured as the rate at which a number of customers discontinue a service during a specific time period divided by the average number of customers over that same time period. A major concern in the communications industry, where customers move from carrier to carrier in search of better deals, churn is prevalent in every business that relies on long-term relationships to drive profitability.

Figure 1.2 Reducing the problem of customer churn (reproduced by permission of Diamond Management & Technology Consultants, Inc.)
Source: Factiva

individual product(s) that the customer buys. This can lead to all kinds of changes in product and pricing strategies as well as promotion, delivery, and service levels. A great example of product development aimed at a long-term relationship with the customer is Pampers'® development of a series of products for babies and toddlers (www.pampers.com). The mother is offered a series of products as the baby grows up: 'Products for every baby stage' (Figure 1.3).

New Baby
Created specially
for newborns.
Uniquely designed
to absorb wee and
a newborn's soft poo.

Active Fit
Wriggling, jiggling,
bouncing or crawling,
your baby can find their
own unique moves with
Pampers Active Fit
3-WAY FIT.

Easy Up Pants
Help your little ones to
feel a bit more grown
up, with super leakage
protection and even
stretchier sides.

Feel'n Learn
Advanced trainers
help your little ones
to understand dry, by
first understanding
wet.

Figure 1.3 Pampers® – products for every baby stage (reproduced by permission of Procter & Gamble)
Source: www.pampers.com

Product profitability is out...

The shift towards relationship marketing has had a profound impact on the way that companies think about the drivers of profit. A major implication of relationship marketing is that marketing decisions should be about optimizing the long-term value of the customer. Consequently, accounting for marketing has shifted from the traditional product profitability approach to a customer profitability focus.

> A major implication of relationship marketing is that marketing decisions should be about optimizing the long-term value of the customer.

To see why this is so, think for a moment about pricing. In a transactional situation, pricing tends to be done relative to a single deal or a single project. In a relational situation, the customer manager will consider the entire relationship that the customer has with the company and all the products or services that the customer already buys or may buy. The price of one product or service could be reduced in order to secure a deal – but the product affected might not be the one that the customer is buying. Rather, it might be a better deal on something that the customer already owns. This can affect the apparent profitability of different products in unexpected ways, but the point is that overall customer profitability will be improved.

...customer profitability is in

Customer profitability is affected by four factors:

- revenues (which goods or services the customer purchased; prices, quantities, and discounts);

- cost to make the goods or deliver the services;
- costs to serve (marketing, sales, customer service, administration);
- customer-specific overheads (dedicated packaging, warehousing, logistics, on-site customer teams, etc.).

The new focus on customer relationships has revealed that customer profitability is principally determined not by the cost of the products that the customer buys, but by the costs of managing the customer relationship (costs to serve). Let's just examine that again for a moment: the profitability of your customers depends on

> The profitability of your customers depends on the marketing, sales, and service package that surrounds and supports the product, not on the cost of manufacturing the product itself.

the marketing, sales, and service package that surrounds and supports the product, not on the cost of manufacturing the product itself. This is a vitally important point, which is still not fully appreciated by many businesses. Increasingly, customers want service. It is more and more difficult to sell even basic products without some form of supporting service. In many businesses the cost of manufacturing or supplying services is falling because they have moved to lower-cost manufacturing environments. In contrast, the service element of even basic products is increasing.

Consider the service surround that Amazon places on standard products such as books and DVDs. First, there is some personalization of the website, with a named greeting and a selection of ideas about what you might buy based on your previous interaction with the website. Second, there are the book details and often the opportunity to search the table of contents. You can choose to buy the book new or second-hand, with details of the condition of second-hand items. There are book reviews by readers and the opportunity to post such a review yourself. The service surround does not end with the book itself. Amazon lets you know what other people bought with that book, and provides you with details of any offers associated with the book you are buying. There is easy 'one click' purchasing, and an email trail to let you know where your purchase is. You can also get information about the status of your purchases through the website.

Amazon delivers these impressive service levels through the use of web technology. Although the investment may be huge, the numbers of customers managed through that website are very large, and so the per-customer investment is not so great. However, in a business-to-business context, the increasing service demands from customers often have to be met through allocating additional face-to-face or telephone servicing, and this is expensive. The bigger and more powerful the customer, the more they can command a disproportionate share of the supplier's resources.

Where a supplier has a large but demanding customer, we typically see two different cost trends. Direct costs (per unit) may fall, but costs to serve may rise. Direct costs may fall because there are lower unit costs associated with long production runs for a large customer, unless the customer is demanding substantial customization. Similarly, providing business-to-business services is more cost-effective on larger contracts because of higher utilization rates for the consultants and managers who are providing the service.

Although direct costs may be lower with larger customers, costs to serve and customer-specific overheads may rise disproportionately because of the complexity of the relationship and the need to provide substantial resources in the form of key account managers, customer service, dedicated warehousing and logistics, and even promotional or brand support. Rising costs to serve can become a major issue in business-to-business markets, in which substantial proportions of sales and marketing resources may be allocated to individual customers. Table 1.1 gives you a quick diagnostic to check what is happening in your own business.

Table 1.1   Sales and costs trends diagnostic

Tick a box to indicate what the sales and costs trends in your business have been in the past three years and what you expect them to do in the next three years. Use two ticks if the trend is strongly in a particular direction.

Item	Past 3 years			Next 3 years		
	Rising	Static	Falling	Rising	Static	Falling
Revenues						
Cost of manufacturing/ service delivery						
Costs to serve (sales, marketing, customer service, admin)						
Customer-specific overheads (if incurred)						

How to interpret your results: *In many businesses, costs to serve are rising faster than other costs. This could compromise the business's profitability unless carefully managed so that sales and marketing costs are directed at customers who will produce a positive return for you on your marketing investment.*

- **Revenues are rising faster than costs:** *Excellent – your business performance is improving.*
- **Costs of manufacturing are rising fast:** *Your manufacturing base might have to be made more efficient or raw materials sourcing changed. Talk to procurement.*
- **Costs to serve are rising fast:** *This is typical but needs careful management. You need to analyse the profitability of your customers and consider where you are spending your marketing effort.*
- **Customer-specific overheads are rising fast:** *Are you over-investing in customer relationships? You need to analyse the profitability of your customers and consider where you are spending your support effort.*

If you can't complete the table: *You don't have the information you need to value your customers or to manage customer relationships profitably. See Chapter 2 for more information about the components of customer profitability.*

Many companies have relatively good information about the direct costs associated with customers, but rather poor or incomplete information about costs to serve. This information asymmetry might lead them to overestimate the profitability of their largest customers, because they associate large customers with lower direct costs per unit and fail to appreciate the considerable costs to serve that may be involved in looking after them.

Managing costs

The main area of cost that sales or marketing people can influence is costs to serve. As we have seen, this area of costs is often the area that most affects the profitability of customers. Sales and marketing people need to be aware that their customer attraction and customer management activities have a major impact on the profitability of customers. The problem here is that it may be difficult to track these costs or attribute them to specific customers. Therefore, customer managers may struggle to tackle some fundamental questions about costs, such as: How much sales time is spent on customer A, compared to customer B? How much customer service does customer C get, and how much does it cost?

> Sales and marketing people need to be aware that their customer attraction and customer management activities have a major impact on the profitability of customers.

Marketing and sales people also need to be aware of the effect on customer profitability of offering customer-specific services. Thus, a key account manager should think very carefully before offering category management or dedicated warehousing to a customer. These kinds of offers should never be made unless the key account manager understands the profitability of that customer and the impact that these dedicated overhead services might have on future profitability. The problem here is that the costs of customer-specific services like these are borne by other departments, and so the incentives for sales people or customer managers to offer them are high because they will not directly have to deal with the cost and resource issues.

Overspending on customer retention can mean that retained customers are not necessarily more profitable. Put simply, unless you are careful you can easily find that you are paying your customers more to stay with you than you will make from them in return. This is a trap that is particularly easy to fall into with bigger and more powerful customers. Because the company is keen to hold on to its high-profile relationships, and because the stronger customers are better able to negotiate keen deals, the cost of retention can outstrip the benefits.

The danger of overspending on retention is a good reason why you should never measure *just* customer retention on its own. After all, this is an easy metric to beat: you can always 'bribe' your customers to stay by making them fantastic (but unprofitable) offers that buy their loyalty. Certainly, it is good for companies to reduce

> You should never measure *just* customer retention on its own, because of the danger of overspending on retention as opposed to focusing on customer profitability. What you want is *profitable* customer retention.

customer churn, so long as this reduction in churn does not cost so much that it reduces the profitability of the business. However, you should never measure *just* customer retention on its own, because of the danger of overspending on retention as opposed to focusing on customer profitability. What you want is *profitable* customer retention.

> **Note**
>
> Find out what proportion of your sales and marketing spend is on customer acquisition versus retention, and make sure these proportions are correct for what you are trying to achieve in the business.

Marketing is a science, not an art

The rising cost of servicing customers has acted as a wake-up call in marketing. Marketing is no longer considered to be an art form in which aesthetics and creativity are all-important and it is uncouth to ask questions about the financial returns. Instead, some serious misjudgements that companies have made about marketing spending have spawned an era in which marketing is regarded as a measurable science and, more specifically, questions are being asked about the returns on marketing spend. No organization got it more wrong than Hoover, with its 1992 'Free flights to America' marketing campaign. Initially, the offer was two free return flights to Europe if customers bought a £100 Hoover. Later, despite difficulties experienced by Hoover's travel agents in meeting demand for the Europe offer, the campaign was extended to offer two free return flights to the US. Irate customers struggling to claim their flights formed the Hoover Holiday Pressure Group that, at the height of the protests, had 8000 members. Customers sued Hoover and the company found itself repeatedly in court. The eventual cost to Hoover was £48 million, but the real damage was to the company's reputation.

The more companies learn about the value of their customers, the greater the insight they get into the value of their business. One striking finding has been about

> The value of customers is related to the value of the firm.

how companies are valued by the stock market (and, indeed, by potential acquirers). Stock market valuations and the price of a company's shares are notorious for their fluctuations, making it hard to see what a business is worth. More recently, it has been suggested that the value of customers is related to the value of the firm and that understanding the value of the firm's relationships is actually a better guide to its overall worth than other valuation techniques.

Marketing and sales are increasingly measured by profit

In addition to its link to the value of the firm, two further factors have focused attention on the value of customer relationships. One, as we have seen, is the call for greater accountability in marketing and for a more scientific view of the returns

> Key account managers are usually measured on margin or customer profitability rather than on volume.

to marketing spending. As a consequence of these demands for greater accountability in marketing, there has been a shift in the way in which sales and marketing performance is measured. Historically, for example, sales people were measured on volumes or revenues. This sometimes resulted in sales people making low-margin sales in order to make their volume targets, particularly if they were also allowed to give discounts. Increasingly, sales people are measured on margin. An illustration of this trend is the development of Key Account Management (KAM), the management of relationships with a company's biggest business-to-business customers. Key account managers spend more of their time relationship building rather than selling and they are usually measured and often rewarded on margin or customer profitability rather than on volume.

Another factor making the valuation of customers a hot topic is the increased availability of information through the advent of sophisticated customer relationship management (CRM) systems. These are IT systems that support the management of customer relationships, but which also make it possible to measure the value and the costs of looking after customers. CRM systems are helping to remove one of the barriers to valuing customer relationships, which is the data requirement. A CRM system can provide vital information about products that the customer has bought in the past, costs to serve, indications of future purchases, and support the profitable management of customer relationships.

The bad news is that the CRM system does not do it for you. This book is about how to gather, analyse, interpret, and use the information that you need to value your customers and manage them more profitably.

How to value customer relationships

So far, we have seen that customers (not products) drive revenues because it is customers who buy goods and services and customers who pay invoices. We have also seen that there are costs associated with this approach. These costs are the costs of providing the goods or services, the costs to serve the customers (sales, marketing, customer service, administration, etc.), and customer-specific overheads. We have also seen that there has been a shift to relationship marketing and building longer-term relationships with customers. This shift allows us to recognize that investment in a customer relationship at one time may not pay off until a later time.

Taken together, these new concepts indicate that customer relationships can be
thought of as assets in which a company
invests its sales and marketing resources
with a view to optimizing its returns
on that investment. In fact, customer

> Customer relationships can be thought of as assets in which a company invests its sales and marketing resources.

relationship assets are analogous to a portfolio of products or brands. Companies
actively manage their brand portfolios to develop new brands, invest in the stars,
and downscale the weaker performers. Brand managers think about the return on
investment in their brands. They routinely make decisions about how to optimize the
return on their brand investment, and they understand how to value the company's
brand assets. Why, then, should a company not value and manage its portfolio of
customer relationship assets in the same way?

Valuing customer assets

In fact, the notion of valuing customers as assets has been gaining ground for the past
few years. However, a portfolio of customer assets is rather different from a portfolio
of products or brands in two important ways. The first is that customers, unlike
brands, have minds of their own and can decide to arrive or leave unexpectedly.
The second way in which customer assets differ from product or brand assets is that
some customers can affect the value of other customers through activities such as
advocacy (word of mouth) or profile. Customers can also affect the value of the
supplier company by suggesting and/or testing new product ideas or by sharing
information or knowledge with the supplier.

These differences have meant that two schools of thought have emerged on how
to value customer assets. The first is a financial approach based on the profitability or
lifetime value of the customer. In this approach, the analogy between the customer
portfolio and other asset portfolios is clear, although the valuation of customer
portfolios is more complex because customers can decide for themselves when
they will arrive in or leave the portfolio. Broadly speaking, there are three financial
methods of valuing customers (customer profitability analysis, customer lifetime
value, and customer equity), which have different advantages and disadvantages.
Customer profitability analysis will be examined in Chapters 2 to 4, customer lifetime
value in Chapters 5 and 6, and customer equity in Chapter 7.

However, the financial approach to valuing customers tends to ignore or downplay
the relational benefits from customers. As we will see in Chapter 8, the reason for
this is that relational benefits can be more difficult to track and measure and may not
affect the value of the customer directly. Some marketers have taken the view that
relational benefits are in fact very important and this has led to the development
of a second method of valuing customer assets, which is a relational approach.
The relational approach suggests that companies obtain value from their customer

relationships in ways that are not directly related to the financial value of those customers.

As we examine the two approaches, we will find that the truth lies between them. In fact, the true value of a customer asset is the financial *plus* the relational value (Figure 1.4).

Figure 1.4 The true value of a customer

Summary: managing customers as assets

The emergence of relationship marketing has had a profound impact on the way in which companies manage their customers. It has led to an increased focus on the value of the customer relationship, rather than the individual transaction. This, in turn, has made marketing and sales managers think about their relationships with customers as an asset of the business in the same way that brands, etc. are marketing or business assets.

New ideas about customers as assets, about customer portfolio management, and about the true value of a customer asset having both financial and relational value are vital to understanding how to value customer assets. In the first section of the book we examine different methods of valuing customers and understand how to place both a financial and a relational value on a customer asset.

In the second section of the book, we will move on to consider how best to manage customer assets based on their financial and relational value, and how to optimize the return on the overall customer portfolio.

The third section of the book contains an in-depth look at some of the strategies that have the biggest impact on the profitability of customers: selective customer acquisition and retention; pricing; and the development of powerful value propositions.

Where to find out more

Christopher, M., Payne, A. and Ballantyne, D. (2002) *Relationship Marketing*, second edition, Butterworth-Heinemann, Oxford. *The second edition of this best-selling book brings relationship marketing up-to-date and focuses on the link between the management of customer relationships and the generation of shareholder value.*

Ryals, L.J. (2005) 'Making CRM work: The measurement and profitable management of customer relationships', *Journal of Marketing*, 69(4), pp. 252–261. *Presents two case studies – one business-to-business and one business-to-consumer – and shows that strategies to manage customers more profitably pay off. Also discusses the ways in which these companies measured the profitability of their customers.*

Chapter 1: Q & A

	Question	Answer
1	Why are so many companies adopting relationship marketing?	As markets mature and growth slows, it gets harder to acquire new customers. In addition, it is generally less efficient to focus purely on customer acquisition (like trying to fill a leaky bucket). Retained customers are generally more profitable, although care needs to be taken not to overspend on customer retention as this can result in lower profits.
2	What are the three main types of customer costs?	• Direct product or service costs. These are the costs of manufacture, raw materials, operations, salaries, etc. • Costs to serve. These are the costs of marketing, sales, KAM, administration, customer service. • Customer-specific overheads. These do not apply to all customers, but might include dedicated warehousing or category management.
3	To what extent can customers be thought of and managed as a portfolio?	The customer portfolio is a powerful new concept associated with longer-term relationships, which encourages managers to think in terms of allocating their sales and marketing spend as though it were an investment in customer relationships, and to think about optimizing the return on these investments. However, customer portfolios are not like brand portfolios. Customers can choose to enter or leave the portfolio at will. They can also add value in other ways.
4	In what ways do customer assets create value for organizations?	Financial and relational. Financial value consists of profit or lifetime value. Relational value is more difficult to measure but might include profile, advocacy, learning and information, and new product development.

2 Customer profitability analysis

What's in this chapter

- Two-minute chapter summary
- Why companies are switching to customer profitability analysis
- Bottom-up or top-down: how to decide on granularity
- What to use customer profitability analysis for
- Customer dependency, skew, and the bell-shaped curve
- Small print: the limitations of customer profitability analysis
- Where to find out more

Key concepts in this chapter

Bottom-up analysis	Calculation starts from the bottom of the customer base (i.e., individual customers) and builds up from there.
Customer dependency	Measures the degree to which a company is dependent on a few customers. The 80:20 rule is often cited here, which is that 80% of sales often come from 20% of customers. If dependency is high (as a general rule, if more than 80% of sales come from less than 20% of customers), this is generally considered to be risky and careful management of the most important customer relationships will be needed.
Customer profitability	The actual profit generated by a relationship with a customer during a defined period, usually a year. In practice, usually calculated as customer revenues minus direct costs, costs to

	serve, and any customer-specific overheads. General overheads are usually disregarded, and so the calculation should strictly be called 'customer contribution'.
Granularity	The level at which the analysis takes place. The greater the granularity, the smaller the 'granules' in the analysis. In other words, higher granularity examines the customer base in 'close up', looking perhaps at individual customers or very small groups. Lower granularity looks at larger groupings, perhaps at whole segments, which gives a bigger picture but in less detail. The decision about what level of granularity to use will depend on what the analysis is trying to achieve. Granularity might depend on the marketing and sales strategy of the firm, the structure of the marketplace, and the availability of information.
Normal distribution	Occurs when a population is balanced about the mean so that the values plotted form a bell-shaped curve.
Profit	The absolute amount of money made; the difference between revenues and costs (can be negative). Historic.
Profitability	Technically, the proportion of money made, expressed as a percentage. In practice, the term 'customer profitability' is often used to describe the absolute profit made from a customer, usually in the preceding period.
Servicization	The addition of a 'service wrapper', even to quite standard products, to differentiate it from the competition. Customers increasingly demand a high service element, and servicization is an increasing trend across all markets.
Top down analysis	Calculation starts from the top of the customer base (i.e., the entirety of customers) and drills down from there.

Key tools in this chapter

- Granularity: The level of detail at which the customer profitability analysis is to be carried out. High granularity = high detail, possibly even analysing the profitability of individual customers. This is a good idea for key accounts, where the company has relatively few customers, or where a high proportion of business comes from a small number of customers (business is highly concentrated). Low granularity = low detail, possibly calculating customer profitability by segment, channel, or some other form of customer grouping. This is appropriate where there are larger numbers of customers, distinct segments with different behavioural characteristics, or distinct channel or regional differences. High granularity has the advantage of giving lots of detail but can be confusing and expensive if lots of customers are to be analysed. Low granularity is cheaper to implement but gives less detail.

- Customer dependency: The degree to which the firm depends on a few major customers for most of its business. The Pareto rule, or 80:20 rule, suggests that 80% of revenues might come from 20% of products. This rule can also be applied to customers. However, firms can vary widely in their customer dependency and also in the degree to which they are comfortable with a high concentration of business in a few customers. Industry structure affects the degree of dependency. For example, suppliers to automotive or aircraft manufacturers tend to have high dependency, because there are relatively few car and aircraft manufacturers in the world and the customers are very large. By contrast, firms selling into business-to-consumer markets such as retailing and banking tend to have lower dependency because there are millions of customers. Calculating the distribution of customers relative to the average, and comparing this with the normal distribution curve, is a good way of checking for dependency in a customer portfolio.

- Normal distribution curve: Another way of looking at customer dependency is to analyse the spread of customer numbers, revenues, or profitability about the mean (average). A normal distribution will form what is known as the 'bell-shaped curve'. However, the distribution might be skewed in one direction or another. A positive skew (to the right) suggests dependency on a few, larger customers. A negative skew (to the left) suggests disproportionate numbers of smaller or less profitable customers, perhaps indicating that there is too much emphasis on customer acquisition rather than on maximizing the returns from a customer relationship.

Two-minute chapter summary

As markets mature, companies can no longer grow rapidly through customer acquisition. Thus, they turn to customer retention (reducing customer churn) and selling more to their existing customers. It therefore becomes more important for them to be able to value their customer relationships.

Sales and marketing activities that build and maintain customer relationships should be thought of as investments, not as costs. This is part of the 'portfolio concept' of customers as assets that need investment.

For most companies, the journey to managing their customer portfolio more effectively begins with customer profitability analysis. Customer profitability is defined as the historic value of the customer – in other words, the profit or cash flow they delivered in the previous year.

Before the customer profitability analysis begins, an important decision needs to be made concerning the level of granularity. Should the customer profitability analysis take place bottom up, starting with individual customers and working up from there? Or, should it take place top down, starting with the entire customer base and drilling down? If the latter, to what level of granularity should the analysis drill down?

Where the customer base is dominated by a few, large customers, there is a clear case for high granularity and a profitability analysis customer by customer. Where there are hundreds of thousands of customers, it is not feasible to calculate customer profitability individually for each, and a lower granularity is more useful. In the latter case, customer profitability might be calculated by segment, tranche, or some other customer grouping.

Customer profitability analysis is based on actual data about previous customer purchases and associated costs. It is useful for evaluating:

- customer dependency (the degree to which the firm depends on a few, large customers);
- balance between customer retention and customer acquisition activities;
- payback period to customer acquisition.

Customer dependency or skew in the customer base may be identified by comparing the distribution of customers in the firm's customer base with the normal distribution curve, also known as the bell-shaped curve. When they carry out a customer profitability analysis for the first time, most companies find that a proportion of their customers are unprofitable.

Why companies are switching to customer profitability analysis?

As we saw in Chapter 1, many organizations still take a product profit approach in their management accounts even though, as more and more firms switch to a relationship marketing approach to customer management, there are increasing pressures to think in terms of customer, not product, profitability. So why is product profitability so widely used?

One reason is inertia: companies have always done it like this, so why change? Of course, this simply moves the argument back one step. Why do organizations do this? Why were their management accounts set up like this, in the first place? Unfortunately, it seems that the reason most organizations measure product profitability is that it is easy to do. Historically, most companies were organized around some kind of manufacturing unit. Therefore,

> The reason most organizations measure product profitability is that it is easy to do.

it was straightforward to measure the amount of raw materials that went in to each of these units and the costs of the people actually doing the manufacturing, and to count the number of products that came out. In this way, the gross profits made by each manufacturing unit could be measured and it made sense to organize the management accounts in this way. Another advantage of product profitability measurement was that the profitability of different manufacturing units could be compared with each other. Weaker units could be benchmarked against stronger units and, in this way, corporate performance could be improved.

In this scenario, activities such as sales and marketing were handled by Head Office and were seen as an overhead. When times got tough, managing directors tried to

> Sales and marketing: an overhead, or an investment?

reduce overheads. Thus, sales and marketing activities would be squeezed during an industry downturn, because they were regarded as part of the overheads of the firm.

In fact, this is exactly what happened during the tougher economic conditions during the 1980s. Some companies slashed their marketing budgets, including cutting back on advertising and promotions. Sadly for them, when economic conditions

> Smart companies recognize that their sales and marketing activities are an investment that creates value for them.

improved, the companies that had cut their marketing budgets found themselves at a disadvantage compared with competitors that had continued to market themselves. The latter companies had maintained customer recognition of their brands and, when customers had money to spend, they turned to the brands and products they remembered. The lesson to be learned from this experience is that sales and marketing activities that build relationships with customers should be thought of as an investment, not as a cost. Some managers still think of sales and marketing as overhead activities that are parasitic upon the 'real' business of the company, which is making widgets or whatever. This is out-of-date thinking. Smart companies recognize that their sales and marketing activities create value for them, just as making world-class widgets creates value. Companies need to invest in making products or delivering services, sure, but they also need to invest in marketing and selling them.

Globalization and the importance of customer relationships

Another change that has challenged the notion of sales and marketing as overheads has been the maturation of markets in the Western hemisphere (the US, UK, and Western Europe). As markets mature, growth slows down. Fewer new customers enter the market, and more customers have already got the products they need or are already spending as much of their income as they are able or willing to on consumer goods.

We can witness this phenomenon by comparing growth rates in the emerging markets of China, India, and Brazil, where there is rapid growth in disposable income and spending, with growth rates in the US, the UK, and Germany. Where there are fewer new customers, companies cannot sustain their growth by customer acquisition. Instead, they have to nurture and grow the relationships with their existing customers. A good example of this is the mobile phone industry, which has reached saturation point in many Western markets. In some markets, such as Finland and the UK, penetration is already over 100% (that is, there is at least one mobile phone per person). To grow their business, the mobile phone providers are turning to new growth markets such as Africa, but they are also trying to manage their relationships with existing customers better. In mature markets, telecom providers are extending the range of services that they provide and offering user contracts and tariffs designed to reduce 'customer churn', the problem of customers leaving for competing providers.

As well as slower growth in mature markets, companies in both business-to-business and business-to-consumer markets also have to contend with globalization. In a business-to-business context, globalization has resulted in the emergence of fewer, larger customers with powerful centralized purchasing functions and the need for international supply and service. Suppliers to

> In a business-to-business context, globalization has resulted in the emergence of fewer, larger customers with powerful centralized purchasing functions and the need for international supply and service.

these global customers are under pressure to provide internationally standardized products and harmonized prices. Many of these customers have also introduced tiered supplier status and now require the Tier 1 suppliers to manage other supplier relationships on behalf of the customer, as well as providing complete assemblies rather than individual products. Consider, for example, the car manufacturing industry, which is dominated by four global players and where the number of suppliers who still have direct access to the global customer has plummeted.

In business-to-consumer markets, the emergence of global markets means that consumers can and do source their products from suppliers anywhere in the world. So, visitors to Amazon in Germany (www.amazon.de) can purchase books in German or English. Visitors to TopGear's website in the UK (www.topgear.com/

> In business-to-consumer markets, the emergence of global markets means that consumers can and do source their products from suppliers anywhere in the world.

content/buyersguides) can obtain information about how to import a car from abroad. Consider also the contact and shipping details for iwantoneofthose on www.iwantoneofthose.com. This London-based business, selling toys, household goods, and gadgets over the Internet and winner of the 2006 customer service awards, has a separate telephone number for international sales, customer service,

Help & Customer Services Pages
Contact details

Sales – 24 Hour Dedicated Order Line Service:

You can now place an order via the telephone 24 hours a day! Please note, however, that this is for orders only – for any other queries please contact Customer Services during office hours.

0870 241 1066 (UK)
+44 870 241 1066 (International)

Customer Services:

For order or despatch questions, or if you simply feel like a chat, please call us during office hours.

0870 241 1066 (UK)
+44 870 241 1066 (International)

American Customers

Our Customer Support team, based in London, are also available by telephone on: +44 870 241 1066 at the following times:

Eastern Time: 4am–1pm

Central Time: 3am–12 noon

Mountain Time: 2am–11am

Pacific Time: 1am–10am

Finance Dept.:

0208 655 7595 (UK)

+44 208 655 7595 (International)

9am–6pm GMT Monday to Friday

Fax: 0870 220 2149

Figure 2.1 iwantoneofthose – selling consumer goods in global markets (reproduced by permission of www.iwantoneofthose.com)

Source: www.iwantoneofthose.com

and for its finance department. It even provides details of its customer service opening hours in four different American time zones (Figure 2.1).

So, customers now have more choice of supplier than ever before. Greater customer choice, plus mature markets in which fewer new customers are entering the marketplace, means that new customers are more difficult to acquire and therefore the loss of a customer is more serious. Given these conditions, it is not surprising that many industries have experienced 'servicization'. This is the addition of considerable service elements to what were standard products. Taking all of these trends together, we can see why the costs to serve customers are increasing far faster than the actual cost of making goods. Instead of being a relatively minor afterthought, a company's sales, marketing, and customer service activities are now essential to its success and companies are now spending proportionately more than previously on these activities.

Increased competition and customer choice (even, some would argue, customer confusion), coupled with the increased complexity of many products, have resulted in an increase in customer acquisition costs. In addition, costs to serve have increased as a proportion of company budgets and information about customers has increased.

> Rather than treating sales and marketing as an overhead, we are now in an era in which these costs are regarded as an investment in a long-term relationship.

At last, companies can see that the costs of acquiring and servicing customers are so high that they may need to retain the customer for years before they begin to make a profit on the relationship. Thus, rather than treating sales and marketing as an overhead, we are now in an era in which these costs are regarded as an investment in a long-term relationship. From there, it is only a short step to asking just how much money a company makes from its investment in a customer relationship.

Getting started on valuing customers

The starting point for most companies who set out to value their customer relationships is customer profitability analysis. Customer profitability analysis is about the historic value of a customer relationship, usually the profit that the company made from the customer in the last year.

Technically, 'profit' is the absolute amount of money that a firm makes whereas 'profitability' is the proportion it makes. Thus, it would probably be more accurate to talk about 'customer profit analysis' although customer profitability analysis is the accepted term.

There is a well-known saying:

cash is fact, profit is opinion

This saying indicates an important fact about customer profitability analysis, which is that it is not strictly about cash flow. Instead, customer profitability analysis is about an accounting concept: profit. It is worth bearing in mind that accepted accounting practices can differ between countries and they can also change over time. Hence the saying that 'profit is opinion'. Managers need to be aware that, because accounting practices may differ between countries, a customer profitability analysis carried out in one country may not be strictly comparable with that carried out elsewhere.

Bottom-up or top-down analysis?

The first decision that has to be made is whether the customer profitability analysis should be 'bottom up', calculating the profitability of individual customers, or 'top down' by customer tranche or segment. Table 2.1 defines these terms and sets out the advantages and disadvantages of each.

Granularity

The alternatives set out in Table 2.1 help with a decision about the level of 'granularity' of the customer profitability analysis: generally, the higher the level of granularity, the more useful the information. High granularity means more detail, so the bigger

Table 2.1 Bottom up versus top down

Method	Explanation	Advantages	Disadvantages
Bottom up			
Individual customers	Calculates the profitability of individual customers separately. Based on that customer's overall relationship with the firm or business unit.	Very high level of detail. Gives a picture of overall relationship. Clearly defined. If customer acquisition costs are known, indicates how long it takes for a customer to become profitable. This is useful information when setting objectives for customer retention.	If many customers are to be considered, the time and resources to carry out individual customer by customer calculations can be extremely high.

Table 2.1 *Continued*

Method	Explanation	Advantages	Disadvantages
Top down			
Customer tranche or segment	A customer tranche is a 'slice' of the customer base. This could be a behavioural segment (showing profitability of frequent purchasers versus low-frequency purchasers, for example). Or it could be demographic segmentation (profitability of younger versus older customers) or geographic segmentation. Business-to-business, this could be by industry sector.	Easier to calculate for large numbers of customers. Indicates how dependent the firm is on particular customer segments. Useful for comparison purposes. Helps measure the success of past marketing or sales campaigns.	Does not explain *why* the profitability differs from segment to segment. Useful differences may be concealed. Segment profitability may be affected by marketing actions to that segment. Quality of output depends on how good the original segmentation was (segmentation is a problem area for many companies).

the grouping of customers, the lower the granularity. The highest granularity is the individual customer view. Looking at the profitability of the entire customer base gives the lowest granularity.

Table 2.2 is a quick audit tool to help managers decide what level of granularity would be most useful to them when carrying out a customer profitability analysis. This is an important decision: if the granularity is too low, the analysis will not give sufficient information to support the development of marketing and sales strategies.

Table 2.2 Auditing the appropriate level of granularity

High granularity (analyse individual customers or small groups) if:	Current company situation
Fewer than 30 customers are to be included in the analysis	
We have good information about individual customer relationships	
We have a lengthy and/or complex sales process	
We have a few large customers	
Our bigger customers are more profitable	
Losing one of our larger customers would be disastrous for our annual performance figures	

Table 2.2 *Continued*

	Current company situation
Lower granularity (customer tranches or segments) if:	
Customer acquisition costs are strongly driven by channel	
We spend disproportionate amounts of time and effort on smaller customers	
We have hundreds/thousands of customers	
We have customer loyalty (or retention or churn reduction) targets	
We have a useful segmentation model	
We use segmentation in our marketing campaigns	
We target certain clearly-defined segments with our sales efforts	
There are definite behavioural differences between our customer segments	
We can map our segments to our customer base, so we know which customers are in which segment	

If the granularity is too high, the overall picture might get lost in the detail, and the project might prove needlessly expensive.

Note: Granularity

Before starting on customer profitability analysis, determine what level of granularity would be most useful for you.

The advantages of customer profitability analysis

Customer profitability analysis has the advantage of being based on actual historic data about customer revenues and costs, rather than on forecasts. Customer lifetime value, as will be seen in the following chapter, is based on forecasts. Thus, there is generally greater certainty about the reliability of customer profitability analysis data.

What to use customer profitability analysis for

Customer profitability analysis is used to help companies make three kinds of marketing observations:

- customer dependency;
- balance between customer retention and customer acquisition activities;
- payback period to customer acquisition.

Customer dependency

Customer dependency is a useful concept, particularly in business-to-business situations where a company might have relatively few customers. It is based on the idea that marketing managers should monitor which customers their profits come from, in order to see how dependent they are on a few, very profitable customers. In other words, customer dependency looks at how heavily profits are skewed towards a few customers. Figure 2.2 shows a normal distribution curve. In this customer portfolio, a few customers are highly profitable and a few customers are unprofitable, but most are moderately profitable.

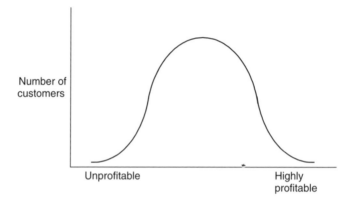

Figure 2.2   Normal distribution of profitable customers within a portfolio

Customer dependency here is low, because very few customers are highly profitable. The description of this as a normal distribution curve is related to statistics, rather than it being 'normal' in the sense that most companies have this pattern. An illustration of the statistical meaning of the normal distribution curve would be if the horizontal axis in Figure 2.2 represented people's height and the vertical axis represented the number of adults in the US. Then the normal distribution curve would show us that there are a small number of very tall adults and a small number of very small adults, but that most people are of moderate height somewhere in the middle.

If the actual customer profitability curve is different from the normal distribution curve then it is described as skewed. A skewed curve can tell us something important about a company. In fact, many companies (particularly those doing most or all of their work business-to-business) report that they have high customer dependency. High customer dependency means that a high proportion of profits is generated by a small proportion of customers. In other words, the distribution curve is skewed to the right. Figure 2.3 illustrates a skewed portfolio in which a very few customers are highly profitable.

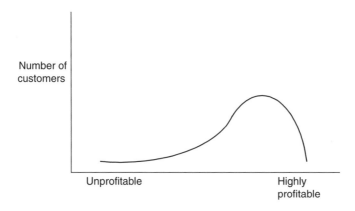

Figure 2.3 Skewed portfolio indicating high customer dependency

High customer dependency indicates a degree of risk, because the loss of a small number of customers could greatly damage the company's overall performance. Where the distribution curve is closer to normal, the chances are greater that a lost customer is only moderately profitable, so the damage caused by losing a typical customer is far less.

As Figures 2.2 and 2.3 imply, customer profitability analysis can also reveal that a proportion of customers is unprofitable. The discovery that a certain proportion of customers is unprofitable often comes as something of a surprise to companies when they first carry out a customer profitability analysis, although it should not. More and more studies using customer profitability analysis have found that a proportion of customers is unprofitable, and the proportion can be surprisingly high. Some researchers have found that only 30% of US retailing banking customers are profitable, and others have suggested that UK mobile phone companies make money out of only about half of their customers.

As a result, some companies are withdrawing certain products or services from less profitable customers or beginning to charge for these services. In the case of retail banking, low-balance current account holders who have no other products with the bank are relatively unprofitable, even where the bank's costs are low. The first major UK bank to do this was First Direct, a telephone and online bank. In February 2007 First Direct imposed a charge of £10 per customer for the approximately 195,000 current account customers who did not have any other products such as home insurance, a credit card, or a personal loan. Alternatively, customers had to have a minimum salary deposit of £1,500 ($3,000) per month into the account, equivalent to the UK average wage.

As the First Direct example illustrates, the discovery that a proportion of customers is unprofitable can have an impact on the balance of a company's customer acquisition and customer retention activities.

Balancing customer acquisition and retention

The discovery of unprofitable customers in the portfolio means that companies have to think about which customers they acquire and which they retain. Many marketing and sales managers do not appreciate that a proportion of their customers are unprofitable and that this implies that the profitable customers are subsidizing the unprofitable ones. One reason why managers do not realize this fact is that the 80:20 rule is often incorrectly applied.

Credited to early 20th century Italian economist Vilfredo Pareto, the Pareto Principle or 80:20 rule broadly states that 80% of the results come from 20% of the causes. In the case of the profitability of the customer portfolio, this means that 80% of a company's profits come from 20% of its customers. The 80:20 rule is well-established and has been found to be a useful general rule in many different applications ranging from economics to computing.

What is of interest to marketing and sales managers, however, is not just the 20% of customers who account for 80% of profits. The other 80% of customers, who account for just 20% of profits, are a major concern. Often, diagrams showing the 80:20 rule are drawn so as to suggest that the remaining 80% of customers are diminishingly profitable (Figure 2.4). In this comfortable but purely theoretical world, each customer produces a small amount of profit and the company should go on acquiring customers until the marginal profit generated by the next customer is zero.

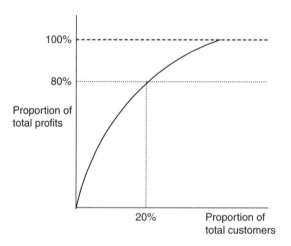

Figure 2.4   Erroneous application of 80:20 rule

In reality, as shown earlier, a customer profitability analysis typically reveals that a proportion of customers is unprofitable. In this real-world situation, the marginal profit of a customer can be negative and acquiring more customers could reduce profits. The cumulative profits curve for most customer portfolios does not curve smoothly towards 100%. Instead, it overshoots 100%, perhaps indicating that 60% of customers actually account for *more than 100%* of total profits and the remaining 40% are unprofitable (Figure 2.5)

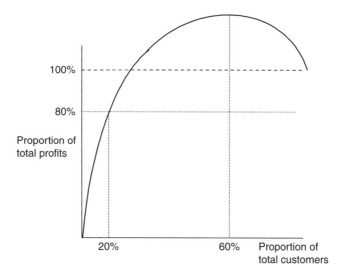

Figure 2.5 A proportion of customers is unprofitable

This finding from a customer profitability analysis, that a proportion of customers is unprofitable, can reveal some startling differences in profitability, as US heating systems company Kanthal discovered:

Kanthal's 225:20 rule

20% of customers = 225% of profits
70% of customers = breakeven
10% of customers = *minus* 125% of profits

The Kanthal customers generating the greatest losses were among those with the largest sales volume ... You can't lose large amounts of money on a small customer.
Source: Cooper, R. and Kaplan, R. (1991) 'Profit priorities from activity-based costing', *Harvard Business Review*, May–June, p. 134

In this case, the observation that some customers can be highly unprofitable is a useful one. The sales force, for example, needs to understand that it should not be acquiring customers at any price and that the customers it aims to acquire should be carefully selected. The marketing department needs to realize that loyalty or advocacy campaigns aimed at highly unprofitable customers might in fact be very damaging to the business. Customer profitability analysis can therefore provide very useful input into business decisions about the balance between customer acquisition and customer retention activities.

> **Note**
>
> Compare our customer distribution with the normal distribution curve. Does the analysis reveal anything of concern, or are we happy with the distribution the way it is?

Part of the decision about customer acquisition versus customer retention will have to be made based on the payback period.

Payback to customer acquisition

The payback period is the length of time (usually measured in months) that a newly-acquired customer takes to become profitable. In most cases, because of the costs of customer acquisition (sales and marketing costs, credit checks, etc.) new customers are not immediately profitable. Calculating the month by month profits generated from that customer enables a company to find out how long it has to keep the customer in order to make a net profit.

However, in some industries and for some products and services the cost of customer acquisition is greater than the annual profits from that customer. This is a particular problem where the product or service being sold is highly complex, or where the selling process itself is very formal and prolonged.

> In some industries and for some products and services the cost of customer acquisition is greater than the annual profits from that customer.

For example, it has been estimated that customers buying personal pensions do not become profitable for up to seven years because they are so costly to acquire. In complex business-to-business transactions such as those that take place in the defence industry, the tendering process can take many months and cost tens of millions of dollars. The eventual winners can expect to make a profit over the life of the contract, but it may take some months or years before the customer becomes profitable.

Part of the decision about whether to accept an ITT (Invitation to Tender) or an RFP (Request for Proposal) from a potential customer is the payback period. A company that takes on too many complex tenders is investing a great deal of its capital. If the payback period is very lengthy, this could cause cash flow problems. Understanding customer profitability analysis can help a company to get the balance right and not to take on too much customer acquisition activity. Similarly, one of the reasons for a high proportion of unprofitable customers in the customer base might be that customer churn is relatively high, so that many customers are gained and then lost again before they have stayed long enough to become profitable. If the customer profitability analysis reveals that this is likely to be the case, the marketing managers should put more effort into customer retention than customer acquisition, to increase customer retention and allow the customer base to 'mature' into greater profitability.

> **Note**
>
> What is our customer payback period? Do we some-
> times tender for/pitch for business that we then
> cannot deliver profitably?

Customer acquisition and customer retention strategies are the subject of Chapter 13.

Small print: the limitations of customer profitability

When companies analyse their customer base period by period they often discover that a proportion of their customers is unprofitable. Sometimes these are larger customers, as in the Kanthal example earlier.

However, there are only a few applications for which a customer profitability analysis can be used, as discussed earlier in this chapter (understanding customer dependency, payback periods, and the balance between customer acquisition and retention). The reason is that customer profitability analysis has certain limitations.

Limitation #1: the 'rear view mirror' problem

Customer profitability can fluctuate considerably from period to period. In customer relationships, the past is not a good guide to the future and relying on historical data can be dangerous, reducing the usefulness of customer profitability analysis for marketing decision making. For example, a customer might be low profit in years 1 and 2 but highly profitable in year 3. Looking only at the poor returns on this customer relationship in year 1, a company might be tempted to reduce service levels to that customer. This could threaten the future value of the relationship. Short-term service reductions could result in longer-term damage in the future. This problem is the 'rear view mirror' problem.

> **The 'rear view mirror' problem**
>
> Customer profitability analysis is based on historic data and the past may not be a good guide to the future. Looking only at customer profitability is analogous

to driving looking only in the rear view mirror. You get a good view of what happened in the past, but for decision-making purposes it is a lot more useful to look out of the front windscreen to see what might be happening in the future.

Limitation #2: 'Ready, Fire, Aim'

A danger of customer profitability analysis is what action the gung-ho marketing manager takes to deal with low profit or unprofitable customers. A customer profitability analysis that reveals unprofitable customers could persuade companies into thinking that they could improve their performance by cutting costs to these unprofitable customers or even by getting rid of them altogether.

The problem is that such actions may damage the organization. For example, a large volume but unprofitable customer might be important because the volume of business that it brings in keeps the average production costs down or enables the supplier to exercise purchasing muscle by buying in bulk. It could be that the customer is making a contribution to overheads, without actually being profitable. This is certainly a short- to medium-term consideration, although it would be dangerous to retain a long-term unprofitable customer unless there were very good reasons for doing so. Or the customer might be a new customer that had not yet been retained long enough to become profitable.

Another reason that a customer profitability analysis might persuade marketing managers to 'jump the gun' and reduce service to, or get rid of, unprofitable customers is that customer profitability analysis does not take account of the relational benefits of a customer. So, it might be worthwhile

> It may be worthwhile for a company to have a certain number of unprofitable customers if they are high-profile enough to attract others.

for a company to have a certain number of unprofitable customers if they are high-profile enough to attract other customers.

That said, in the longer term unprofitable customers could be more damaging to a company than might at first appear. To see why this is so, consider Figure 2.5. Year by year, profitable customer relationships have to subsidize unprofitable customer relationships. This has the overall effect that the profitable customers receive slightly poorer service than they should, because the company has to divert some of its money to servicing the unprofitable relationships. The unprofitable customers, conversely, receive slightly better service than they should. The longer-term results are likely to be that the more profitable customers will tend to migrate away from the supplier, because they can get better service from a competitor who does not have to 'carry' so many unprofitable relationships. Moreover, less profitable customers will tend to migrate towards the supplier as word gets round that service levels are better than the unprofitable customer has the right to expect.

The cross-subsidization issue is one that affects many different kinds of companies, from utilities to financial services to chemicals manufacturers. The normal mechanism to reduce the problem is to increase prices or reduce (or cease) services to the customers that are unprofitable, although regulation in certain industries such as utilities may prevent differential pricing.

> **Note**
>
> Check whether cross-subsidization is occurring in our customer base, and whether we are happy to manage the customer portfolio that way.

Summary: the use of customer profitability analysis

Customer profitability analysis helps a company to:

- appreciate its portfolio skew and whether it is heavily dependent on a relatively small number of customers;
- calculate the payback period on an acquired customer;
- understand how long a customer takes to become profitable, which can be helpful in alerting marketing managers to the necessary balance between acquisition and retention activities.

Customer profitability analysis has the advantage of being based on actual data about customer revenues and costs, rather than on forecasts. It helps a company to understand whether it is heavily dependent on a relatively small number of customers and to calculate the payback period on an acquired customer. In some industries the cost of customer acquisition is greater than the annual profits from that customer. Understanding how long a customer takes to become profitable can be helpful in alerting marketing managers to the optimal balance between acquisition and retention activities.

The starting point for customer profitability analysis is to decide on the appropriate level of granularity – will the analysis be bottom up, at the level of the individual customer, or top down?

Once that decision is made, the customer profitability analysis can be carried out. A straightforward method for calculating customer profitability is set out in Chapter 3.

Where to find out more

Cooper, R. and Kaplan, R. (1991) 'Profit priorities from activity-based costing', *Harvard Business Review*, May–June, 69(3), pp. 130–135. *Two leading US professors tell the story of how US heating wire company Kanthal applied activity-based costing to its customer profitability calculation and discovered that some of its largest customers were also the most unprofitable.*

For more detail about costing systems by the same authors, see Kaplan, R. and Cooper, R. (1997) *Cost and Effect: Using Integrated Cost Systems to Drive Profitability and Performance,* Harvard Business School Press Books, Boston, MA.

Dunn, S. (2007) 'Romance is dead with First Direct', *Independent on Sunday,* 11 February 2007, p. 23.

Chapter 2: Q & A

	Question	Answer
1	Why might the globalization of markets encourage companies to switch to customer profitability analysis?	There are several reasons for this. One is that globalized markets are associated with the emergence of fewer, more powerful customers that can use their power to put pressure on their suppliers. Also, selling internationally or globally has cost implications including logistics, legal, and regulatory compliance, translation, etc. In addition, global customers may have subsidiaries trading under many different names, and it is important to identify where these actually relate to a single customer so that the importance of that customer is understood. Plus, a global customer may demand price harmonization across markets whereas, from the supplier's point of view, the costs may be very different.
2	Why is skew an issue in customer portfolio management?	Normally, in the distribution of returns in a portfolio, we find a 'bell-shaped' or normal distribution curve. So, some investments have very high returns and some have very low (or negative) returns, but most are around the average. If the distribution of returns is not bell-shaped, it is said to be skewed. In a customer portfolio, there might be a few very profitable customers and a few very unprofitable customers, with most somewhere in between. This would be a normal distribution. If there are many highly-profitable customers, the portfolio is skewed to the positive, and the company should focus on retaining those customers. If, however, there are many low or unprofitable customers, the portfolio is skewed to the negative and is likely to be damaging the financial performance of the business. The company should think carefully about its customer acquisition strategy.

Calculating customer profitability

3

What's in this chapter

- Definition of customer profitability
- Customer revenues: where to get the data
- Cost of goods and services
- Costs to serve
- Customer-specific overheads

Key concepts discussed in this chapter

Customer revenues	Income received from the customer during a specific period. Comprises the amount of each product sold, multiplied by the price.
COGS	Cost of goods or services sold. The direct costs of making a product or providing a service.
Cost of capital	Where a firm has capital tied up in a particular investment (in this case, in a customer relationship), the cost of capital is the annual cost of providing that capital. For example, when a bank lends to a customer, regulations say it has to increase its reserves proportionately. The cost of doing so would be its cost of capital. In general, cost of capital is calculated as: (Proportion of debt × cost of debt) + (proportion of equity × cost of equity). This calculation gives the firm's WACC (Weighted Average Cost of Capital). The cost of capital is affected by the perception of the credit-worthiness of the borrower.

CTS	Costs to serve. The costs of the service surround, which might include sales, customer service, technical support, administration, logistics, etc.
Customer-specific overheads	The overheads of the firm are the functions it needs simply to be in business. They include the rental and running costs of buildings and the support functions such as IT and HR. Customer-specific overheads occasionally arise where there are premises or support facilities dedicated to a particular customer. For example, a vendor-managed inventory (VMI) system might involve fencing off a section of the warehouse so that it can be used only for one customer. The costs relating to the rental, heating, lighting, and running of this part of the warehouse can be designated as a customer-specific overhead so that the costs of providing VMI to that customer are fully understood.

Key tools explained in this chapter

- Activity-based costing: An approach to calculating costs based on the amount of time (activity) involved, multiplied by the per-hour costs of the employees carrying out the work. Useful for calculating costs to serve, where the amount of service time varies considerably from customer to customer. Also useful in high service environments or project work, such as legal or professional services or consultancy, where customer profitability is strongly influenced by the way in which the project is staffed. Using capable but lower-paid and more junior staff often results in a more profitable outturn.
- Standard costs: An approach to costing for small repeated operations. Standard costs are the average or typical cost of performing the operation (for example, the typical cost of preparing an invoice or a statement for a client). The actual cost per year is then the standard cost multiplied by the number of times the operation was performed (e.g., 10 invoices were sent at a standard cost of £40 per invoice, total cost of invoicing £400). Standard costs do not reflect the *actual* cost of preparing a particular invoice or statement.

Two-minute chapter summary

Customer profitability is measured as the revenues, minus product costs and costs to serve, that the company received from the customer in the previous year. If relevant, customer-specific overheads should also be taken into account. Some companies allocate part of their general overheads to customers when calculating customer profitability, although this has little relevance for sales and marketing decision making. Product costs, or COGS (Costs Of Goods and Services), are the direct costs of providing physical products or services to customers. Service businesses also have 'product costs', in the sense that they have to meet the costs of the people who actually deliver the services to their customers. COGS are usually supplied by the operations department, although for an accurate customer profitability analysis it is important to understand what is included/not included in COGS.

Costs to serve (CTS) are the indirect or support costs of dealing with customers. CTS include sales and marketing, key account management costs, administration and customer service, and may even include logistics costs if these are not included in product costs. CTS is a large cost component and should be taken into account. It is not sufficient simply to pro-rata CTS according to the size of the customer. Instead, the actual costs should be determined on an activity-cost basis. This is because different customers use widely different amounts of service time, so the pro-rata method can give a seriously misleading picture of relative profitability.

Customer-specific overheads are mainly relevant for very large business-to-business customers. They might include keeping a manager or team on-site at the customer or a branch office in the customer premises (if this is not already recognized as part of COGS or CTS), or the costs of holding customer-specific stock, or the cost of capital used to finance stock holding or support major customer-specific transactions.

Definition of customer profitability

By now, the first decision about customer profitability analysis should have been made, which is the level of granularity (level of detail) of the analysis. Generally, the greater the granularity (looking at more specific groups of customers or even at individual customers), the more useful the marketing information is but the more complex the analysis becomes. The lower the granularity (larger or less specific groups of customers), the less useful the information is for marketing and sales purposes but the easier the analysis becomes.

Two approaches have been identified:

- Individual bottom-up customer profitability analysis.
- Top down customer profitability analysis.

Carrying out a customer profitability analysis is where most companies start the process of managing customers profitably. Before we begin, a quick reminder of what customer profitability analysis is: it is the calculation of the historic profit (or, more often, the contribution before overheads) of a customer during a preceding period, usually a year.

> Definition of customer profitability:
>
> A 'snapshot' of the profit or contribution from a customer (or group of customers) during a previous period, usually a year.

Technically, if the calculation includes a full allocation of overheads (such as IT, HR, other central office functions, etc.), it is a true customer profitability analysis. In practice, most or all overheads are outside the control of the sales or marketing functions and moreover their inclusion in customer profitability analysis makes the analysis extremely difficult to complete. For these two reasons, most overheads (except customer-specific ones) are often left out of the customer profitability analysis. In this case, it would be more correct to speak of a customer contribution analysis rather than a customer profitability analysis, although most managers use the latter term.

Individual customer profitability analysis

The building block of customer profitability is individual customer profitability analysis. This literally means customer-by-customer analysis of revenues and costs. Individual customer profitability analysis is the most appropriate method where an organization has a few large customers ('key accounts'). Even where there are thousands or even millions of customers, the calculations can still be carried out, but this will need to be done by the customer relationship management (CRM) system rather than manually.

The basic calculation of customer profitability is as follows:

Customer profitability = customer revenue − (costs of goods sold + costs to serve + customer-specific overheads)

Thus, customer profitability (CP) during a specific period such as the previous year, t0, equals the revenues obtained from that customer (CR) during the period, less the total customer-specific costs. There are three elements of customer-specific costs: the cost of goods sold (COGS); the costs to serve (CTS); and customer-specific overheads (CSO). COGS could be the direct product costs, or the costs of delivering services, or both. CTS is likely to include sales, marketing, customer service, and customer management costs. CSO might be the cost of providing dedicated warehousing space for a customer. CSO will probably only be incurred for the largest customers.

So, the approach to customer profitability analysis used here can be summarized as

$$CP_{t0} = CR_{t0} - (COGS_{t0} + CTS_{t0} + CSO_{t0})$$

Customer profitability analysis can be tricky to calculate, so there is a general rule that will be used throughout this calculation: fit for purpose.

Fit for purpose

The objective of carrying out a customer profitability analysis is to make better-informed marketing and sales decisions. This means that the customer profitability analysis has to be fit for purpose. It does not have to be perfect.

A 'fit for purpose' customer profitability analysis tells you *accurately* what the relative profitability of your customers is, and *approximately* what their absolute profitability is.

Many customer profitability analysis projects get bogged down in detail. Aim for 80% right. Get all the big numbers correct (the large elements of cost) and estimate the smaller, less important cost elements.

Figure 3.1 illustrates how customer revenues can be broken down into four elements:

- cost of goods sold (direct cost of goods or services);
- costs to serve (sales, marketing, customer service and management);
- customer-specific overheads;
- profit from that customer (what is left when the costs have been deducted).

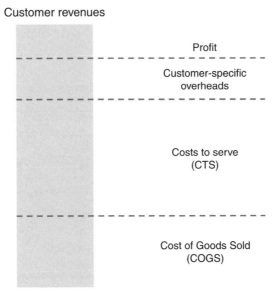

Figure 3.1 Customer revenues, costs, and profitability

The situation illustrated in Figure 3.1 is typical of what many companies find when they analyse customer profitability, which is that the largest element is the costs to serve the customer. This is because of a trend known as 'servicization'. Increasingly,

> Costs to serve are often the most sizeable element of costs, and are rising faster than other cost elements.

customers demand a higher service level from their suppliers. In business-to-business markets, for example, suppliers have had to implement key account management (KAM) processes that might include international harmonization of service standards. This has driven up their costs to serve, particularly for larger and more demanding customers. In business-to-consumer markets, companies are under pressure to provide integrated multi-channel access to their products, involving considerable investment in CRM systems. Research in the US has revealed a similar pattern: costs to serve are often the most sizeable element of costs, and costs to serve are rising faster than other cost elements.

As Figure 3.1 indicates, profit is what is left from customer revenues (CR) when the three cost elements (COGS, CTS, and CSO) have been deducted. So, to calculate customer profitability, we need to determine what customer revenues are and then look at how to calculate the three cost elements.

Customer revenues

The starting point when calculating customer revenues is to find out the number of each type of product that the customer bought during that period, and then multiply it by the product price (Table 3.1).

Table 3.1 Illustrative customer revenue calculation

Customer:..			
	A	**B**	**C**
Product	**Quantity purchased in period**	**Price (£)**	**Revenues (A x B) (£)**
Product X	10	100	1000
Product Y	10	50	500
Product Z	10	10	100
		Total customer revenues:	1600

Table 3.1 shows that this customer bought 10 units of Product X at £100 each, 10 units of Product Y at £50 each, and 10 units of Product Z at £10 each, giving a total customer revenue of £1600.

Where to get customer revenue data

Broadly speaking, customer revenue data come from invoices. Sadly, this is a deceptively simple explanation and there are a number of points that need attention:

- Is the customer picture complete?
- Do all invoices include the same information?
- What about returns?
- What happens if the revenue hasn't been received yet?

Is the customer picture complete?

Although the customer revenue concept is straightforward, it can be difficult to identify all of a customer's purchases during the year.

In business-to-business markets, identifying customer revenues is complicated by two issues, one internal and one external. The internal issue is that the supplier may be divided into several business units, so that information on customers is held in multiple business units. There may even be a reluctance to share customer information on the basis that 'it's *my* customer'. This led to a serious problem for one business-to-business supplier of building and engineering services.

> The information on customers may be held in multiple business units and there may even be a reluctance to share customer information between business units.

Failing to recognize the importance of a customer

This building and engineering company had grown both organically and by acquisition, resulting in a complex organizational structure comprising 25 business units. There was little internal cohesion and a complex transfer pricing mechanism that meant some business units actually preferred to bid for projects with competitors rather than with partner business units, because they felt they 'made more money'. The result was that the organization was heavily silo-based and not able readily to identify its largest overall customers.

Several years ago, the company completed an out-of-town retail development for a major global retailer. Many of the business units were involved in
the development, including the roofing division. Two weeks after the retailer
moved into its new store, the roof began to leak.

The retailer approached the roofing division to complain about the roof. The
roofing division, regarding the retailer as one customer among many, refused
to take responsibility on the grounds that the retailer had signed off on the
work. Eventually, the exasperated retailer brought in another contractor who
fixed the roof.

Over the subsequent four years, the retailer spent many hundreds of millions
of dollars on developing new sites around the world. How much of this work
did the building and engineering company get? Absolutely none! Moreover, it
took some serious diplomacy and apologies from a main Board director of the
supplier before the retailer would even talk to them again.

The external (customer) issue in business-to-business markets is that customers
may trade under different business names, and so the revenue data collection process needs to recognize and allocate the revenue correctly. This problem can be
particularly acute where the supplier trades with an international customer; it is
not uncommon for global companies to have a multiplicity of trading names and
business identities. If the customer has very different trading names in Kansas and
Kazakhstan, this can make it difficult for the supplier to identify that both sets of
business come from a single customer.

In business-to-consumer markets, the problem is usually one of data cleansing
and de-duplicating. Customer records can get confused and/or duplicated where
customers change name, move house, or some other details about them change or
have not been correctly recorded. Problems can even arise for some companies if
customers buy through more than one channel. Any of these confusions can result
in the creation of an additional customer record, or even of several duplicates.
The supplier now thinks it has two or more customers when, in fact, it has one.
Data cleansing and de-duplication is one of the big areas needing attention when
companies install CRM systems. The fact that cleansing and de-duplication services
are such big business indicates the extent of the problem.

The suspicious case of the elderly customers

Several years ago, as part of its CRM system installation, a leading UK retail
bank asked a data consultancy to cleanse and de-duplicate its customer data.
The consultants reported back that 10% of the customer base appeared to be
well over 90 years old! Not only this, but all of them had been born on the

same day: 11th November, 1911. It turned out that branch and call centre staff that had to enter data into this field were often embarrassed about asking a customer's date of birth. They soon found they could enter pretty well any number and the system would accept it. So, they simply keyed in 11/11/11 and the customer base became suspiciously elderly . . . .

The examples of the engineering company and the retail bank are a warning that customer revenue data may not be as straightforward to collect as it seems. There can also be different invoicing practices between different business units or international divisions that need to be considered.

Do all invoices contain the same information?

Even within the same company, there can be different invoicing practices. This is something that needs to be considered when trying to calculate the customer profitability of a large business-to-business customer. The invoice price (shaded in Table 3.2 below) may not in fact be the actual, or realized, price. Moreover, the invoice price may include or exclude different aspects of revenue. These points are illustrated by the PaperCo* example.

What is included in the invoice price?

PaperCo* is a Scandinavian manufacturer of paper products. It has operations in the USA, Western and Eastern Europe, and Latin America (the latter mostly through local agents). The company is divided into three major geographical regions.

As part of a customer profitability study, PaperCo asked managers to examine customer revenue information from invoice data in each of these three main regions. However, it quickly became clear that there were differences between the information included on the invoices. The Finance Director summarized the differences in invoicing (Table 3.2).

Table 3.2 shows some important differences between what is and what is not included on the invoices of this company across three international divisions. Not only are there multiple discounting structures, there are also different campaigns and special offers to be taken into account and, in Latin America, the agents' commission is treated differently to the way it is treated in the US. In addition, in the US, the loyalty discount is incorporated into the invoice price, whereas in Europe and Latin America it is taken 'below the line'.

Table 3.2　Differing invoicing practices within PaperCo*

US	Europe	Latin America
PaperCo list price	PaperCo list price	PaperCo list price
Customer negotiated price	**Customer negotiated price**	Agent-negotiated discount
	Product mix discount	**Customer negotiated price**
Agent-negotiated discount	**Invoice price**	Special offer on one product
Agent fee	Free goods supplied	Other discounts
Logistics discount	Loyalty discount	Campaign discount
Repalletizing fee	Special offer discount	Clearance discount
Lead time discount	Delivery credit	Quantity discount
Loyalty discount	Loyalty discount	**Invoice price**
Trade advertised discount	Campaign discount	Customer-specific discount
Environmental charge	Other discounts	Product mix discount
Invoice price	**Realized price**	Loyalty discount
Other discounts		Co-load discount
Realized price		**Realized price**

*The name of this company has been changed for reasons of commercial confidentiality.

Strictly, when analysing customer profitability, price discounts should be treated as reducing customer revenue (rather than increasing costs). Thus, it is the revenues after price discounts that should be used in the calculation. Other forms of discount, though, such as early payment discounts or rebates, should be treated as increasing the cost to serve (rather than as revenue reductions).

What about returns?

Returns (goods or entire deliveries) that are sent back by the customer need to be considered in some customer relationships. For example, two business-to-consumer examples would be mail order and Internet ordering (excluding food), where the proportion of purchased items that are returned can be very high. Some research suggests that up to 30% of catalogue-ordered clothing may be returned. Returns may need to be netted off from the customer revenue, because they are effectively 'negative revenue' if a refund is to be given. If replacement goods are to be provided, the revenue can still be recognized although the costs to serve may be higher because of the double delivery.

The situation is somewhat different in business-to-business, where returns or refused deliveries are likely to be for quality reasons or because the supplier has missed its delivery slot. Often, the revenue will still be countable in the customer profitability analysis calculation because the customer will expect redelivery.

In business-to-business services, such as management consultancy or legal services, there can be considerable uncertainty about what the actual customer revenues (as opposed to the invoiced amounts) will turn out to be. This problem will be discussed further in the next section.

What happens if the revenue hasn't been received yet?

There are two kinds of circumstances in which customer revenues may be extremely uncertain: multi-year projects, such as those that characterize the construction industry; and professional services such as legal services.

Multi-year projects are often paid for in stages. The problem is that stage payments may distort the apparent annual revenues from a customer (in fact, this problem is one of the limitations in the use of customer profitability analysis for marketing and sales decision making). Depending on the project milestones, there might be two big payments in one year and then nothing the next. Sometimes there will be an initial payment up-front, before the supplier has done much work, in which case measuring customer profitability would make the customer appear very profitable at the beginning of the relationship and much less profitable in later years.

Accountants deal with the timing problem by using the concept of 'accruals'. In addition to the *actual* customer revenue received during the year, the accrued revenues (work done but not yet paid for) could be recognized as part of customer revenues. Accruals are a standard concept in profitability measurement but they do not relate to cash flows.

There is a more general problem in many businesses of work done or goods sold that have been invoiced but the customer has not yet paid. Again, because it is profit that is being measured here, the accruals concept can be invoked and the amounts can be recognized as part of customer revenues for the year[1].

In *business-to-business professional services*, such as legal, consultancy, or professional services[2], there are some complex issues relating to the way in which such services firms invoice and also how they measure performance. In these cases, there is no tangible product and it may be difficult to ensure consistency of performance. Different people may tackle the same task in different ways and, indeed, the same individual may complete the same task in different ways on different occasions.

---

[1] Technical point: this may lead to double-counting of accrued revenue where customer lifetime value is also to be calculated.
[2] I am indebted to Chris Howe, Divisional Business Director for Addleshaw Goddard, the major legal practice, for advice and input into the section on customer profitability analysis in professional services.

For this reason, professional services firms tend to measure the input of hours spent on a task and then cost that in terms of a standard cost for an individual of a certain pay grade. Thus, they measure the number of hours they spend working on a particular customer's business and then multiply this number by the hourly rate for that level of employee (associate, junior partner, senior partner) and the total presented to the client. The hourly rate will include a percentage profit margin, although market forces may affect the profit margin that a professional services firm can obtain. Interestingly, this can mean that staff of different grades are differentially profitable, and it is not necessarily the case that partners or directors commanding higher hourly rates are more profitable for the business. Therefore, the way in which a job is resourced and staffed can substantially affect its profitability.

Obviously, a system in which firms charge by time spent is hardly conducive to tight control of costs. This is even more so where the internal performance measurement of the professional services firm is based on the number of hours that the lawyer, accountant, architect, consultant, etc. bills to the client, meaning that they have an incentive to bill as many hours as possible. Moreover, the client will sometimes take the view that certain work carried out in relation to a legal case is background or overhead work, which should be carried by the law firm, rather than work that should be billed to itself.

Therefore, some clients insist on a fixed price for a job. The supplier will then use the standard rate for the job and the number of hours to evaluate whether this is 'good' or 'bad' business to win.

The performance of professional services firms, and important inputs into their customer profitability calculations, is based on an assessment of utilization, realization, and recovery.

Utilization is an internal performance calculation of resource usage – whether the firm has enough people for the work available. Utilization is calculated as

$$\text{Utilization} = \frac{\text{Hours booked on work}}{\text{Total hours available}}$$

The 'total hours available' calculation is based on 7 or 8 hours a day, 5 days per week. This means that utilization can be more than 100% where people are working long hours or at weekends.

Utilization is widely used as a performance measure in, for example, management consultancy firms, but it does have certain drawbacks. For example, just because a person or a department has high utilization, this does not mean that they are engaged on profitable work. Moreover, excessively high utilization can be damaging not only to the health of the individual but also to the future prospects of the firm. For example, the development of new products, services, and client relationships requires non-billable time that reduces apparent utilization, unless the system is administered carefully to take account of business development activities.

The problem with utilization is that it measures how busy people in the firm are, not how profitable their activities are. Utilization is about volume, not profits. In fact, there could be a temptation for less-busy employees to 'pad' their time with low value work in order to reach utilization targets. The firm itself can also suffer from over-fixation on inappropriate volume targets. High utilization does not mean that the firm is actually making any money on its business. Customer profitability analysis may reveal that customers who pay higher prices or buy more expensive products are more profitable, even if there is a higher proportion of 'down time' (lower utilization). Utilization is a useful measure of performance but it should not be used in isolation without an accompanying profitability analysis.

To help overcome this potential pitfall, many legal and professional services firms measure realization[3]. Realization is the price achieved (what the client actually paid, per hour) compared to the standard rate. It is usually expressed as a percentage:

$$\text{Realization} = \frac{\text{Actual per-hour rate} \times 100}{\text{Standard rate per hour}}$$

If there is a difference between the actual and standard hourly rates, this can be thought of as a price discount (if the standard rate is higher than the actual rate) or as a price premium (if the actual rate is higher than the standard rate).

Realization is widely used by professional services firms as a proxy for profitability. Generally, a higher percentage realization is associated with higher profitability. However, care needs to be taken when comparing one client or job with another. Just because the firm achieves higher realization on one client compared to another, does not necessarily make the first client more profit-generating. It will depend how much profit was incorporated into the standard rate, and the mix of resources used on each. Professional services firms that have been successful in driving up client – and firm – profitability have often done so through changing the resource mix, using a higher proportion of junior staff to deliver work and carefully managing the delivery of results through robust quality processes.

Note
Begin the customer profitability analysis with a customer revenues calculation. Be careful about where the revenues information comes from, ensuring that you are happy with the way that returns, etc. are treated.

Once the customer revenues have been calculated, there are three cost elements that need to be subtracted to determine the profitability of that customer:

- direct cost of goods or services sold;
- costs to serve; and
- customer-specific overheads.

Each of these three cost elements, and how to calculate them, will now be examined.

---

[3] Some firms refer to this as 'recovery'.

Cost of goods or services sold

Having established per-customer revenues, the next step is to find out how much (directly) the products that the customer bought actually cost to make, or how much the services purchased directly cost to deliver. Thus, these costs are sometimes referred to as 'direct costs'.

For manufactured products, direct product costs are usually calculated as the direct costs of production divided by the number of items produced. Raw materials and manufacturing labour costs would be considered to be direct costs of production. Packaging, too, would be typically considered to be part of the direct cost of manufactured goods, because it is unlikely that a product could be delivered without packaging and the packaging costs usually vary closely with the amount of product sold.

For services businesses, direct costs largely comprise people costs. So, the direct costs of services are typically calculated as the number of hours or days worked, multiplied by the hourly or daily rate of that person. As well as salary costs, 'on-costs' may also be added in. On-costs are the costs of employing someone, such as pension and national insurance contributions, their holiday pay, and sometimes the physical cost of their office space, etc. A general rule for on-costs is that they are about 40% of basic salary, although this varies according to individual company and regulatory environment.

Sometimes, associates (non-employees or subcontractors) are used to deliver a piece of work. In this case, the direct costs are usually clear, because they are the amounts invoiced by the associate. On-costs are usually assumed to be zero, because most associates do not receive company pensions, although some companies add on an administration charge that covers the company's costs of finding and processing the associate.

The components of COGS

The basic rule for calculating direct COGS is that it measures what is used up in the production of goods and services. So, raw materials and time are clearly used up and are important components of COGS. However, the detailed components of COGS may vary, and it is important that the main components of COGS specific to each company are identified so that a reasonably accurate picture of customer profitability can be built up (Table 3.3).

> To build up a reasonably accurate picture of customer profitability, it is important to identify the main components of COGS that the company takes into account.

Table 3.3 sets out some of the items that are usually, although not always, included in COGS and provides a checklist to help you to determine how COGS is defined in

Table 3.3 The components of COGS

COLUMN A		COLUMN B	
Checklist for physical goods and products	**Included**	**Checklist for service businesses**	**Included**
Order processing		Order processing	
Raw materials		People/time costs	
Processing costs		Subcontractor costs	
Technical service/consultancy		Technical service/consultancy	
Special grades/sizes		On-costs	
Special finishing		Administration costs relating to people or associate costs	
Packaging			
Customer-specific equipment costs			
Logistics			

your company (bearing in mind that COGS data are usually collected already under the heading of 'product profitability'.

Three elements (order processing, logistics, and technical service) may or may not be included in COGS. Order processing can be calculated on an activity costing basis, or it could be taken as the average or standard cost of processing an order, multiplied by the number of orders the customer has placed during the period. Occasionally, order processing is considered to be part of costs to serve. The same is true of logistics and technical service, which some companies treat as part of direct COGS, whereas other companies think of logistics costs as part of costs to serve.

Where there are special finishes to the product, or where equipment is specific to a customer, these costs are likely to be treated as part of COGS, as is packaging.

Using COGS

Because there is no hard and fast rule about which costs are direct and which are indirect, it is important to gain an understanding about which cost components are included in COGS and which are not. This is particularly true of logistics costs for manufactured or assembled goods, because these can vary considerably from customer to customer

> Logistics costs for manufactured or assembled goods can vary considerably from customer to customer and have a substantial impact on customer profitability.

and can have a substantial impact on customer profitability. Table 3.3 is designed to help sales and marketing managers determine how COGS is defined in their firm. Space is provided for additional cost components that may be included. Use column A for physical product COGS, and column B for services COGS; use both columns if the firm provides both to the customer.

Cost elements listed in Table 3.3 that are *not* included in COGS should either be recorded as N/A (not applicable) or they should be considered under costs to serve (see Table 3.4). Sales and marketing managers are advised to discuss the composition of COGS with their finance department or operations managers.

$$\frac{\text{Direct costs of production}}{\text{Number of items produced}} \times \text{No of items customer bought}$$

This means that the manufacturing division or finance department add up, usually for each separate product line, the direct costs of raw materials and manufacturing labour costs that were used in the manufacture of a product. The packaging costs would typically be included as part of the COGS, because it is unlikely that a product could be delivered without packaging and the packaging costs usually vary directly with the amount of product sold.

Costs to serve

Costs to serve (CTS) are the indirect costs that are incurred in providing goods or services. CTS are vital to the development and ongoing management of the relationship, but they are not directly related to a specific product or transaction.

Broadly speaking, costs to serve are about sales, marketing, and customer service. Therefore, CTS is about pre-, during-, and post-transaction costs. Customer-specific logistics costs may also be included if they were not already taken into account as part of COGS.

CTS are also known as 'Sales, Administration and General' or 'SAG' costs.

Most companies find that costs to serve are a large cost element and are also growing fast as customers demand higher service levels. This is particularly true in key account relationships, where the cost of the key account manager or KAM team may be considerable.

> Allocating CTS to customers according to the amount of business that the customer does is likely to give a seriously misleading picture of their relative profitability.

A common mistake that companies make when carrying out customer profitability analysis is to calculate their overall costs of sales, marketing, etc. and then allocate these costs to customers according to the amount of business that the customer does (revenues or volumes). This is a dangerous practice because it is likely to give a seriously misleading picture of the relative profitability of different customers. Although it is generally true that larger customers cost more to service than smaller customers do, it is absolutely not the case that each large customer or each small customer takes up equal amounts of resource. As every salesperson or customer manager knows, some customers are comparatively straightforward to do business with while others need a lot of 'hand holding', either through the sales process or in terms of post-purchase support. Pretending that customers need support that is proportional to their purchasing amounts is likely to lead to poor allocation of sales and marketing resources.

> You get some customers who want their hands held for every single process and that can end up taking hours and hours of extra work . . . The fact of the matter is, we don't really want to have to have one person who sits there and 'hand-holds' somebody unless that particular customer is so valuable to us, that it makes it worth that expenditure of resource.
>
> Key account manager, business-to-business insurance

Some customers buy in a very efficient manner, using low-cost channels, placing their orders quickly in large order quantities, requiring centralized delivery of standard products, etc. Other customers use up a lot of sales or service time or they may have non-standard requirements such as customized products or particular invoicing arrangements. Although some of these additional costs (such as the direct additional costs of customized products or packaging) may be picked up as part of COGS, there may be some additional development or service time that also needs to be added in.

Service businesses also find that the costs to serve certain customers differ from others and that this is not related linearly to the size of the project or fees. Thus, some customers have longer sales cycles that require greater expenditure of effort by the sales team; or they have complex tendering processes; or they make frequent changes during the life of a project that not only affect the direct cost of delivery but also require additional administration or project management time to implement.

It cannot be stressed strongly enough that costs to serve are an important determinant of customer profitability, and that allocating them proportional to customer revenues is simplistic and likely to be misleading. Customers behave differently in their relationships with suppliers, and these differences profoundly affect their relative profitability. CTS need to be taken

> Costs to serve are an important determinant of customer profitability.

seriously and, as far as possible, need to be allocated to the customers to which they relate. Table 3.4 lists the main components of CTS.

Table 3.4 The components of costs to serve (CTS)

Physical goods and products	Service businesses
Marketing materials	Marketing materials
Sales costs: sales visits, tendering, contracts, etc.	Sales costs: sales visits, tendering, contracts, etc.
Order processing, if not included in COGS Channel costs	Commission or third party payments if not included in COGS
Administration costs (desk-based account management, letters, statements, raising contracts, invoicing, credit notes, etc.)	Administration costs (desk-based account or project management, telephone support, letters, statements, raising contracts, invoicing, credit notes, etc.)
Key account management (dedicated manager or team that supports larger or more important customers)	Key account management (dedicated manager or team that supports larger or more important clients)
Senior management time supporting account relationship	Senior management time supporting account relationship
Other marketing (during and after-sales service, technical support, training)	Other marketing (during and after-sales service, technical support, training)
Product development/technical	Specialist advice

The components of costs to serve for manufacturing and for services are relatively similar. Some of the components (such as KAM) are specific to business-to-business relationships but others (such as order processing) are common to business-to-business and business-to-consumer.

Table 3.4 illustrates another aspect of costs to serve, which is that some costs are much bigger than others, and are also more likely to vary between customers. Thus, invoicing costs – the costs of actually raising an invoice – are relatively small and are pretty much the same whether the customer is large or small (although the actual number of invoices raised may be very much greater for a bigger customer). For calculating these smaller, repetitive, and relatively standard operations, a process called standard costing is used. Other costs shown in Table 3.4, such as key account management, represent bigger 'chunks' of cost and also differ more between customers. For example, medium sized and smaller customers are not offered key account management and so these costs are not allocated to them. For larger and more variable cost items, the precise cost of the activity for each customer needs to be worked out using an activity-based costing approach.

> For smaller and more standard operations, use **standard costs**.
>
> For larger and more variable costs, use **an activity-based costing approach**.

The following two sections demonstrate how to apply the two approaches to calculating costs to serve (standard costs and activity-based costing).

Standard costs

The standard cost of an operation such as invoicing is the average or typical cost of doing it. Standard costs are used in calculating customer profitability where the cost item is relatively small but the same item recurs frequently, such as raising invoices or credit notes, sending statements, or sending letters or emails.

The standard cost of an item can be calculated by considering a set of such activities, such as raising a series of invoices, and then dividing the total cost by the number of invoices in that batch to give an average cost per invoice. So, if on a typical day an administrator takes the whole day to raise 10 invoices and the cost to the company is £80 per day, the standard cost for raising an invoice is £80/10 or £8. The standard cost does not necessarily reflect the actual cost of raising a particular invoice, but it is an approximation and accurate enough on smaller items. In this case, half of the invoices might have been pages long and taken twice as long as the others to raise, but the difference in cost (perhaps £12 for a long invoice versus £6 for a short one) is so small that it will make very little difference to the overall profitability of the customer, and so the standard cost is used.

There are recognized techniques for calculating standard costs that are outside the scope of this book, but the standard costs that need to be used for customer profitability analysis can be obtained from the finance director.

Once the standard cost is known, all the sales or account manager has to do is to find out how many letters, invoices, credit notes, and statements were sent to the key account during the period and multiply the number sent by the standard cost of each (Table 3.5).

For service businesses with a very large customer base, such as a bank, customer administration may also be treated as a standard cost of £X per year, rather than worrying about small variations in administration costs across millions of customers.

Table 3.5   Applying standard costs

Item	Standard cost (£)	Number of items sent to customer during period	Total item cost (£)
Email	5	20	100
Invoice	8	10	80
Credit note	15	1	15
Statement	5	12	60
		Total:	£ 255

Activity-based costing approaches

Activity-based costing (ABC) is used for the larger and more variable elements of costs to serve, such as key account management or complex sales processes.

ABC is about calculating the actual costs associated with performing certain tasks or delivering services. It is useful where an activity varies from customer to customer, such as with a complex business-to-business sales process for which standard costs would not be appropriate.

Usually, ABC is associated with the time that people spend on servicing a particular customer. Thus, the activity-based cost of key account management is calculated as the number of hours spent by each person in the KAM team multiplied by their hourly rate (but, if the key account manager is dedicated to a single key account, the activity-based cost is simply that manager's annual cost).

Full ABC projects are complex and sophisticated, and provide very detailed and accurate information. However, for most sales and marketing purposes, a simpler form of activity-based approach is more than adequate. Two examples of simple activity-based approaches are given in the following box.

Simple activity-based costing approaches

A financial services company that had only introduced key account management (KAM) a year before, decided it wanted a 'quick and dirty' view of the costs of its KAM operation to make sure that costs were not getting out of hand. On the face of it, this was a complex KAM operation with 5 KAM team members and a number of administrators looking after 18 key accounts. To his relief, the business unit director quickly discovered that the staff involved fell into three pay grades – administrator, key account manager, and senior manager. He was able to work out the approximate day rate for each role. Then, he asked some administrators, the key account managers, and the senior manager to keep a diary of where they were spending their time. They were asked to note down major activities and chunks of time – days and half-days spent in meetings or on client visits, for example. After three months, the diaries were analysed. By focusing on the big chunks of cost, this director was quickly able to attribute about 80% of his sales, marketing, and admin costs to specific clients.

A small software company had recently been spun off from its parent company in a management buy-out. Most of the business still came from the former parent company, but the company had had some success in attracting a limited number of new accounts. The management team was anxious to ensure the correct balance of activity between managing the relationship with the parent company, managing new key accounts, and working on customer acquisition activities. This was a very IT-literate company and so it used data from electronic diaries, combined with a staff survey, to create a spreadsheet showing what percentage of their time the managers were spending on a variety of duties. Each quarter the managers were sent an email listing the proportions of time they had previously reported and asking them to update the record. This system was moderately expensive in time and effort to set up, but very quick for the managers to update. Consequently, the response rate to the quarterly questionnaire was very high. The tracking system meant that the quality of activity-based data improved over time.

Technology can help provide activity-based costing information. Many call centre management packages incorporate a feature that allows for the tracking of both inbound and outbound calls. This feature

> Technology can be used to help identify where the salesperson spends his or her time.

can be used to allocate the costs of desk-based account managers or support staff between the clients they service. Similarly, some Sales Force Automation IT packages can provide data about where salespeople spend their time. Useful customer profitability data are also available through some enterprise or CRM systems such as SAP.

Note

Consider implementing a simple activity-based system for capturing cost to serve information. This is particularly useful where a few customers are taking up a disproportionate amount of time. It may be worth sharing some of this information with the customer, and investing in processes to reduce the amount of time spent on the customer.

By this point, the main elements of a customer profitability analysis are in place: customer revenues, cost of goods and services, and costs to serve. The general overheads of the business, such as heating, lighting, rent and rates, other premises costs, Head Office costs, IT costs, and HR costs, are disregarded here because they do not affect relative customer profitability, and it is relative profitability that is most useful for sales and marketing decision making.

However, there is one additional cost element that needs to be considered in business-to-business relationships with larger customers: customer-specific overheads.

Customer-specific overheads

Customer-specific overheads are only relevant where the acquisition of a new customer would result in additional overheads for the business. For most customer profitability analysis calculations this is not the case although there are a few instances where the acquisition of, for example, an important new key account, would involve the company in some additional overhead expenditure.

> Customer-specific overheads are only relevant where the acquisition of a new customer would result in additional overheads for the business.

Customer-specific overheads might include a branch office within a key account's premises, or an on-site team, or customer-specific stock in a dedicated area of the warehouse. Because customer-specific overheads can involve substantial investment on the supplier's part, they should be included in the calculation of customer profitability.

The way in which the costs of customer-specific overheads are calculated will depend on the precise service that is offered. For example, an on-site team at the customer could be calculated on an activity cost basis, taking into account the salaries of the team and any additional costs the supplier incurred. Customer-specific stock might include some activity-based costs, such as a proportion of the warehouse manager's time, but there may also be a pro-rata element in terms of rent, rates, heating, lighting, and handling the customer-specific stock that is taken to be a percentage of the total rent, rates, etc.

Where there is customer-specific stock that cannot be used for other purposes, it may also be appropriate to include a cost of capital charge, because the supplier has to tie up money in holding the customer-specific stock that it could otherwise use elsewhere in the business. This could be calculated as:

> It is appropriate to include a cost of capital charge where the supplier has to tie up capital that it could otherwise use elsewhere in the business.

$$\text{Cost of capital charge} = \text{Value of stock} \times \text{Cost of Capital}$$

The value of stock and cost of capital figures are readily available from the finance department. However, it should be noted that the cost of capital charge derived in this way is unlikely to reflect the real risk, which includes a risk that the customer-specific stock remains unused or becomes damaged or obsolete (or is even stolen) and eventually has to be written off by the supplier. Supply chain professionals use a general rule for total stock holding costs (including handling, storage, damage, obsolescence, etc.), which is that the value of stock depreciates by 25–30% per annum. It may be worth comparing that figure to the cost of capital charge. If large amounts of customer-specific stock are held, the actual costs of doing so may be understated using the cost of capital charge method.

The cost of capital issue is also one that affects services businesses such as insurance and banking. Here, large contracts with customers may have to be supported by ring-fencing some of the supplier's capital. Sometimes this could be for regulatory reasons relating to capital adequacy. In other circumstances, customers themselves may require evidence of financial backing. Again, cost of capital figures can be obtained from the finance department.

Completing the customer profitability calculation

At this point, the four elements of the customer profitability analysis calculation are in place:

- customer revenues;
- COGS;
- costs to serve; and
- customer-specific overheads (if relevant).

To complete the customer profitability analysis calculation, the cost elements need to be subtracted from customer revenues (Table 3.6, in which some notional figures are included for illustration purposes).

The customer in Table 3.6 generated revenues of $1000 last year (time period −1). The cost of goods and services was $350 and so a supplier that looked no further than this and failed to take costs to serve into account might conclude that this was a valuable customer. In fact, this is a difficult customer and the costs to serve are $550, far exceeding the direct costs of goods and services. In addition, there are some customer-specific overheads of $50, meaning that the bottom line for this customer is a relatively modest $50.

Table 3.6 Completing the calculation of customer profitability

Period t = −1	Customer
	. . . .
Revenues	1000
Costs of goods and services (COGS)	(350)
Costs to serve (CTS – sales, marketing, key account management, logistics, customer-specific admin)	(550)
Customer-specific overheads (stock held for customer, branch at customer site, cost of capital)	(50)
Customer profit	50

Once the customer profitability analysis has been completed for all customers, it can be used to help with three marketing decisions, as described in the previous chapter:

- customer dependency;
- balancing customer acquisition and customer retention;
- understanding payback period.

Note

Now you can get started on your customer profitability analysis using the worksheets on the following pages!

Worksheets for customer profitability analysis

CUSTOMER PROFITABILITY ANALYSIS

Customer: [   ]   Year: [   ]

A. Customer revenue calculation

Product or service line	Revenues

Total revenues: [   ]

Insert a formula in the total revenues box that will sum the revenues. In a spreadsheet this will update automatically. In a Word table, it will need to be updated manually by right-clicking on the box and selecting 'update field'.

B. Customer COGS calculation

Cost of goods or services	Costs
Order processing	
Raw materials	
Processing costs	
People/time costs	
On-costs	
Subcontractor costs	
Admin relating to subcontractors	
Technical service/consultancy	
Special grades/sizes	
Special finishing	
Packaging	
Customer-specific equipment costs	
Logistics	

Total COGS:

Modify the list of costs as appropriate for each customer.

Insert a formula in the total COGS box that will sum the COGS.

C. Customer CTS calculation

Cost to serve	Costs
Marketing materials	
Sales costs	
Order processing	
Channel costs/commission	
Admin costs	
Key account management	
Senior management time	
Other marketing costs	
Product/Technical/Specialist	

Total CTS:

Modify the list of costs as appropriate for each customer.

Insert a formula in the total CTS box that will sum the CTS.

D. Customer-specific overheads calculation

Customer-specific overheads | **Costs**

Customer-specific overheads	Costs
On-site manager or team	
Customer-specific stock	
Cost of capital	

Total customer-specific overheads |

Modify the list of costs as appropriate.

Insert a formula in the total customer-specific overheads box that will sum the overhead costs.

Where to find out more

Wilson, C. (1996) *Profitable Customers: How to Identify, Develop and Retain them*, Kogan Page, London. *One of the earliest books on customer profitability analysis but does contain some useful and clear guidelines, especially in Chapter 4 (pp. 49-60).*

How to calculate customer profitability for large customer numbers

4

What's in this chapter

- Top-down customer profitability analysis
- Customer profitability decision trees
- The factors that drive customer profitability
- Using top-down customer profitability analysis

Key concepts discussed in this chapter

Classification data	Data that describe and classify individuals or companies. Classification data for individuals in a business-to-consumer analysis might include their gender, age, postcode, income bracket, socio-economic group, how they use the product or service, whether there are other family members who are also customers, their satisfaction level or other attitudinal data, and how they are classified in the company's existing segmentation. Classification data in a business-to-business analysis might include size of customer firm, location, number of employees, industry sector or SIC code, purchasing process, attitudinal data, and segment classification.
Customer payback period	The number of months or years that it takes for a customer to become profitable, once the costs of acquiring the customer have been taken into account. So, if the customer generates profits of £10 per month and the acquisition cost of this customer was £100, the payback period is 10 months.

Decile	Divides the customer base into 10 equal tranches, from the biggest 10% of customers to the smallest 10%.
Decision tree	Way of mapping the possible decisions or combinations of factors, in this case the drivers of customer profitability
RFM/RFA	Recency, Frequency, and (Monetary) Amount: a tool developed to understand the drivers of revenue generation by customers. Does not take account of product mix purchased, which also affects customer revenues (see Chapter 3). Also, does not take account of costs.

Key tools explained in this chapter

- Decision tree analysis: A sophisticated analysis tool that is used here to think about what drives customer profitability and to create a map of the possibilities. The map takes the form of a tree, which begins with a single driver but rapidly branches out.
- Decile analysis: A less sophisticated but less useful approach that divides the customer base into 10 tranches, each with an equal number of customers, and then looks at how much profit each tranche delivers.

Two-minute chapter summary

Understanding individual customer profitability is vital for a company's largest and most important customers (its key accounts). However, individual customer profitability is cumbersome to calculate for large numbers of customers. In these circumstances it may be more effective to calculate top-down customer profitability.

One way to do this is to develop a 'decision tree', which identifies the factors that determine customer profitability. The data can then be analysed along these lines.

Decision trees do have the drawback that they branch time and time again, and so they can quickly become very complex. However, with a project team that includes IT support, the analysis can be carried out.

It is also useful to collect classification data such as age, income, and gender (or industry sector and customer firm size in business-to-business), so that customer profitability can be overlaid on to the classification data. If the company has an existing segmentation, it is also possible to compute the profitability of each segment by including the segment membership in the classification data.

The data can then be used to examine customer dependency, the balance between acquisition and retention activities, and the payback periods to a customer relationship.

Top-down customer profitability analysis

Individual customer profitability analysis gives a high level of granularity and provides a detailed and accurate picture of individual customers. It is particularly useful for looking at relationships with larger customers and key accounts. Individual customer profitability analysis is particularly important in these circumstances because key accounts are likely to use large amounts of sales, marketing, and customer service resource, and may also have customer-specific overheads. This means that simply looking at the basic costs of goods and services would not give any useful guide to the real profitability of these customers.

However, individual customer profitability analysis may be too detailed, or too time-consuming to calculate, for any other than the top few customers of the firm. For larger numbers of customers, or where less accuracy about individual customers is needed, a 'top down' approach may be preferred.

> For larger numbers of customers, or where less accuracy about individual customers is needed, a 'top-down' approach may be preferred.

The top-down approach starts from the total customer base and works down to the profitability of groups of customers. Thus, it gives a lower granularity and less detail, but can handle larger numbers of customers. This contrasts with individual customer profitability analysis, which is 'bottom up' – starting from individual customers. The sum total of all the individual customer profitability analyses would be the same as the total profitability of the firm. This latter point is the starting point for top-down customer profitability analysis.

This chapter describes a process for calculating top-down customer profitability analysis. It should be emphasized that, if the top-down approach to customer profitability analysis is used in a company that also has key accounts, the profitability of each key account should still be calculated 'bottom up'. In this case, the starting point for the top-down analysis of the rest of the customer base would be total profits minus the key account profits.

Customer profitability decision trees

The approach to top-down customer profitability analysis for large numbers of customers that will be described in this chapter is based on the idea of a decision tree.

Decision trees are a way of describing a series of decisions (in this case, about the factors driving customer profitability) that branch out as more and more decisions are made.

The decision tree approach to customer profitability analysis should be structured as a project. The project team should include sales and marketing, finance, and ideally, IT and market research people.

> Decision trees are a way of describing a series of decisions that 'branch out' as more and more decisions are made.

The project falls into four stages:

1. Identify the factors that drive customer profitability.
2. Decide the start point and the logical order for the factors.
3. Agree a pilot data set and test the tree structure.
4. Collect and use data.

Each of these four stages will now be described.

The factors that drive customer profitability

The first stage of the top-down customer profitability analysis project is to brainstorm the factors that drive customer profitability.

A good start for this brainstorming process is to think about the RFM factors: Recency, Frequency, and Monetary Value (RFM is also sometimes known as RFA, for Recency, Frequency, and Amount). RFM has been widely used in the past as the

> There is some research that shows that frequent purchasers are more likely than occasional purchasers to repurchase.

basis for customer profitability analysis of larger numbers of customers and it still represents a useful benchmark. Recency refers to how recently the customer purchased. It also helps to signal whether a customer account is still active (that is, whether the customer has been retained). Frequency refers to the number of times that a customer purchased within a certain period and is also thought to indicate loyalty. Certainly, there is some research that shows that frequent purchasers are more likely to repurchase than occasional purchasers. This has been demonstrated, for example, with gym membership, where people paying monthly are both more likely to use the gym and more likely to renew their membership than others who pay the same amount but as an annual lump sum.

Monetary Value, or Amount, is the revenues that customers generate. This in turn is affected by their frequency of purchase, so the two factors are not fully independent. Monetary value is also affected by the product mix, because customers buying more expensive products will tend to generate higher revenues.

The RFM model does not examine costs, and so these also need to be factored into the tree. For example, the channel through which the customer is acquired or managed may be an important factor in business-to-consumer markets. There will also be product costs and costs to serve (such as administration) to take into account.

Another cost that might become significant when considering large numbers of smaller customers is credit rating, because there is a cost to having customers credit rated and also because customers with poorer credit ratings may require more administration as more of them may get into difficulties with payments. Again, some of these factors may be interdependent. For example, customers through one channel (face-to-face, for instance) might have a better payment track record than customers through another channel (e.g., telephone call centre).

Table 4.1 lists some of the possible factors that might be taken into account when preparing the decision tree.

Table 4.1 Factors affecting customer profitability

Factor	Affected by	Relevant/not relevant
Recency	Product usage; purchasing patterns; procurement strategy	
Frequency	Product usage; need; reason for purchase	
Monetary value/Amount	Purchase mix; size/wealth of customer	
Product cost	Raw materials costs; manufacturing/ operations costs	
Costs to serve	Complexity of customer; relationship; purchasing patterns and behaviours	
Credit rating	Financial status of customer; other borrowing	

Ordering the factors

Once the factors are agreed, the basic shape of the tree needs to be agreed. This discussion may affect the factors that are thought to be important. The start point for the decision tree may not be obvious. For example, rather than starting with revenue drivers, as would be the case for a standard customer profitability analysis, it might be more useful to start with the channel that the customer mainly uses, or with their credit rating. It may take several iterations to arrive at a tree framework that can be used.

Figure 4.1 shows what such a tree framework might look like before it is populated. This tree is based on a simplified version of an actual customer profitability tree for a personal loans provider. The company makes loans from $1000–30 000 to individuals for purchases such as cars, holidays, home extensions, etc.

In this simplified version of the tree, three factors are thought to determine customer profitability. The credit rating of the customer affects the price at which the lending is done, the amount that is lent, and the likelihood that the customer will repay. The second factor, size of the loan, affects revenues. Performance is about what happens during the year – whether the customer pays off the loan or whether they renew it. Because of space limitations, not all of the branches of the tree are shown. On the 'size of loan' line, there are nine possible combinations. Since all of these could be either paid off or renewed, there should strictly be 18 customer tranches along the bottom of the tree, giving 30 tranches in total.

Agree a pilot data set and test the tree

It is good practice to test the tree with a small subset of the customer data, to ensure that the results it gives will be useful. An important aspect of this testing process is to select a subset of the data that is likely to be representative of the data set as a whole. So, for example, the data subset should not be selected from a period when particular promotions were running, because this would be likely to distort the results and make them unrepresentative of the rest of the year.

The results of the pilot should be reviewed by the team to see whether the tree will give useable results or whether the factors themselves or the order in which they are present in the tree needs to be reshaped.

Once the testing process is complete, the full data set can be run.

Using customer profitability data

Before the tree is run on the full customer data set, it is useful to decide what classification data are needed to help interpret the results.

> **Note**
>
> Before running the analysis, agree on the classification data that will also be needed. Without classification data, it will not be possible to fit the customers to the decision tree, or to identify key trends.

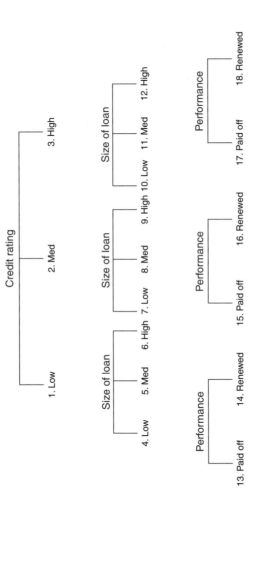

Figure 4.1 Customer profitability tree skeleton

Classification data are data that describe and classify the individuals or companies that are the subject of the customer profitability analysis. Thus, classification data for individuals in a business-to-consumer

> Classification data are data that describe and classify individuals or companies.

customer profitability analysis might include their gender, age, postcode, income bracket, socio-economic group, how they use the product or service, whether there are other family members who are also customers, their satisfaction level or other attitudinal data, and how they are classified in the company's existing segmentation.

Classification data for business-to-business customer profitability analysis might include size of customer firm, location, number of employees, industry sector, purchasing process, attitudinal data, and segment classification (Table 4.2).

Table 4.2 Classification data checklist

Business-to-business		Business-to-consumer	
Factor	Relevant (Y/N)	Factor	Relevant (Y/N)
Customer firm size		Gender	
Number of employees		Age range	
Location		Postcode	
Industry sector		Income bracket	
Purchasing process		Socio-economic group	
Attitude to us		Product usage	
Segment		Links to other customers	
		Attitude to us	
		Segment	

Once the data have been collected, they can be analysed. Here, the classification data can also be useful. For example, the profitability data can be overlaid against the current segmentation used within the company to calculate the profitability of existing segments.

Figure 4.2 illustrates what the completed customer profitability tree might look like.

Although this customer profitability tree is simplified and should have 30 customer tranches if all the branches in the tree were fully described, Figure 4.2 does help to illustrate some important features of the top-down approach.

The first thing to note is that each line of the tree should sum to the total data set. So, there are 100 000 customers in total, generating $25m in revenues and $15m in profit, as shown at the top of the tree. Each line (Credit rating, Size of loan, and Performance) has a number of tranches but in each case these sum to 100 000 customers, $25m of revenues, and $15m of costs. For example, on the credit rating line there are three tranches containing, respectively, 10 000, 75 000, and 15 000 customers (10k + 75k + 15k = 100k).

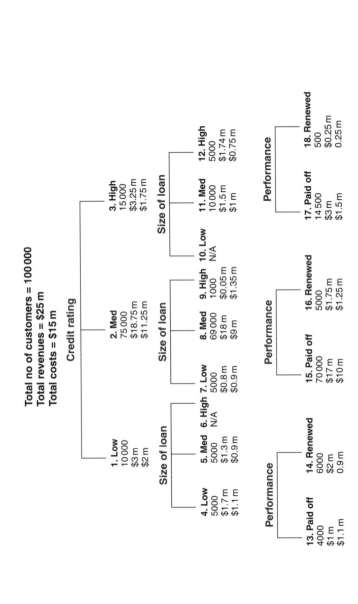

Total no of customers = 100 000
Total revenues = $25 m
Total costs = $15 m

Credit rating

1. Low
10 000
$3 m
$2 m

2. Med
75 000
$18.75 m
$11.25 m

3. High
15 000
$3.25 m
$1.75 m

Size of loan

4. Low
5000
$1.7 m
$1.1 m

5. Med
5000
$1.3 m
$0.9 m

6. High
N/A

7. Low
5000
$0.8 m
$0.9 m

8. Med
69 000
$18 m
$9 m

9. High
1000
$0.05 m
$1.35 m

10. Low
N/A

11. Med
10 000
$1.5 m
$1 m

12. High
5000
$1.74 m
$0.75 m

Performance

13. Paid off
4000
$1 m
$1.1 m

14. Renewed
6000
$2 m
0.9 m

15. Paid off
70 000
$17 m
$10 m

16. Renewed
5000
$1.75 m
$1.25 m

17. Paid off
14 500
$3 m
$1.5 m

18. Renewed
500
$0.25 m
0.25 m

Figure 4.2 Customer profitability tree with data

A second feature of this tree is that not all the customer tranches have any customers in them. Thus, there are no customers with low credit ratings who have large loans (tranche 6), because the loan company will not lend large amounts of money to poor credit-risk customers. There are also no customers with high credit ratings but small loans (tranche 10). The lender would happily lend money to them because they are low risk, and so presumably the reason here is that customers who have better credit ratings tend to be better off and don't need to borrow smaller amounts of money to pay for a holiday. Instead, they will borrow larger amounts of money for a new car or for a home extension.

Another useful feature of the tree is that it illustrates how misleading the notion of an 'average customer' can be. In this example, the average customer would have revenues of $250 and costs of $150. The only tranche of which this is true is tranche 2 on the top line, which contains 75% of the customer base. In fact, average revenues range from $500 in tranche 18 down to $50 in tranche 9.

The tree also makes it possible to see that some tranches generate zero or negative profit. Although the average revenues in tranche 18 are high, the average costs are the highest in the tree and the tranche generates zero profit. This immediately suggests that the cost of persuading high-rated, large loan customers to renew makes this a poor use of resources. Tranches 7 and 13 are marginally unprofitable and tranche 9 is very unprofitable. In absolute terms, the company makes the largest amount of profit in Tranche 15, which is also by far the largest tranche with 70 000 customers. The size of this segment indicates that this is the loan provider's mainstream market.

However, the highest average profit is in tranche 12, where there are only 5 000 customers. The loans provider could improve its overall performance if it could acquire more customers like these (high credit rating, large loans). The drawback of this strategy is that these customers are likely to be very attractive to competitors and the loans provider might in fact like to balance its customer acquisition activities with acquiring more customers in tranche 14, which has the second-highest average profit but is a larger tranche and likely to be in a very different part of the market (low credit rating customers with low or medium size loans who re-borrow during the period).

Using top-down customer profitability analysis

A problem with the decision tree approach is that the multiple tree branches can result in a very large number of profitability tranches. So, some attention must be paid to the analysis of the data for use in sales and marketing decision-making.

A problem with the decision tree approach is that the multiple branches can result in a very large number of tranches.

Chapter 2 outlined three applications of customer profitability analysis:

- evaluating customer dependency;
- balancing customer acquisition and customer retention;
- understanding the payback to customer acquisition.

Customer dependency can be examined by generating a chart of the number of customers against their profitability. This chart will help to identify visually whether there is a 'skew' or dependency on a few more profitable customers in the customer portfolio. Statistical tests, such as the standard deviation (which measures the width of the distribution curve) or kurtosis (which measures the height of the curve) can also help identify dependency.

Another excellent visual representation of the customer base is a decile analysis. The decile analysis takes each 10% of the customer base, from the biggest 10% to the smallest 10% in terms of revenue, and then shows for what percentage of total profits each decile accounts (Figure 4.3).

Figure 4.3 shows that this company loses money on its smallest customers and, more surprisingly, also loses money on the largest 10% of customers. Its most profitable deciles are its major accounts in deciles 2 and 3. This 20% of customers accounts for 65% of all profits.

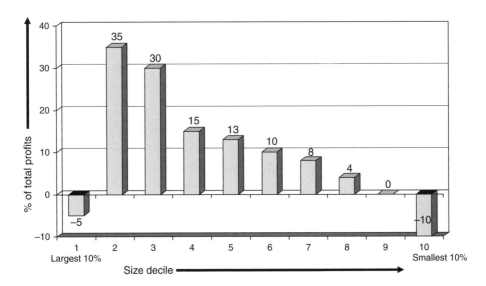

Figure 4.3 Decile analysis

This kind of analysis is the starting point for *balancing customer acquisition and retention*. Figure 4.3 presents a top-down customer profitability analysis by customer size. If this was re-presented in terms of greatest profitability, the company could look at its cumulative profitability as described in Chapter 2. In particular, the very large customers that are costing the company money (decile 1) need to be re-examined to see whether too much resource is being poured into retaining them. There are also some small customers that seem to be very unprofitable. In some cases, these might be new customers that have not yet 'matured' into their full profitability. In other cases, these are perhaps customers that should be passed on to distributors or other, cheaper channels to improve their profit performance.

Some more very interesting analysis could be carried out if customer retention is known by segment or by other factor. It would then be possible to plot the relationship between retention and profitability. This might reveal that, for example, customers acquired through the Internet channel were likely to be short-term profitable but have low retention, whereas customers acquired through the branches or by the field sales force tended to have lower profitability but higher retention. The company would then need to decide what the appropriate balance between acquiring and retaining its customers should be.

Part of the decision about balancing customer acquisition and retention is related to the cost of acquisition and the *customer payback period*. Although the cost of customer acquisition is not explicitly included in the customer profitability analysis calculation, it is possible to estimate it from the data that have already been collected on channel costs, sales, and key account management costs, etc. Then, the customer profitability analysis can be used to establish the profits that might be expected in a typical year from a customer of that type. The payback to customer acquisition can then be calculated in terms of the number of years that the customer will take to become profitable.

$$\text{Payback period on customer} = \frac{\text{Acquisition cost}}{\text{Typical annual profit}}$$

So, if a customer costs €100 to acquire and would typically (in that tranche) generate €50 per year in profit, the payback period is 100/50, or two years. In some industries, for example complex financial services products such as pensions, the customer acquisition costs are extremely high by comparison with the typical annual profits and hence the payback periods are very long (seven years or more). Where payback periods are longer, companies need to concentrate on customer retention so that they keep the customers long enough for the relationship to mature into profitability. Where payback periods are shorter, it makes sense for companies to acquire as many customers as they can in order to maximize their overall profits.

> Where payback periods are longer, companies need to concentrate on customer retention so that they keep the customers long enough for the relationship to mature into profitability

Summary

Top-down customer profitability analysis is useful where there is a large number of customers. Some IT input may be helpful in modelling the drivers of customer profitability. Once the drivers of customer profitability have been identified, these can be developed into a customer profitability tree. This gives information about the profitability of different customer tranches.

A drawback of customer profitability analysis using the decision tree format is that the number of possible branches to the tree increases rapidly with the number of profitability drivers that are considered. Not all these tranches will actually have customers in them, but the complexity might require some computing resource to resolve it.

Alternatively, the approach of thinking about customer profitability drivers might reveal that the analysis could be based on existing segmentation or channels. This is one reason why classification data are important.

Another approach is the decile approach. This approach plots the size of customers (based on their revenues) against the proportion of the firm's profits that they generate. The decile approach is much more straightforward to implement but has very little explanatory power.

Where to find out more

Van Raaij, E.M., Vernooij, M.J.A. and van Triest, S. (2003) 'The implementation of customer profitability analysis: a case study', *Industrial Marketing Management*, **32**(7), pp. 573–583. *Includes an interesting case study showing the results of a top-down customer profitability analysis and the degree of skew that the analysis uncovered.*

Chapter 4: Q & A

	Question	Answer
1	What is the value of a RFM analysis?	RFM – Recency, Frequency, and Monetary Amount – can be useful as a way of thinking about customer revenues. It also offers some insights into the way that customer purchasing patterns differ between segments, and may therefore be used to help decide on particular offers to certain customer groups. However, it does not include information about costs, and so these would have to be calculated separately.

2	Why are customer payback periods important?	In many industries, whether business-to-business or business-to-consumer, the costs of customer acquisition may exceed the first year's profits from the relationship. The longer and more complex the customer acquisition process, the greater the per-customer acquisition costs are likely to be.
		This means that the period at which a customer finally generates overall profits greater than the cost of acquisition is important. If this period is long, having an aggressive customer acquisition policy could be unacceptably costly to the firm. For this reason, the firm's sales strategy should include a mention of the customers that the firm does *not* want to acquire. Moreover, any firm should think carefully about whether it wants to accept all the invitations to tender (ITTs) that it receives, because there are important cash flow implications.
		Generally, firms should establish a sales and marketing strategy that balances customer acquisition and customer retention.
3	Are classification data useful?	Classification data are the factual data about customers. Usually, classification data can be directly observed (gender, age range) or quickly established (location, industry sector, likely income group). Classification data are unlikely to offer much of a competitive edge on their own, because they are easy to collect and other suppliers will also know them, but they can be useful in combination with other information such as customer profitability analysis. In particular, collecting classification data about new customers will make it easier to decide to which segment they probably belong.

5   Customer lifetime value

What's in this chapter

- Why companies need to measure customer lifetime value
- The four components of customer lifetime value
- What to use customer lifetime value for
- Lifetime value and key account management
- The limitations of customer lifetime value

Key concepts discussed in this chapter

Customer lifetime value (CLV)	The stream of profits or cash flow generated by a customer over the remaining lifetime of the relationship, expressed in present-day money. Can therefore be thought of as the NPV of a customer relationship.
Discounted cash flow (DCF)/net present value (NPV)	DCF is the process of using a discount rate to adjust forecasts of future profits or cash flows so that it can be expressed in terms of today's money. The total DCF gives the NPV, which is the current value in today's money of this future income.
Key account management (KAM)	The process of managing certain larger and more complex customers in a differentiated way. Also known as 'strategic account management'.

Segmentation	The process of identifying groups of customers with similar needs. It is used where a company has a large number of customers, which can then be grouped into a manageable number of segments. Given that each segment has different wants or needs, it is usual to develop a slightly different value proposition for each segment.
Weighted average cost of capital (WACC)	The weighted average of the cost of debt and the cost of equity, giving the true overall cost of borrowing for the company. The WACC would then be used in place of the discount rate to calculate NPV.

Key tools explained in this chapter

- Customer lifetime value calculation process: A four-step process consisting of the forecasting of remaining lifetime, future revenues, costs, and then the calculation of the net present value of these future amounts.
- Gateway criteria: The criteria that define what constitutes a key account or a potential key account (the former is a current customer; the latter is not). There are usually relatively few of these, say four or five factors. They might include financial factors, such as the potential to generate a certain amount of revenue. There might be relational factors, such as the brand or market position of the customer. Gateway criteria may also include features that a supplier would not want a key account to have, such as needing co-location from its suppliers.

Two-minute chapter summary

There are limitations to customer profitability analysis that reduce its usefulness for marketing decision making. In customer relationships, the past may not be a good guide to the future. Using the past alone as a measure can result in companies misallocating their sales and marketing resources. This chapter discusses how customer lifetime value is a more representative tool for strategic marketing decision making.

Customer lifetime value is the stream of future profits or cash flow generated by the customer over the course of its remaining relationship lifetime, minus the direct costs and costs to serve, and minus customer-specific overheads if incurred.

There is a four-step process for identifying customer lifetime value:

1. Forecast the remaining customer lifetime (in years).
2. Forecast the year-by-year revenues, based on assumptions about future products purchased and price paid.
3. Estimate the costs of delivering those products or services.
4. Discount the future amounts back to the present day.

Customer lifetime value has two major advantages over customer profitability analysis for marketing and salespeople. The first advantage is that it enables the customer relationship to be managed as an asset that might require investment in one period that will not pay off until future periods. The second advantage is that it enables sales and marketing managers to monitor the impact that their customer management strategies have on the value of those customer assets.

Customer lifetime value is also a useful tool in segmentation, where it can be used to adjust proposed value propositions to ensure that the supplier also benefits. If the supplier develops value propositions for its customers without properly understanding their value, it can 'give away the farm' (that is, create value that is then delivered to customers at zero profit or at a loss).

Customer lifetime value is also useful in the identification of key accounts, where it may be one of the gateway criteria. Gateway criteria are the factors that define a key account; clearly, a particular level of future profits from the relationship could well be an important gateway criterion below which a customer or potential customer is not considered to be a key account.

Two limitations affect customer lifetime value calculations. One is forecasting accuracy. The other is that it can be difficult to track customers over time so that if they leave and then return they may be treated as new customers for valuation purposes. Even something as simple as customers changing addresses or names may make it difficult to track them and hence to understand their lifetime value.

Why companies need to measure customer lifetime value

Although customer profitability analysis is the usual starting point for valuing customer relationships, it has certain quite serious drawbacks that limit its value for sales and marketing decision making. The profitability of a customer can fluctuate considerably from period to period. It will be affected by short-term fluctuations in the customer's industry, and by the customer's own buying decisions during the year. In addition to these factors, the profitability of a customer will also be affected by the investment that the supplier has made in that customer relationship during the year. Much of the sales and marketing investment made during a year will not pay off until future years. Increasing the focus on a particular customer and allocating a greater proportion of sales and marketing resources during the year may increase the longer-term value of that customer, but will reduce the short-term profitability.

These periodic fluctuations in the needs, purchasing patterns, investment in, and value of, a customer mean that the past is not necessarily a good guide to the future. Relying on historical data can be dangerous, which reduces the usefulness of customer profitability analysis for marketing decision making.

> Relying on historical data can be dangerous, which reduces the usefulness of customer profitability analysis for marketing decision making.

If the past, in the form of customer profitability analysis, is not a good guide to the future, in terms of the potential value of that customer, there is a distinct danger in using customer profitability analysis to make marketing decisions. A customer profitability analysis that indicates, for example, that 20% of customers are unprofitable, may persuade companies into thinking that they could improve their performance by cutting costs to these unprofitable customers or even by getting rid of them altogether. The problem is that such actions may damage the organization in the longer term. Newly-acquired customers, for example, may be currently unprofitable because all the investment of time and money in the early development of the relationship has not yet paid off. However, these customers could have considerable potential.

Future potential is not captured by customer profitability analysis because it is backward-facing. So, companies wanting to match their sales and marketing investment to customer potential prefer the forward-facing lifetime value measure for marketing decisions. Although many companies begin the process of customer asset management by calculating

> Although many companies begin the process of customer asset management by calculating customer profitability analysis, it is not long before they recognize the need to take future potential into account.

customer profitability analysis, it is not long before they recognize the need to take future potential into account. This is where customer lifetime value comes in.

Definition of customer lifetime value

Customer lifetime value has become an important concept in marketing because of the growing notion of customers as assets and the need to track the supplier's investment in that customer asset over time. In business-to-consumer, the supplying company's investment mainly involves sales and marketing effort. In business-to-business, the investment in the customer might include product or service customization, dedicated logistics, and tailored paperwork, as well as the customer management input from sales and marketing. This can amount to a substantial investment in a customer asset so it is important for companies to be able to calculate the payback on that relationship.

If the payback on investing in a customer relationship is defined as the returns minus the cost and effort invested, it becomes clear that there can be considerable risk involved. Part of the risk is that the effort spent on wooing a customer never pays off, because the customer ends up placing his or her order elsewhere. For those investments in relationship building that do pay off, however, the investment may not pay back in the same year. This is true in both business-to-consumer and business-to-business, although the problem is more acute in business-to-business because the size and nature of the investment in the sales and marketing process (including product and service customization, taking part in formal tendering processes, and relationship management) is much greater.

In fact, much marketing and sales activity is risky, based on the expectation of (uncertain) future payback. Therefore, account managers have to make decisions about how to spend their time and budget in order to maximize their returns from managing their customer portfolio. Many of these customer management decisions cannot be evaluated without taking a longer-term view, because the effort expended in the current year will not pay off until future periods. Customer profitability analysis will not give them this information. For this reason, sales and marketing managers have to make their decisions to invest in a customer relationship by looking at the potential return to the business over the lifetime of that customer relationship. In other words, they have to consider customer lifetime value.

Customer lifetime value is the expected value of the future relationship with that customer. When companies talk about customer lifetime value, they generally mean the future value of an individual customer.

> Customer lifetime value is the expected value of the future relationship with that customer.

For some purposes, it is more useful to look at the potential value of a group of customers or of the entire customer base. To avoid confusion, the latter will be termed 'customer equity' and considered in Chapter 7.

The four components of customer lifetime value

The calculation of customer lifetime value has four components: relationship duration, cash in, cash out, and the discount rate (Figure 5.1).

To calculate customer lifetime value, marketers should forecast the likely length (duration) of the relationship lifetime and then the profits or cash flow each year. The cash flow consists of cash in, in the form of net revenues, and cash out, in

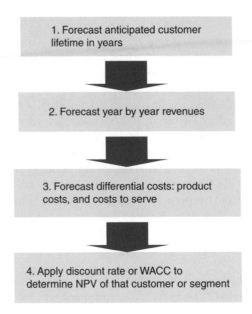

Figure 5.1   Four step process for calculating customer lifetime value

the form of costs of goods and services and costs to serve. If there are cash flows associated with customer-specific overheads these, too, can be included. General business overheads are usually disregarded for the purposes of customer lifetime value calculation, as they are not customer-specific.

Short technical note: profits versus cash flows

Profit is an accounting concept based on a change in value over a period. Thus, profit measures accumulated assets minus liabilities. Both the assets and the liabilities might include accrued amounts that have not yet been realized in the form of cash. This concept was covered in Chapter 3, where the problem of work done but not yet invoiced or paid for was considered. Moreover, the amount of value that has accumulated may be disputed, and the rules on how to measure it may vary over time or from country to country. So, profit is opinion.

Cash flows are, as the name suggests, the tangible cash flows that take place, in this case between the customer and the supplier. Cash flows are not a matter of opinion, because they are tangible. Thus, 'cash is fact'. However, the timing of cash flows may be very different from the commitment to the business. For example, a supplier might sign a very big contract with a customer but not yet have received any payment. It would seem odd to value this relationship as zero, just because no cash flows had taken place.

For calculating customer lifetime value, future profits or cash flow can be used. In either case, the future profits or cash flows must be discounted back to the present day (this concept will be explained later in the chapter).

The commonsense approach to valuing customer relationships taken in this book is somewhere between profit and cash flow (technically, it measures customer contribution, because overheads are not included unless they are customer-specific). So, it can be used for both customer profitability analysis and for customer lifetime value.

Calculating money in minus money out will give a net profit or free cash flow year by year. However, these profits or cash flows are expressed in future values (tomorrow's money). The fourth step is, therefore, to discount the future amounts back to present day values.

As customer lifetime value looks at the future potential of the relationship, historical profits are usually excluded for the purposes of the analysis, as are customer acquisition costs for existing customers (because, by definition, they were incurred in previous periods). However, customer acquisition costs may be included for new or returning customers. Including customer acquisition costs when calculating the lifetime value of customers that the business expects to acquire in the near future will tend to make new customers seem less attractive than existing customers. As this probably reflects the business reality, customer acquisition costs for *potential* customers (but not for existing customers) are usually included.

Because of the time value of money, forecast future customer profits or cash flow must be discounted back to the present day. In other words, the forecast future values must be expressed in today's money, which means using a discount rate that reflects factors such as inflation. For most marketers, the discount rate is a 'given' and is determined either by organizational policy or by the company's weighted average cost of capital (WACC). WACC is used by companies that are measuring shareholder value. It reflects the cost to the company of borrowing money from the bank in the form of debt and of borrowing money via the stock market in the form of equities.

Some marketers have become concerned that the use of a single discount rate may not reflect the risk in certain customer relationships and have developed additional techniques, either adjusting the discount rate or assessing the relationship risk and thus the probability of future profits. The problem of risk to the supplier in customer relationships will be discussed in Chapter 11.

The advantages of customer lifetime value

Customer lifetime value has two major advantages as a tool for marketing and sales decision making. The first advantage is that it takes the future into account, underlining the notion of customer relationships as assets that need to be managed today for payback tomorrow. This

> Customer lifetime value takes the future into account and enables companies to understand the impact of their customer management activities.

positions a firm's sales and marketing activities correctly as investment activities rather than incorrectly as 'cost centres'.

The second advantage of customer lifetime value analysis is that it enables suppliers to understand the impact that their customer relationship management activities have on the value of customers. The lifetime value of customers is not a 'given'. Customer management, including business-to-business relationship management and key account management, affect the value of the relationship. The customer lifetime value calculation enables a marketing manager to calculate, for example, the financial value of a specific loyalty campaign that has succeeded in extending the relationship lifetime of a customer segment.

In fact, the way in which the relationship is managed is just one of the three factors that affect the lifetime value of a customer. The other factors are the actions of competing suppliers and changes in the customer's own circumstances (Figure 5.2).

Thus, customer relationship management activities such as increasing the perceived value of the product or service, running loyalty programmes, or building relationships, will affect customer lifetime value, as will factors such as convenience and cross-selling (there is a known relationship between number of products held and customer retention; the more products a customer buys, generally the more likely they are to be retained). However, lifetime value will also be affected by customer circumstances such as lifecycle stage (in business-to-consumer markets) and industry factors (in business-to-business markets). Moreover, the actions of competitors such as a strategy to enter or exit a particular market or running promotions to attract new customers can affect the value of another company's customers.

Since all three factors have an impact on lifetime value, calculating customer lifetime value should not be seen as a one-off exercise but as dynamic. Similarly, resource allocation decisions should be made on the basis not just of the currently-calculated customer lifetime value, but based on potential and on optimizing returns on marketing investment.

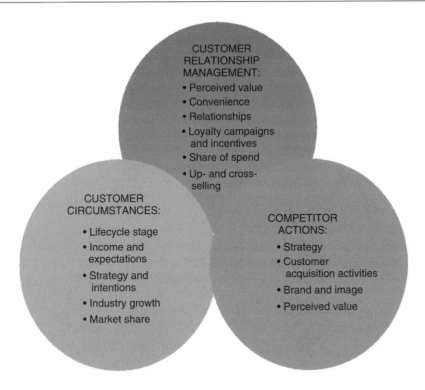

Figure 5.2 Factors affecting the lifetime value of a customer

What to use customer lifetime value for

Customer lifetime value is used to assist sales and marketing managers to make two essential decisions:

- Deciding on appropriate customer management strategies.
- Customer segmentation and differentiation strategy.

Appropriate customer management strategies

Customer management strategies refer to the particular strategies selected to manage a relationship. Customer lifetime value plays an important role in these decisions. Generally, customers with high lifetime value will be preferred targets for retention strategies. Customers with low or negative lifetime values

> Customers with high lifetime value will be targets for retention. Customers with low or negative lifetime values might be better managed through cheaper channels or via a third party.

might be better managed through cheaper channels or via a third party such as a distributor, or offered a lower service package.

Even in the absence of lifetime value information, many customer management decisions are made on the basis of anticipated returns. Thus, companies will aim to target their most valuable customers, or the customers who have the highest potential, with customer retention strategies. However, this can be problematic if the perception of customer lifetime value is not accurate. For example, key account management (KAM) has become a very popular and widespread technique in business-to-business markets for managing the most important customers of the firm. Usually, these are the largest customers, partly because larger customers have more buying power and so can demand higher service levels, and partly because suppliers tend to equate size (customer revenues) with profits. Overall, key account management pays off for suppliers. Study after study shows that introducing key account management increases the supplier's share of spend, and that revenues and growth rates rise.

However, introducing key account management is costly in time and resources and care must be taken carefully to select the customers to which it is offered. Some customers have no intention of entering into partnership relationships with their suppliers, because they are motivated by low cost and engage purely in exploitative relationships. Other customers have policies relating to share of spend with supplier or they have multi-sourcing requirements. In these cases, pouring additional time and resources into the relationship may actually *decrease* the returns. The appropriate customer management strategy to adopt will depend on the cost of the strategy and the impact that the strategy will have on the overall lifetime value of that customer.

> The appropriate customer management strategy to adopt will depend on the cost of the strategy and the impact that the strategy will have on the overall lifetime value of that customer.

Companies that are serious about managing their customer relationships profitably need to calculate the payback on their investments in the relationship. More and more companies now think of their customer relationships as assets that have to be invested in and managed like other assets. Defining appropriate customer management strategies and measuring the impact of these strategies in terms of their impact on customer lifetime value supports this asset management approach.

Customer segmentation and differentiation strategy

Customer lifetime value can be used in conjunction with segmentation to develop a differentiated approach to customers. Customer lifetime value is increasingly the most important factor in the identification and management of strategic key accounts. It is also combined with traditional segmentation to develop service-based segmentation strategies. As both of these are major topics and important applications for customer lifetime value analysis, they will be considered separately in a later section (see 'Segmentation and differentiated strategies').

Customer lifetime value and key account management

Identifying and managing strategic or key accounts is an essential strategy in business-to-business relationship contexts. Key accounts are the most important customers of the organization. In the early days of key account management, the supplier's key accounts were typically identified by size (revenues or volumes). Increasingly, however, key accounts are identified as customers that are strategically important to the supplier and this means in terms of lifetime value and market position. Research shows that strategic account managers are usually tasked to manage not just the revenues but, more importantly, the lifetime profits from their key accounts. Therefore, customer lifetime value is an essential tool for identifying and managing strategic accounts in business-to-business contexts.

> Customer lifetime value is an essential tool for identifying and managing strategic accounts in business-to-business contexts.

Using customer lifetime value to identify strategic accounts

A supplier's portfolio of strategic or key accounts usually includes its biggest customers (by revenues or volume). However, the portfolio of strategic accounts should also include the customers with the highest lifetime value, and these are not necessarily the largest customers. Future profits are clearly of vital importance to the business, so it is essential that customer lifetime value is considered when selecting a portfolio of key accounts. In addition, there are other factors that might affect whether a business-to-business customer is considered to be a key account, such as profile. A high-profile customer may open doors into other industries, or attract additional customers. Alternatively, a customer may be considered strategic because the supplier can learn from them or because they may help the supplier develop new products or services. All of these are about future potential, which may not be connected at all to current revenues.

Three common problems in selecting a portfolio of key accounts are:

- The definition criteria for key accounts are unclear.
- Too many key accounts are selected for inclusion.
- The key account portfolio is not reviewed regularly.

If the criteria defining key accounts are unclear, there is a danger that accounts are included in the strategic account portfolio for reasons that have little or nothing to do with value. For example, customers might be given key account status because they ask for it, or because the account manager wants the status of managing a key account. This can have potentially serious consequences because of the investment that is made in a key account.

> If the criteria defining key accounts are unclear, customers may be included in the strategic account portfolio for reasons that have little or nothing to do with value.

When implementing strategic account management for the first time, it is not unusual for companies to select too many customers for inclusion (the 'we have 200 key accounts' syndrome). The problem here is one of expectations: customers that have been told that they are key accounts form expectations about the levels of service that they will receive. If these expectations are not met – if the supplier has insufficient resources, or if it has to down-grade certain customers to non-key status – the relationship can be dam-aged. A useful general rule is that there should be no more than 30 key accounts.

The third issue in selecting strategic accounts is that the portfolio should be regularly reviewed to ensure that all the accounts in it are still strategically import-ant, and to check that there are no stra-tegically important customers that are not yet in the portfolio. It is easy to add new customers to a portfolio but it is more difficult to downgrade customers

> The key account portfolio should be regularly reviewed to ensure that all the accounts in it are still strategically important, and to check that there are no strategic-ally important customers that are not yet in the portfolio.

that are no longer strategically important. So, suppliers can suffer a form of insidious key account inflation over time, in which the portfolio of strategic accounts gets steadily larger and uses more and more resources.

A useful tool that overcomes the difficulties of key account selection is to develop gateway criteria that identify clearly what constitutes a strategic account.

Gateway criteria for key account selection

Gateway criteria define what constitutes a key account. In other words, customers that meet the criteria pass 'through the gate' into the key account portfolio. They are specific measurable criteria that clarify what constitutes a key account. Regu-lar reviewing of the key accounts within the portfolio and also the potential key accounts that have not yet passed through the gate will ensure that the appropriate customers are treated as key.

Customer lifetime value is one of the most important gateway criteria. Gateway criteria may include:

- turnover/volume;
- customer lifetime value (or a proxy future potential measure);
- relational aspects such as customer profile.

As a general rule, there will be five gateway criteria or fewer.

Gateway criteria should be:

- agreed across the business (strategic accounts should be managed at a firm, not at a divisional, level);
- specific and measurable;
- relate to the future as well as the current value of the relationship.

Table 5.1 demonstrates some gateway criteria for identifying strategic accounts.

Table 5.1 Gateway criteria for a management consultancy's key clients

No.	Criterion	Measure	When (time)
1	Customer's total spend on consultancy, advisory, and risk management services	£10m p.a. or more	Current annual spend
2	Projected lifetime value	£2m or more	Over the next 3 years
3	Buys or is likely to buy from more than one business unit	No. of business units	By the end of year 3
4	Strong market profile/brand presence	At least 1 brand in the Interbrand top 100 listing	Current
5	Does NOT require integrated international services	At least 80% of client turnover is domestic	Current

As Table 5.1 illustrates, the gateway criteria can and should include some measures of potential value, as well as current value. Measures of potential value might reflect growth potential and will enable the inclusion of prospective as well as current key accounts in the portfolio. The inclusion of prospective key accounts is important if the portfolio is to grow and if the key account managers or KAM team are to be correctly focused. The job of a key account manager or KAM team typically includes prospecting and developing new strategic accounts as well as managing the existing ones.

Table 5.1 also shows that gateway criteria can include 'soft' factors such as market profile, although it is always useful to try to define what these mean. The example in Table 5.1 uses the Interbrand listing of the world's top brands to define market profile. Other measures might include market share, innovation rates, media coverage, media spend, etc.

Gateway criterion no. 5 is an interesting one, as it illustrates an important point. The gateway criteria might include *negative* as well as positive criteria; that is, factors that might exclude a customer from becoming a key account. In the case of this consultancy, they have limited international scope despite being a major player in the domestic market, so they are not interested in pitching for work with global customers that would require a wide international support network. Other negative criteria that might exclude a customer from key account status include high risk of takeover, poor business or risk management, incompatible strategic aims between the two businesses, and ethical issues.

There is one criterion that should *not* be included in the gateway criteria: share of the customer's spend. Share of spend (also called share of customer's wallet in business-to-consumer) is the *result* of the customer management strategy and not an input into it. Including share of spend would also make existing customers appear more attractive than potential customers, which may not be the case at all. Share of spend should *not* be a gateway criterion, because it is the result of previous strategies. However, 'potential to increase share of spend' *could* be a gateway criterion.

> Share of spend should not be a gateway criterion, because it is the result of previous strategies. However, future potential to increase share of spend could be a gateway criterion.

Note

If your company is implementing/running KAM, there should be a clear set of gateway criteria that identify which customers are included in the key account portfolio. Key accounts should be regularly reviewed against these criteria.

If the gateway criteria are unclear, the key account portfolio will be poorly defined.

See worksheet at end of chapter for help on defining gateway criteria.

Using customer lifetime value to manage strategic accounts

Customer lifetime value is affected not only by customer circumstances and competitor actions, but also by the way in which the relationship is managed. This was illustrated in Figure 5.2. Measuring customer lifetime value is particularly important in the business-to-business context of key or strategic account management, because the size and complexity of these relationships is so much greater and can have a substantial impact on the overall profitability of the firm.

Having identified which accounts are strategically important enough to be included in the key account portfolio using the gateway criteria, the lifetime value of each key account should be calculated using the process shown previously in Figure 5.1. This calculation is effectively a forecasting exercise and can be performed on a spreadsheet. One such calculation is shown in Figure 5.3.

Figure 5.3 shows the revenues that this business-to-business insurer gets from two streams of business: insurance premiums (the figure shown here includes a group motor policy, buildings and factory cover, liability and key man insurance, and loss of profits); and risk consultancy services. The product costs, in this case, are the cost of the claims that the insurer has to pay, and the costs to serve include the costs of the KAM team, administration, and the costs of putting together complex contracts and proposals. Subtracting the total costs from the total revenues gives a year-by-year profit. This is then discounted back to today's money, showing that a customer with a notional lifetime value of £3 334 389 at a discount rate of 4.8% is actually worth £2 967 952 at today's value.

The calculation of customer lifetime value is a forecast and should be treated in the same way as any other forecast. It should be revisited and revised periodically. If the forecast customer lifetime changes (that is, because a customer becomes more, or less, likely to be retained) this will affect the calculation of customer lifetime value, as well as changes to the customer revenue forecasts that might be triggered by changes in the customer's purchasing needs or perhaps by the introduction of new products on the part of the supplier. Changes in the underlying forecasts of the products that the customer will be buying may also result in a change to forecast product costs, and changes to the customer management strategy may affect costs to serve.

Segmentation and differentiated strategies

Once the key accounts of a firm have been identified and passed over to a KAM team for individual customer management, the sales and marketing managers have to consider how to manage the remainder of the customer portfolio. This is where customer lifetime value and segmentation comes in. Customer segmentation is about recognizing different customer groups in the marketplace. Done well, segmentation can be a powerful business tool to differentiate a company. This important topic, and how it links to the profitable management of customers, are discussed in detail in Chapter 12.

Customer H	Yr 1	Yr 2	Yr 3	Yr 4	Total
Revenues:					
Insurance Premium	2 517 987	2 643 887	2 776 081	2 914 885	
Other Fees	436 411	436 411	436 411	436 411	
TOTAL REVENUES	**2 954 398**	**3 080 298**	**3 212 492**	**3 351 296**	
Costs:					
Claims	1 888 490	1 982 915	2 082 060	2 186 163	
Costs to serve	242 290	266 519	293 170	322 488	
TOTAL COSTS	**2 130 780**	**2 249 434**	**2 375 230**	**2 508 651**	
Lifetime value:					
Profit	**823 618**	**830 864**	**837 262**	**842 645**	**3 334 389**
Discount rate	4.8%	4.8%	4.8%	4.8%	
Net present value	**785 732**	**756 086**	**727 581**	**698 553**	**2 967 952**

Figure 5.3 Customer lifetime value calculation for business-to-business insurer

A marketing segment can be defined as a group of customers with similar needs or characteristics. Once segments have been defined, the next step is to create an appropriate and attractive value proposition that is specifically tailored to appeal to that segment (for information about how to do this, see Chapter 15). However, the company needs to be realistic about how much value it is offering to customers compared to the price it is charging (see Chapter 14). If it offers too much, the customers might be very happy, but the supplier could lose money.

This is where customer lifetime value comes in. If the supplier has a good understanding of the customer lifetime value of its customer segments, it can develop service packages for each segment that will appeal to the customer but also ensure that value is captured by the supplier. This decision is based on the value of those customers.

This approach aims to manage the service levels that customers receive over the relationship lifetime so as to optimize customer lifetime value. It may involve some 'tough conversations' with customers about the amount of resources they are using compared to the value they give back. Customers in less profitable segments might be required to pay for services that more valuable customers get for free.

Small print: the limitations of customer lifetime value

Although marketing managers are increasingly interested in understanding customer lifetime value as a guide to the way they manage customer relationships, forecasting difficulties have limited the take-up of customer lifetime value by practitioners.

Limitation #1: forecasting accuracy

Like any forecast, customer lifetime value can be over- or underestimated. More accurate forecasts of customer lifetime value can be developed by applying standard forecasting improvement techniques, such as comparing forecasts with actual outturns, improving customer information, using statistical techniques within the customer relationship management (CRM) system to assist in predicting future customer behaviour and needs, and even planning jointly with customers.

Limitation #2: returning customers

Another area in which companies experience difficulties with customer lifetime value is in the treatment of customers who leave and then return. Many CRM systems experience difficulty in handling customers with this pattern. It can be difficult to link the previous record with the returning customer, so that returning customers may appear as though they are new customers. If this is the case, their true lifetime value is underestimated because the duration of their relationship with the company appears shorter than it really is.

Summary: the use of customer lifetime value

Customer lifetime value helps a company to:

- Decide on appropriate customer management strategies.
- Identify customer segments and develop a differentiated strategy.
- Identify and manage key or strategic accounts.

Customer lifetime value has the advantage of being based on forecast, rather than on historic, data. This helps the company assess the potential in its customer relationships. As customer lifetime value is affected by the way in which the relationship is managed, it is an invaluable metric when suppliers are deciding on how much time and effort to devote to a particular account. Effectively, once the customer lifetime value is known, a marketing or sales manager can calculate the return on investment in the customer. By monitoring the likely costs of a particular customer management strategy and comparing this to the forecast change in lifetime value, the manager can make informed decisions about how much time and resource should be spent on a particular customer.

Customer lifetime value can also be used in conjunction with strategies for managing that lifetime value, such as segmentation. Customer lifetime value may also be a guide to customer acquisition and customer retention strategies that differentiate the supplier from its competitors. Customers with high lifetime value will be key targets for both acquisition and retention; the use of customer lifetime value data enables the supplier to put together packages that attract and retain such customers differentially. For example, one such package might involve some attractive price offers but linked to longer-term contracts and/or a wider product range purchased. The initial price offer (perhaps based on a single product within the package) is used to attract the high-value customer, and the multi-product package and longer contract encourage customer retention and thus facilitate capture of the lifetime value. Management of customer lifetime value through price, product, and service strategies will be discussed in later chapters.

Note

Use the worksheet on the following page to identify any key accounts in your portfolio/on your list of potential clients.

Worksheet for key account gateway criteria

The purpose of this worksheet is to develop gateway criteria that define what constitutes a key or strategic account of the business

No.	Criterion	Measure	By when
1			
2			
3			
4			
5			

There are typically four or five gateway criteria that define a key account or potential key account. An example might be: Criterion = Potential to generate substantial fees; Measure = $2 million per annum; By when = end of planning period.

Where to find out more

Ryals, L.J. (2005) 'Making customer relationship management work: The measurement and profitable management of customer relationships', *Journal of Marketing*, 69(4), pp. 252–261. *In this paper, I describe how two companies implemented customer lifetime value analysis and the impact that this had on their customer management strategies. The changes in customer management resulted in substantial profit gains.*

6 Calculating customer lifetime value

What's in this chapter

- Estimating customer lifetimes
- Forecasting year-by-year revenues
- STEEP analysis and the Five Forces of competition
- Differential costs: direct costs, and costs to serve
- Discounting future profits

Key concepts discussed in this chapter

Customer lifetime value	A forecast of the remaining financial value of a trading relationship with a customer, stated in terms of its present-day monetary value.
Discount factor	Expresses the discount rate (explained in Chapter 5) as a factor. The factor will be less than 1.0, because future money is worth less than current money. Income or profit expressed in future money is multiplied by the discount factor to convert it to today's money.
Discounting	The process of expressing future monetary amounts in terms of today's money.

Key tools explained in this chapter

- STEEP analysis: Method of analysing the customer or supplier's marketplace and business situation. STEEP is a mnemonic that stands for: Socio-demographic (can be thought of as Structural in business-to-business markets); Technological developments; Economic; Environmental and Ethical; and Political, Legal and Regulatory.
- Porter's Five Forces of competition: A way of analysing the competitive forces acting on a company. Michael Porter said there were five of these: core industry competitors; buyers; suppliers; new entrants; and substitutes. The strength of each force should be considered when analysing the overall competitiveness of the market.

Two-minute chapter summary

Customer lifetime value is a forecast of the remaining financial value of a trading relationship with a customer, stated in terms of its present-day monetary value. It enables the identification of the most valuable customers. The future perspective is important, because there may be reasons why a customer does not seem very important at present but in fact represents a vital future asset for the business.

The first step in calculating customer lifetime value is forecasting the remaining lifetime of the customer. Customer relationship management (CRM) systems may be useful here, because they may indicate the average lifetimes of similar customers.

The second step is to forecast future revenues from the customer, which are driven by product or services purchased and prices paid. Tools such as STEEP analysis and Porter's Five Forces can be useful in forecasting future purchases.

The third step, forecasting costs, looks at direct costs, costs to serve, and any customer-specific overheads for each future year. The final step is to restate the numbers in today's money terms, using a discount factor.

Forecasting customer lifetime value

Customer lifetime value has become an important concept in marketing because of the growing notion of customer relationships as assets. As with other assets, a customer relationship needs initial investment and ongoing care and mainten- ance. For profitable management of the customer relationship, the supplier needs to track the investment in that asset over time. This is where customer lifetime value comes in.

To calculate it, marketers must forecast the likely duration of the relationship and then the customer profitability or cash flow each year. Customer acquisition costs for existing customers are generally disregarded, although they may be included for new or returning customers. Because of the time value of money, these forecasts of future customer profits must be discounted back to the present day so that the lifetime value can be expressed in terms of today's money.

Thus, customer lifetime value is the forecast value of the current and future trading relationship, expressed in today's money terms.

The focus of customer lifetime value is on the direct financial value of a customer relationship through the trading relationship with the supplier. It has been said that there are other sources of value ('relational value') that may be generated from customer relationships, and these will be examined separately in Chapter 8.

> Definition of customer lifetime value:
> A forecast of the remaining financial value of a trading relationship with a customer, stated in terms of its present-day monetary value.

How to identify the most valuable customers

The starting point for calculating customer lifetime value is to examine existing customer information to see what is already known about the customer that might aid forecasting. This information can include historic customer profitability; current products purchased; account plans, customer documents, or sales visit reports that indicate future purchasing intentions; and any information about contractual arrangements that might inform forecasts of relationship duration.

Customer lifetime value focuses on the financial value of an individual customer relationship. It is vitally important where a supplier has a few key customers who account for a major proportion of its business, as in the case of a major international airline (Figure 6.1).

The airline has some 25 000 business-to-business customers in total. These are customers such as travel agents, event management companies, and major corporations who make their own travel arrangements in-house. Figure 6.1 shows that 22 of these customers (less than 0.1% of the customer base) account for 31% of revenues. The dominant strategy for customers like these is to work alongside the customer on joint planning. There is another stratum of 'strategic accounts', by which they mean major, but not key, customers. There are 1200 of these and they account for 40% of revenue; the dominant strategy here is that the airline manages them by sector and makes its own, sector-based plans for these customers. Finally, the remaining 23 750 customers are managed by marketing on a portfolio basis, using segmentation and with a dominant strategy to manage these relationships as efficiently as possible so as to minimize costs to serve.

	No. of customers	% of Revenue	Dominant Strategy
Key Accounts	22	31%	Joint marketing and business plans
Strategic Accounts	1200	40%	Unilateral business plans
Marketing portfolio: other customers	23 750	29%	Minimize cost to serve

Figure 6.1   Identifying key customers at a major airline

Customer lifetime value is also important where the supplier takes on risk or has to invest up-front in the relationship with a customer, in the anticipation of future returns. This is the case, for example, for some financial services products where the returns will not take place for some years, although much of the investment in the relationship takes place before, or at the time of, customer acquisition.

The basic calculation of customer lifetime value is as follows:

Customer lifetime value = stream of customer revenues

− (costs of goods sold + costs to serve

+ customer-specific overheads), discounted back

to the present day

Thus, the customer lifetime value (CV) of a relationship that lasts for a number (n) of months or years, t_n, equals the revenues obtained from that customer ($CRt_{1 \text{ to } n}$) during the period, less the total customer-specific costs (the cost of goods sold ($COGSt_{1 \text{ to } n}$); the costs to serve ($CTSt_{1 \text{ to } n}$); and customer-specific overheads ($CSOt_{1 \text{ to } n}$), discounted back to current day money using a discount rate (d).

So, the approach to customer lifetime value analysis used here can be summarized as follows:

$$CV = [CR_{t1 \text{ to } n} - (COGS_{t1 \text{ to } n} + CTS_{t1 \text{ to } n} + CSO_{t1 \text{ to } n})]^d$$

As we have seen, it is important to remember that customer lifetime value is a forecast, which needs to be monitored and updated. So, the general rule for customer lifetime value is as follows: aim for sufficiently accurate forecasts of lifetime value, and review them regularly.

Forecasting issues

Sales and marketing managers can sometimes be unduly sceptical about the value of customer lifetime value as an analytical and management tool, because they are concerned about the accuracy of their forecasts of future sales to the customer and of costs.

Although it is important to make the best forecasts possible for customer lifetime value, perfect accuracy can never be achieved. Therefore, regular review of the customer relationship and updating of the customer lifetime value calculation should take place.

Some managers who use customer lifetime value also take the view that the *absolute* lifetime values are less important when considering a group of customers such as a key account portfolio, and that in fact it is the *relative* values that are important. As long as the account managers know, with some degree of confidence, which are their most valuable and which are their least valuable customers, they can allocate their time and resources appropriately.

The previous chapter set out a four-step process for calculating customer lifetime value:

1. Estimate remaining customer lifetime (duration).
2. Forecast year-by-year revenues.
3. Forecast year-by-year differential costs (product costs, costs to serve, and any customer-specific overheads).
4. Discount back to the present day.

Figure 5.3 in the previous chapter (page 98) illustrated a customer lifetime value calculation by an insurance company for one strategic account, a chemical manufacturer. The four stages were illustrated in this figure. The remaining relationship lifetime was estimated as four years; the year-by-year revenues and the year-by-year costs were then forecast. The annual profits from the relationship were discounted at the company's discount rate of 4.8% to give a 'current money' customer lifetime value figure of £2 967 952.

Each of the four steps of the customer lifetime value calculation will now be considered in detail.

Step 1: Estimating customer lifetime

The first step in calculating customer lifetime value is to estimate the remaining lifetime in the relationship. This estimation could be carried out based on contractual data, on conversations with the customer, or using database information about the lifetime durations of comparable customers.

For most practical purposes, account managers are not able to estimate details of revenues and costs for more than about four to five years ahead, so this usually limits the estimates of relationship duration[1].

Table 6.1   Step 1 – relationship duration

Customer:..			
	Yr 1	**Yr 2**	**Yr 3**

Table 6.1 shows the first step of the customer lifetime value calculation. This relationship is forecast to last for the current year (shown as year 1 – Yr 1 – in Table 6.1) plus two further years.

> **Note**
>
> Check whether your company has database records that would allow it to forecast customer relationship lifetime with more confidence.

The next step is to forecast the year-by-year revenues.

Step 2: Forecasting year-by-year revenues

The process for forecasting year-by-year revenues is analogous to that used in the calculation of customer profitability (Chapter 4). The products and services that the customer is currently buying form part of the calculation, because this forms the input for year 1. However, the analysis

> Where a company already has considerable amounts of data about its customers, the CRM system may be able to predict what future purchases could be.

---

[1] Where the relationship with the customer is confidently expected to be of much longer duration, it may be necessary to seek help from a management accountant to calculate what is known as the 'terminal value' of the customer.

has to be extended into the future, which involves analysing the likely future needs and buying patterns for the customer. Where a company already has considerable amounts of data about its customers, the CRM system may be able to predict what future purchases could be. Tools such as neural networks may be used to identify products and services that the customer probably buys elsewhere and then the company can devise a sales strategy to persuade the customer to switch.

In addition to the specific knowledge gleaned by the sales force from their conversations with the customer, there are two marketing tools that can help forecast year-by-year revenues: STEEP analysis and Porter's Five Forces of competition.

STEEP analysis

The STEEP analysis is a widely-used tool in strategic and marketing planning. It provides a structured approach to analysing the business or general situation of a customer, whether business-to-business or business-to-consumer. STEEP stands for a series of factors that affects the business situation: Socio-cultural; Technological; Economic; Environmental; and Political/Regulatory.

> STEEP stands for: Socio-cultural; Technological; Economic; Environmental; and Political/Regulatory.

The STEEP analysis is used as a checklist to help sales and marketing managers to identify particular opportunities, threats, or issues that might affect the customer's purchasing patterns over the relationship lifetime. Therefore, the STEEP analysis must be carried out on the *customer's* market or situation. The way to use the STEEP analysis for customer lifetime value analysis is to consider each of the STEEP elements in turn and see whether there are any specific factors under any of the headings that might affect the customer's purchasing behaviours. Examples of such factors in both business-to-business and business-to-consumer markets are shown in Table 6.2.

Obviously, not all the STEEP elements will be relevant to every customer or business situation. The framework is applied here as a structured approach to customer analysis, to see whether there are

> Not all the STEEP elements will necessarily be relevant to every customer or business situation

particular factors that might affect the customer's buying patterns or intentions. For example, for a business-to-business relationship, 'Socio-cultural' changes might involve merger and acquisition (M&A) activity that could profoundly affect a customer's buying behaviour. Business-to-consumer socio-cultural changes in the form of fashion trends or predicted changes in preferences might have a considerable impact on purchasing.

Table 6.2 Using the STEEP analysis to predict changes in revenues

	Business-to-business	**Business-to-consumer**
Socio-cultural	Industry structure; M&A activity; changes in purchasing strategy	Changes in fashion; ageing population; lifestyle and aspirations
Technological	Technological changes	Technological changes
Economic	Financial performance of customer or sector; stock market conditions; interest rates; gearing; exchange rates; customer's raw materials and other costs	'Feelgood' factor; personal disposable income; level of indebtedness; need for product
Environmental	Corporate social responsibility; 'green' policies	Attitudes towards consumption, recycling, etc.
Political/Regulatory	Changes in government and industry regulation	Changes in government policy; changes in regulation affecting development and sales of existing and new products

Another possible series of factors driving future customer purchasing and hence revenues are based on the actions of competitors and the strengths of the forces acting on the customer. A useful framework for thinking about these factors is the Five Forces of competition, developed by strategy guru Michael Porter.

The Five Forces of competition

The Five Forces of competition are particularly useful in a business-to-business context for analysing the forces within a customer's marketplace that might influence their future purchases. Table 6.3 defines the five forces and suggests how they might influence future customer revenues.

As with the STEEP analysis, the Five Forces analysis is applied to the customer's marketplace and, again, there may not be an issue or influence associated with each factor. However, the framework may suggest ways in which the customer's buying pattern might change over the course of the relationship lifetime. STEEP and Five Forces analysis may help to validate the customer lifetime revenue forecasts.

Table 6.3   The Five Forces of competition

Force	Definition of force	Possible impact on customer revenues
1 Current industry competitors	Power of customer's immediate competitors	Changes in customer market share could affect their purchases
2 Potential entrants	Potential new entrants into the customer's market	New entrants could capture market share, reducing customer's need for product
3 Substitute products or services	Other products or services that the customer's customer could buy, that would satisfy that particular need	Switching could reduce customer's need for product
4 Bargaining power of suppliers	Any changes in the balance of power between the customer and its other suppliers	Pressure from other suppliers could reduce purchasing power of customer
5 Bargaining power of customer's customers	Any changes in the balance of power between the customer and its customers	Increasing demands from end consumers could affect product specification and/or service costs

> **Note**
>
> Apply the STEEP and Five Forces analysis and see whether it generates opportunities or threats for the customer. Then, think about the way your firm might help the customer with its opportunities or threats. A threat for the customer might be an opportunity for the supplier!

RFM analysis

Another tool to support customer revenue forecasting is RFM. This stands for Recency, Frequency, and Monetary Amount. RFM techniques use data on previous purchasing patterns to inform forecasts of future purchases. The Recency part of the data analysis helps to indicate whether the customer is still 'live', and to prompt consideration of whether additional orders are likely in the near future. Frequency indicates the possible timing, and Monetary Amount the value, of purchases. RFM can be used in conjunction with a STEEP and a Five Forces analysis to evaluate whether previous purchasing patterns are a reliable guide to the future.

Customer revenue forecasts

Based on the STEEP, Five Forces, RFM, or other historic data on purchases, combined with sales call data, etc., the account manager should be able to make reasonably reliable forecasts of customer future product purchases and, hence, customer revenues (Table 6.4).

Table 6.4 Step 2 – forecast customer revenues

Customer:...

	Yr 1	Yr 2	Yr 3	Notes and assumptions*
Product X	£1000	£1000	£1000	Replacement purchases continue at current levels
Product Y	£600	–	–	Phased out by end of year 1
Product Z	£100	£1000	£1200	Fast rate of adoption across all client strategic business units (SBUs) by end of year 2
New product AA	–	£100	£400	Trial purchase in year 2; 2 divisions buy in year 3
Subtotal: revenues	£1700.00	£2100.00	£2600	

*Details of products/services likely to be purchased, forecast quantities, price and exchange rate assumptions, returns, etc.

Table 6.4 shows a pattern in which the customer continues to buy product X at current levels for the foreseeable future. In year 2, the customer switches from product Y to a new product, AA, which is introduced in that year although the switch is not complete even by the end of year 3. The forecast of customer revenues also assumes that the trial of Product Z, which the customer is testing in the current year, is successful, so that the customer substantially increases its purchases in years 2 and 3.

Validating customer revenue forecasts

The discussion of Table 6.4 reveals some key assumptions that underlie the customer revenue forecasts. It is important that these assumptions are captured and documented, either in the customer account plan or in the customer lifetime value calculation, so that future reviews of the customer lifetime value numbers can evaluate the accuracy of these predictions. Reviewing the customer revenue forecasts on a regular basis (at least annually), including the assumptions on which the revenue forecasts were based, should help to improve the accuracy of forecasting over time.

> Reviewing customer revenue forecasts on a regular basis, including assumptions, should help to improve the accuracy of forecasting.

The best way of validating revenue forecasts, of course, is to discuss with the customer what its likely future spending plans are. This was illustrated by the airline example earlier in the chapter. The airline actively engages its key customers in joint planning discussions that help the airline predict what the level of demand might be from their largest customers.

Measuring share of wallet

Another way in which the customer revenue forecast can be validated is by including share of wallet (also called share of customer spend) as a measure of the relationship. Share of spend is such an important topic that it will be considered in more detail in Chapter 13. The definition of share of wallet/spend is:

> The supplier's percentage share of the customer's
> total spend on these and related products.

Monitoring share of spend helps the supplier to evaluate the strength of the relationship and its closeness to the customer. Where the share of spend is declining, even if the monetary amount of customer purchases is increasing, this is an indicator that the relationship may be weakening and thus that the revenue forecasts may be less secure. Where the share of spend is increasing, this generally indicates a relationship that is becoming more important to the customer and therefore that the revenue forecasts are probably more secure, all other things being equal.

> Monitoring share of spend helps a supplier to evaluate the strength of a relationship with the customer.

Step 3: Forecasting differential costs

Having estimated the remaining customer relationship lifetime and forecast future revenue streams based on anticipated customer purchases, step 3 in the calculation of customer lifetime value is to forecast differential costs. As discussed in Chapter 2 (calculating customer profitability), there are three categories of differential costs that are relevant here:

- direct product or service costs;
- costs to serve; and
- customer-specific overheads.

General overheads (Head Office costs, etc.) are *not* included in the customer lifetime value analysis because they lie outside the domain of influence of the sales or marketing manager and add to the complexity of the analysis without affecting the usefulness of the results.

Chapter 3 on customer profitability analysis contains an extensive discussion of the process for calculating all three categories of costs using historic data, which is useful background when trying to understand forecast costs. Some additional guidelines for forecasting these costs in the future will now be given.

Future direct costs

Future direct costs relate to the direct product costs or the direct costs of providing the services that the customer is forecast to purchase over the remainder of the relationship lifetime. This is why it is important to set out the assumptions that underlie the revenue forecasts (Table 6.4, right-hand column).

Forecast direct costs, or future costs of goods sold (FCOGS) relate to the forecast labour costs, raw materials, packaging, etc. (or, for services, the number of direct person-hours multiplied by the hourly rate) that will be needed to deliver the product or service. Thus, the future cost of goods sold can be forecast as

$$\frac{\text{Direct costs of production}}{\text{Number of items forecast to be produced}} \times \text{No of items customer forecast to buy}$$

For services, the FCOGS might be described as

$$(\text{Forecast hourly delivery rate} \times \text{no of hours required for delivery})$$
$$+ (\text{other hourly rate} \times \text{no of hours required})$$

In fact, there might be a number of different hourly or daily rates depending on the pay grades of the people directly involved in delivery, the need to use associates, any requirement for specialist or technical input, etc.

Forecasting future direct costs should be carried out with input from Operations. Moreover, these forecasts are very sensitive to changes in forecast future product sales, and so the account manager needs to ensure that any changes in the forecast revenues are reflected in changes in the forecast FCOGS. Historic data on purchasing patterns, plus information about current bids and prospective business, are important inputs here, and so the sales team should also be consulted. Finally, for manufacturing companies, the FCOGS may be influenced by changes in raw materials costs or exchange rates, and so the procurement team should also be consulted.

Future costs to serve

Future costs to serve (FCTS) are difficult to forecast, because they depend on the amount of service that the customer demands and the amount of service that the company is prepared to supply. Costs to serve include sales, marketing, admin, and possibly also logistics costs (unless logistics costs have been treated as a direct cost and included in the FCOGS calculation). Clearly, unanticipated events can have a major impact on FCTS. The problems in forecasting FCTS are compounded when new products or services that have yet to be launched are included in the forecasts. It can be very difficult to foresee just how much sales and marketing support a new product or new service might need.

A pragmatic approach to estimating future costs to serve is to look back at historic data about how much time and resources were spent on the customer and then to take a view about whether the historic allocation was too high, too low, or about right in view of the forecast future revenues. Where hard data are not available, it is even possible to examine the diaries and meeting records of the sales team and account managers, to arrive at some estimates. Then, these need to be translated into year-by-year service requirements, taking into account any increases in salaries, future hires, etc. that might affect FCTS in future years (at the very least, an annual increase in line with inflation should be assumed).

Sales strategy and costs to serve

The company's sales strategy can also be an important input at this stage. Questions such as the following will help determine the appropriate service level:

- Is this the kind of account that the company wants to target?
- What channels might the company use to service this customer? (A switch to cheaper channels will reduce FCTS.)

- How fast are future sales forecast to grow (or decline)?
- Are additional salespeople or account managers to be recruited?

If the customer is large enough and friendly enough, it may be worthwhile for the account manager or salesperson to discuss future buying patterns with the customer's procurement team, to see whether any changes are planned to the *way* that the customer buys that might, in their turn, affect the costs of service to this customer. For example, if the customer is contemplating centralizing its purchasing, this may result in fewer larger orders (lower order processing costs, reducing FCOGS), but a more complex sales process (higher FCTS).

Standard and activity-based costs

As for calculating historic CTS, there are two types of FCTS: standard costs and activity-based costs. The same general rule already given in Chapter 3 applies:

> For smaller and more standard operations, use **standard costs**.
>
> For larger and more variable costs, use **an activity-based costing approach**.

Standard costs are the standard (usually, the average) costs of performing a repeated customer support operation, such as the cost of raising an invoice or credit note, sending a letter, preparing a contract, etc. For FCTS, the number of expected invoices, credit notes, letters, statements, contracts, etc. has to be forecast year by year and this number multiplied by the standard cost of the operation. Future standard costs should be checked with the Finance department.

Activity-based costs are the variable costs of servicing customers, usually the people costs of sales, account management, and customer administration and service. As discussed above, these should be estimated on a time spent ('activity') basis, and then multiplied by the hourly or daily rate for that job grade, allowing for likely salary increases and incorporating the costs of any planned new recruits. The supplier's sales strategy should be taken into account here, as well as the products and services that the customer is expected to buy.

> Activity-based costs are the variable costs of servicing customers, usually the people costs of sales, account management, and customer administration and service.

Future customer-specific overheads

In some cases, although not for all customers, there is a third cost element that needs to be calculated. This is customer-specific overheads. As discussed in Chapter 3, customer-specific overheads might include a branch office within a key account's premises, an on-site team, or customer-specific stock.

Input from the sales strategy and from Operations will be necessary to forecast the likely costs of customer-specific overheads. It is important that, if the future revenue figures depend on, say, the provision of vendor-managed inventory within two years, the costs of providing this service must be included in the customer lifetime value forecast. A general rule is that the cost of holding customer-specific stock is approximately 25–30% of the value of that stock, per year. See Chapter 3 for a more detailed discussion of customer-specific overheads.

Table 6.5 Step 3 – forecast future costs

Customer:..

	Yr 1	Yr 2	Yr 3	Notes and assumptions*
Subtotal: Revenues	£1700	£2100	£2600	
Direct costs (FCOGS)	£500	£600	£800	Take-up of new product AA will increase production costs in the short term
Costs to serve (FCTS)	£250	£650	£550	Customer acquires company Q in year 2; considerable additional sales effort needed then and in year 3
Forecast customer-specific overheads	£0	£200	£200	Assumes we become category captains for product P in year 2 for 3 years
Subtotal: Costs	£750	£1450	£1550	
Year-by-year profit	**£950**	**£650**	**£1050**	

Table 6.5 illustrates the forecast costs, year by year, in each of the three categories. It also records the assumptions on which these forecasts were based, so that the forecasts can be revised if the assumptions prove incorrect. In this case, some key assumptions relate to the take-up of product AA, some acquisition activity on the part of the customer, and an assumed increase in customer closeness resulting in the supplier being selected as category manager of product P.

Once the year-by-year costs have been forecast, the total costs need to be subtracted from the forecast revenues to give the year-by-year profits (Table 6.5, bottom row). In the example in Table 6.5 there is a dip in profitability in year 2 because of the increased investment in sales effort by the supplier that year; the investment pays off with higher profits in year 3. It is interesting to note the difference between the customer revenues (which show a pattern of steady growth) and customer profitability (which is considerably more variable). This is an illustration of the impact that servicing and customer management decisions can have on the bottom-line returns from customers and also shows why relying on customer revenue data can be highly misleading.

> **Note**
>
> Focus the customer lifetime value analysis on the differential costs that the sales and marketing managers can influence. These are the direct product costs, the costs to serve, and any customer-specific overheads.

However, as discussed in Chapter 5, this year-by-year profit is actually expressed in future money terms. To determine the present-day value of this customer, the future profits need to be discounted. The discounting process is the fourth and final step of the customer lifetime value calculation.

Step 4: Discounting future profits

Factors such as inflation mean that future profits are not worth as much as profits in the hand today. Therefore, the future profits calculated in steps 1 to 3 need to be discounted back so that customer lifetime value can be expressed in today's monetary values. This is done using a discount rate or the company's weighted average cost of capital (WACC).

> Future profits are not worth as much as profits in the hand today. 'Discounting' is the process used to express future money in terms of its value today.

Most companies currently use a discount rate for working out the current value of future projects, investments, etc. The discount rate is, to some extent, determined by company policy and it can be obtained from the finance department.

Using the WACC is an alternative to using the discount rate, used by certain companies who have a stock market listing. It is gaining in popularity as more and more companies become interested in shareholder value management, because the WACC measure not only reflects company funding policy (whether the company has a lot of debt) but also takes account of the cost of equity and of debt funding. Thus, it is an appropriate measure for companies that fund their business partly from bank lending (debt) and partly from shareholders' funds (equity). The proportion of debt to that of equity is also known as the company's gearing ratio: the higher the proportion of debt funding, the higher the company's gearing.

The WACC is defined as follows:

(Proportion of debt funding × cost of debt) + (Proportion of equity funding × cost of equity)

Books on shareholder value management contain detailed instructions on how to calculate the WACC. For the purposes of the sales and marketing manager, it is enough to know that there is a difference and that, if the company is using some form of shareholder value measurement system (such as economic value added), the rate that the finance department should provide is the WACC.

Calculating net present value

The discount rate or WACC takes the form of a percentage. This needs to be converted into a discount factor before it can be applied to the customer lifetime value calculation. The formula for doing this is as follows:

$$\frac{1}{(1+i)^t}$$

where i is the discount rate and t is the time period. The equation can be explained in words as

$$\frac{1}{(1+ \text{discount rate})^{\text{time period}}}$$

It is important to understand that this is *not* the same as reducing the future year profit number by the discount rate percentage. So, if the discount rate was 5%, the current-day value of the profits from the customer shown in Table 6.5 at the end of year 1 is *not* £902.50 (£950–5%). This is a vital point, because calculating the net present value of these future profits incorrectly will lead to a cumulative error that will substantially mis-state the true value of the customer. Instead, the calculation should be carried out as shown in Table 6.6.

Table 6.6 How to calculate a discount factor

	Yr 1	Yr 2	Yr 3
Calculation of discount factor	$\dfrac{1}{(1+0.05)^1}$	$\dfrac{1}{(1+0.05)^2}$	$\dfrac{1}{(1+0.05)^3}$
Discount factor	0.952	0.907	0.864

The example shown in Table 6.6 is for a discount rate of 5%. The expanded version of the discount factor calculation is as follows:

$$\text{Year 1} : 1/(1.05)$$

$$\text{Year 2} : 1/(1.05 \times 1.05)$$

$$\text{Year 3} : 1/(1.05 \times 1.05 \times 1.05)$$

The discount rate is expressed as a decimal, and so a discount rate of 5% becomes 0.05, a rate of 10% becomes 0.1, of 4.5% becomes 0.045, of 8.25% becomes 0.0825, etc.

Once the discount factor has been calculated, the future profits are then multiplied by the discount factor for that year. This gives the net present value (the current-day value) of the future profits. The total of these is the lifetime value of that customer, expressed in terms of today's money (Table 6.7).

Table 6.7 Step 4 – discount future profits back to the present day

Customer:..

	Yr 1	Yr 2	Yr 3	Notes and assumptions
Year-by-year profit	£950	£650	£1050	
Discount factor	0.952	0.907	0.864	Based on discount rate of 5% per annum
Present value of future profits	£904.40	£589.55	£907.20	
Total: Customer lifetime value			**£2401.15**	

The line in Table 6.7 showing the present value of future profits demonstrates why the discounting process (step 4) is so important. Expressed in terms of future profits, it appears that year 3's profits are much higher than profits in year 1. However, when the present value of year 3 is compared to the present value of year 1, there is actually very little real growth in profits. This should send a signal to the salespeople and to the account manager to monitor the resources they spend on this customer very carefully to ensure that there is a real payback to the year 2 investment in future years. As things stand, the investment of additional sales time in year 2 and the new product launch of product AA in year 2 has merely resulted in 'station keeping'.

That's fine, if that was indeed the sales strategy for this customer or if there are prospects of real growth in profits beyond the existing forecasting period. At the moment, though, this supplier should not persuade itself that it is making much progress with the customer, because the figures simply do not support such an argument.

Summary

The calculation of customer lifetime value has started to raise some interesting and important issues about how the customer relationship can be managed profitably. These issues are the subject of later chapters. Before that, we have to consider the case of the company with thousands or millions of customers, where the calculation of 'bottom up' customer lifetime value is inappropriate. Instead, companies in this situation tend to adopt a 'top down' or customer equity approach. How to use and calculate customer equity is the subject of the next chapter.

> **Note**
>
> Now calculate customer lifetime value for an individual customer using the worksheet on the following page.

Worksheet: customer lifetime value

	Yr 1	Yr 2	Yr 3	Yr 4
Customer revenues	☐	☐	☐	☐
Direct product or service costs	☐	☐	☐	☐
Cost to serve	☐	☐	☐	☐
Customer-specific overheads (if any)	☐	☐	☐	☐
Future profits	☐	☐	☐	☐
Discount rate	☐	☐	☐	☐
Discount factor	☐	☐	☐	☐
Present-day value of future profits	☐	☐	☐	☐
Total customer lifetime value:	☐			

Where to find out more

For a reasonably technical discussion of the calculation method, see the following classic: Berger, P.D. and Nasr, N.I. (1998) 'Customer lifetime value: marketing models and applications', *Journal of Interactive Marketing,* **12**(1), pp. 17-30.

Again a fairly technical discussion, but a rare example of research that deals with the problem of valuing customers who leave and then subsequently return: Calciu, M. and Salerno, F. (2002), 'Customer value modelling: synthesis and extension proposals', *Journal of Targeting, Measurement and Analysis for Marketing,* **11**(2), pp. 124-147.

Calculating and using customer equity

7

What's in this chapter

- Getting started on customer equity
- Granularity
- The four components of customer equity
- What to use customer equity for
- The limitations of customer equity
- How to calculate customer equity: revenue and cost drivers
- Improving forecasting using the Delphi Panel technique

Key concepts discussed in this chapter

Cost drivers	Factors that drive the direct costs and costs to serve of customers. Most interesting here are the costs to serve, because there may be customer demands that affect these, or customer location; there may also be cost drivers that relate to actions taken by the supplier.
Customer equity	The total lifetime value plus potential value of a group of customers, such as a customer segment, or of the total customer base.
Customer retention	Measures the extent to which relationships with customers endure from one period to another; the inverse of customer churn. Often expressed as a percentage of total customers in that segment or customer group. Interestingly, it is a more difficult topic to define than might appear, because customers may become dormant or move most of their business elsewhere while still appearing in the database and apparently retained.

Delphi Panel	A forecasting method that involves establishing a panel of experts (within and/or outside the firm) and asking their opinions about a range of future issues. The results are fed back to the panel members and further iterations take place. Usually, the panel's views start to converge. Proponents claim it performs better as a forecasting measure than normal trends forecasting.
Revenue drivers	Factors that drive the revenues from customers over time. Usually related to the size of the customer, its financial ability to buy, and its willingness or propensity to buy. Also affected by product mix and prices.

Key tools explained in this chapter

- Revenue and cost drivers: Factors driving customer revenues and costs. Identified by comparing high and low revenue segments; and high and low cost segments. Process of comparing segments continues until no new drivers are identified. Identification of revenue and cost drivers is important in understanding customer equity and also in managing it.
- Delphi Panel: A panel of experts used in an iterative forecasting process as follows:

  - Assemble a panel of experts.
  - Develop a Delphi questionnaire, generally numerical (Round 1).
  - Collect responses from all participants and produce an anonymous summary.
  - Repeat, looking for convergence rather than unanimity.
  - The panel should close at the end of Round 3 even if convergence has not been reached.

Two-minute chapter summary

Customer equity can be thought of as the total customer lifetime value of a group of customers, including the potential value that might come from these relationships. The lowest granularity for customer equity is to look at the entire customer base; in this context, customer equity is of interest in merger and acquisition situations where some researchers have suggested that it provides a better guide to the real value of a company than some more traditional valuation methods (see the 'Where to find out more' section at the end of this chapter for more information).

The four components of customer equity are:

- forecast revenues;
- additional potential;
- forecast costs;
- customer retention.

Customer equity is a portfolio measure and is associated with the idea of customer relationships as assets that companies should manage in the same way that they would manage a portfolio of products or brands.

Because customer equity is a forecast relating to a group of customers, customer relationship management (CRM) systems may provide useful general data about the way that these customers are likely to behave (their retention rates, for example). Tools such as STEEP and Porter's Five Forces, which were explained in Chapter 6, can also be very helpful in forecasting.

Context: the adoption of customer equity

The case for the adoption of future-based forecasts of the value of customers was made in Chapter 5. Increasingly, firms are recognizing that they need to measure the value of their customers. The starting point is usually to look at historic customer profitability (see Chapter 4) but, for companies that are serious about the management of their customer relationship assets, measures that look forward rather than backwards are vital. Where the company has a small number of key customers, the value of these should be calculated bottom up, using the method set out in Chapter 6. However, where the company has larger numbers of customers, it would be too onerous to work out the individual lifetime value of each customer. In this case, customer lifetime value is used to examine the value of individual key accounts and customer equity is used to calculate the value of the rest of the customer portfolio.

> Where the company has larger numbers of customers, it would be too onerous to work out the individual lifetime value of each customer. In this case, customer equity is used.

Technically, customer equity is the total of all the customer lifetime value and potential value in the customer portfolio. Using the term in this sense, some research has found that customer equity is a better guide to the value of a business than market capitalization, so it has become important to companies contemplating a takeover bid. The role of customer equity in valuing a company for takeover purposes underlines the strategic importance of customer relationships as assets that need to be measured and managed.

In the context of managing customers profitably, however, the term 'customer
equity' will be used to mean the total lifetime value and potential value of a group
of customers, such as customer segments.
Comparing the customer equity of different
segments can provide very useful data for
sales and marketing managers. Customer

> Customer equity is one of the
> building blocks of customer
> asset management, in which the
> customer base is a portfolio in
> which the company invests for
> future returns.

equity is one of the building blocks of customer asset management, which considers
the customer base as a portfolio in which the company invests its efforts in the
expectation of a stream of future returns.

Getting started on customer equity

Customer equity can be thought of as the lifetime value of a group of customers,
and so the techniques for calculating it are similar to those of customer lifetime
value (see Chapter 6). However, because there are larger numbers of customers,
calculating customer equity often involves the use of CRM systems and data mining tools. The larger amount of data makes it feasible to include some modelling
techniques that predict potential value as well as extrapolating current values
(this notion was touched on briefly in the discussion of customer lifetime value
in Chapter 6).

Moreover, because whole groups of customers are being considered, it makes
sense to incorporate customer acquisition/retention modelling into the customer
equity calculation, although this makes the forecasting more complicated. Data gathering and manipulation techniques such as decision calculus, regression analysis,
neural networks, Delphi panels, or Markov techniques may be used to calculate customer equity. Many of these techniques are rather specialist for use in sales and
marketing and are mainly of interest to IT managers. However, the Delphi panel is
an interesting tool that has application to forecasting, and so this tool is discussed
in more detail later in the chapter.

Deciding on the granularity of the customer equity calculation

To get started on customer equity, the company needs to decide how to group its
customers. The grouping will depend on what level of analysis and what kinds of
results are most useful for the development of sales and marketing strategies.

Granularity was discussed in Chapter 2 in relation to customer profitability analysis. It refers to the degree to which the customer base is to be broken down.
If the granularity ('graininess') is high, this means that the customer base is to be

divided into a large number of small groups. The ultimate granularity in this context is the analysis of individual customers. So, if the customer base was divided into its individual parts for a customer equity analysis, this would be the same as calculating customer lifetime value for each individual customer.

Because very high granularity is expensive and time-consuming where a company has a lot of customers, and because grouping customers together may reveal useful patterns of behaviour, customer attributes, etc., customer equity involves a lower level of granularity. Lower granularity means that the customer base is divided into fewer, larger groups. The detail of individual customers is lost, but overall trends and patterns may emerge. The ultimate lowest level of granularity for customer equity would be to treat the entire customer base as a single unit and to try to calculate its customer equity. Although treating the customer base as a single unit may be technically feasible, it is likely to be a rather difficult forecasting exercise because the sales and marketing managers will have to generalize about the likely future purchases of a broad group of customers. Where the customer base is small(ish) and relatively homogeneous, it may be feasible. In most cases, however, the sales and marketing managers make a decision to use an intermediate level of granularity, dividing up the customer base in some way that is useful and informative for forecasting purposes.

Some companies calculate customer equity based on existing customer segments because that allows them to compare the value from one segment to another, and then to allocate their marketing and sales resources appropriately. Other companies take approaches based on channels, industry sectors, geographical location, or even a simple stratification (large, medium, small). Figure 7.1 illustrates the granularity options.

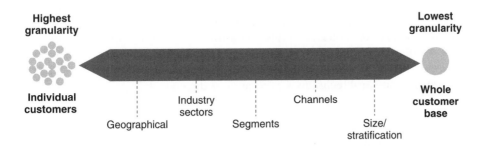

Figure 7.1 Indication of granularity levels

Starting at the lowest granularity, which is the entire customer base on the right-hand side of Figure 7.1, one approach is stratifying the customer base into simple size or other general attributes. Usually this will result in two or three large groups of customers.

Moving to the left, customer equity can be calculated by grouping customers into channels. This is a useful approach for some companies, where the customer characteristics differ between channels and where the costs to serve are different. Many businesses will have three or four channels (call centres, Internet, field sales force or branches, desk-based account management).

> Customer equity can be calculated by channel. This is a useful approach for some companies, where customer characteristics differ between channels and where the costs to serve are different.

Calculating customer equity by segment can also be useful for businesses that have useful segmentation methods; there tend to be more segments than channels, as a general rule, and so the granularity is usually higher. Many organizations will recognize between five and nine segments. Customers can also be valued by industry segment, and there are many different SIC (Standard Industrial Classification) codes that provide a potentially high level of granularity. However, it is unclear whether industry sector would be a useful way to consider the value of customers, because there may be differences in the lifetime value of customers from the same industry sector. Geographical segmentation can provide a very high level of granularity – supermarkets, for example, often use detailed postcode data to develop their marketing strategies – although the level of granularity of this kind of analysis would be too high for most marketing strategy development. The supermarket is unlikely to develop a marketing strategy for each postcode group in its catchment area!

This review of the approaches to granularity shown in Figure 7.1 illustrates why most organizations take a mid-level approach to granularity and calculate customer equity based on some form of segmentation. A useful general rule about granularity is that, if the company is planning to use any statistical analysis techniques, the customer groups should comprise at least 30 customers. A sample of 30 is considered by statisticians to be sufficient to use techniques based on the notion of the normal distribution curve (Chapter 2). Below 30 customers per group, it becomes difficult to draw robust inferences about the group because the influence of outliers is disproportionate. Useful information may still come out of the analysis, but the output from statistical techniques becomes less dependable.

The four components of customer equity

If customer equity is considered from the perspective of a group of customers such as a segment, there are four main components: forecast revenues, additional potential, forecast costs, and retention. These four components are illustrated in Figure 7.2.

> There are four main components of customer equity: forecast revenues, additional potential, forecast costs, and customer retention.

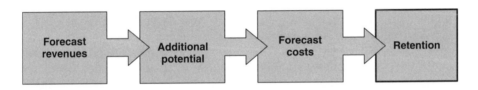

Figure 7.2 The four components of customer equity

The first component is forecast revenues based on the trend for this segment or group of customers. However, there may be additional potential that could be obtained through changes in the segment itself, or through the way it is managed. These changes might take the form of changes in tastes or fashions, or by cross- or up-selling. Thus, the second component of customer equity is additional potential. The third component is the forecast costs associated with the forecast revenues and additional potential. The fourth element is the retention element. When considering a customer segment or other group of customers, it is not the individual relationship lifetime that is relevant; it is more useful to think about the proportion of customers retained.

Once financial values have been placed on all four components, a discount rate or WACC will need to be applied to express the customer equity in terms of today's money (see Chapter 6 for a detailed discussion of how this can be done).

The advantages of customer equity

Customer equity has the same advantages as customer lifetime value as a tool for marketing and sales decision making. First, it takes account of the future, and supports asset management of customer relationships. This enables the company to manage its sales and marketing activities as investments into the customer portfolio. Second, customer equity calculations can be used in close conjunction with CRM so that the company can calculate the impact of its sales and marketing actions on the value of the customer segment. The impact of sales and marketing actions on the components of customer equity may result in higher future revenues, increased potential, reduced costs to serve, or changes in the probability of retention.

> Customer equity can be used in conjunction with CRM so that the company can calculate the impact of its sales and marketing actions on the value of a customer segment. The result may be higher future revenues, increased potential, reduced costs to serve, or changes in the probability of retention.

Some strategies might impact more than one of the components of customer equity. An example would be cross-selling strategies that increase the number of products that customers in a certain segment hold. Typically, the result of cross-selling is an increase in revenues, because the customer is spending more with that supplier (cross-selling may also be associated with a higher share of wallet, which again drives revenues). Research also shows, however, that the greater the number of products that a customer buys, the lower the likelihood of switching (because it is more trouble to change to another supplier). So, cross-selling may *both* increase revenues and increase retention.

An advantage that customer equity has over customer lifetime value is that it is more useful where there are larger numbers of customers to be managed. Typically, a key account management (KAM) department would manage a small number of key accounts (it is unusual for an organization to have more than 30 key accounts) and in these circumstances it is both feasible and useful to calculate the lifetime value of each key account individually. The customer lifetime value is then used to determine the appropriate customer management package customer by customer.

Where there are larger numbers of customers in the portfolio, as there are for many business-to-consumer and indeed business-to-business companies, it is more useful to divide up the customer base in some way that enables the organization to develop strategies and plans for *groups* of customers. To develop appropriate customer management strategies, the company needs to understand the customer equity of each segment or sector (or other grouping).

Thus, the overall customer portfolio might comprise some key accounts, measured in terms of individual customer lifetime value, and some customer sectors and/or segments for which customer equity is calculated group by group. Figure 7.3 illustrates a typical customer management structure for a business-to-business supplier with a range of different types of accounts.

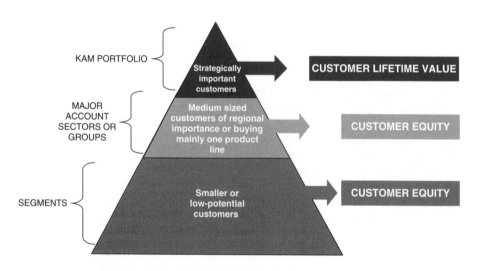

Figure 7.3 Valuing a customer portfolio

At the peak of the customer portfolio are the key accounts or strategic accounts. These are customers of strategic importance, usually as a result of their size. It is likely that they will buy from more than one business unit of the supplier. They are managed by a key account manager, whose management strategy is based on the key account's individual customer lifetime value.

There is then an intermediate layer of customers that are not quite large enough to be key accounts but that are perhaps regionally important or who would be major accounts for a particular business unit. These accounts may be managed by industry sector teams, or by divisional major account managers. Here, the management strategy for the sectors or regions would be based on the customer equity of that group of customers.

At the bottom of the customer portfolio are the very many smaller customers. These are segmented and then managed through segment plans that relate to the customer equity of that segment.

> **Note**
>
> At this point, you need to decide whether customer equity could be a useful approach to analysing your customer portfolio.

What to use customer equity for

Customer equity is a portfolio-based measure and is strongly associated with the notion of customers as assets that companies should measure and manage as they do other assets such as brands. The marketing applications of customer equity relate to budget setting and allocation, balancing customer acquisition and retention activities, and profitable customer management. These uses of customer equity will be considered in more detail later in the chapter.

Small print: the limitations of customer equity

Like customer lifetime value, customer equity has certain limitations that relate to the fact that it is a forecast, rather than historic data. Unlike customer lifetime value, however, the existence of CRM systems can help to mitigate these limitations.

Limitation #1: forecasting accuracy

The accuracy of customer equity forecasts depends on the amount and quality of the customer data that are available and the ability of the company to interrogate its CRM system so as to provide useful input into the forecasting process. Customer equity calculations are less likely to be affected by specific factors affecting a single customer, because the calculation is based on a group of customers or on a segment. That said, some companies do experience difficulties in identifying which customers are in which segment (particularly when it comes to new customers) and there can be gaps and inaccuracies in even the best of data warehouses.

Limitation #2: the problem of potential

Probably the most contentious issue in calculating customer equity is in the potential that is ascribed to the segment. Even small inaccuracies in estimating potential additional sales can scale up to substantial amounts where the customer equity of a large group of customers is concerned. This limitation can affect, for example, the accuracy of overall sales forecasts. As well as actual amounts, the timing of the additional potential sales might be incorrectly forecast so that, for example, the take-up of a new product might be rather slower than expected. Again, data mining tools may help improve the accuracy of forecasting. The company should also ensure that data from market research, focus groups, customer panels, and industry trend monitors, are also used to inform the customer equity forecasts.

How to calculate customer equity

Because customer equity is about the total lifetime value of the customer base, many of the forecasts and assumptions relate to groups of customers. For convenience, it will be assumed in the discussion that follows that the analysis will be carried out at the segment level, although it could be that customers are grouped in other ways (for example, by sector or by geographical region). The same calculation procedures apply.

In addition to thinking about the way in which customers are grouped for customer equity calculations, there is another issue that becomes important in calculating customer equity: the proportion of customers acquired/lost during the period. In customer lifetime value calculations, where a single customer was being considered, the first step was to calculate the remaining customer lifetime in years (see Chapter 6). In the calculation of customer equity, where groups of customers are to be evaluated, it is the average customer lifetime for that segment that needs to be considered. It is likely that there will be different customer lifetimes (retention rates) in the different segments. It should be noted that customer retention can be measured in different ways, and this issue will be considered later in the 'Customer acquisition and retention' section. Note, however, that retention also affects anticipated revenues.

> It is likely that there will be different customer lifetimes (retention rates) in different segments or groups of customers.

Forecasting revenues

Revenue forecasts involve making assumptions about the numbers of products sold (which may be based in turn on a forecast of the percentage of a customer group that will buy the product), the product mix, and the price at which each product is sold. Any discounts or special terms that are likely to be taken up by a particular segment also have to be taken into account.

Chapter 6 discussed techniques such as the STEEP, Five Forces, and RFM (Recency, Frequency, and Monetary Amount) that can be helpful in calculating customer lifetime value. These techniques are also of interest when considering customer equity. In particular, the RFM technique may prove useful when considering a group of customers. Consider, for example, a company with two customer segments (A and B). Analysis of the customer base reveals some clusters of data around Recency, Frequency, and Monetary amount. Table 7.1 summarizes the RFM data.

Table 7.1   Using RFM to calculate customer equity

	Segment A (%)	Segment B (%)
Recency		
within 6 months	60	30
6 to 12 months	20	40
more than 12 months	20	30
Frequency		
average 3 purchases per year	10	40
average 1.5 purchases per year	90	60
Monetary amount		
average £2000 per purchase	70	50
average £5000 per purchase	30	50

Table 7.1 suggests that segment A tends to contain a higher proportion of recently-purchasing customers. This may be an indication that there are more new customers in this segment than in segment B. This would also explain why segment B customers tend to buy more frequently (if there are more 'first time buyers' in segment A, there will be a higher proportion of customers who are trialling the product). Segment B customers also spend considerably more, on average, than segment A customers.

Table 7.1 is a very simplified example, but it does illustrate that segment B is likely to generate more customer equity than segment A, all other things being equal. Once the number of customers in each segment is known, and incorporating repurchase forecasts based on historic frequency of purchase, it is relatively straightforward to calculate the probable future revenues for each of the two segments and also to estimate the timings of these purchases, which affects their present-day value because of the time value of money (see Chapter 6).

As the foregoing discussion indicates, the RFM analysis implicitly involves consideration of customer retention (discussed in the section on retention later in this chapter). For now, it is enough to note that the RFM analysis is incomplete without a consideration of retention. However, RFM is not the only technique that can be used. Where the company has a large number of customers and a CRM system, so that there are large amounts of customer data, the system itself can be used to forecast customer revenues. The same basic processes apply, but a big database can probably produce forecasts of greater accuracy. Moreover, a CRM system can also incorporate lifestage and behavioural data to enable it to forecast additional potential as well as retention.

Understanding revenue drivers

Even companies without a CRM system can improve the accuracy of their forecasting by identifying the drivers that determine customer revenues, through a comparison of high revenue customers and low revenue customers.

Identifying revenue drivers

A useful exercise in developing customer equity models is to identify the revenue drivers – the factors that drive customer revenues. To do this, sales and marketing managers can brainstorm in small groups. First, they identify a number of high and low revenue customers. The identification should be based on potential as well as actual revenue. It is best if these are named customers (company names), but types of customers might be used (e.g., large national distributors versus small local 'mom and pop' stores; high net worth individuals versus home office customers). It is not necessary to know the precise details of the revenues, as long as the group agrees that the customers are at opposite ends of the revenue spectrum.

Then, the brainstorming group compares pairs of one high and one low revenue customer and examines why they are different. The reasons should be the revenue drivers. The comparison of the high/low pairs continues until no new revenue factors are driven out.

Typical revenue drivers for business-to-business customers include:

- size of customer company;
- product mix purchased;
- volume;

- share of their spend;
- discounts[1].

Typical revenue drivers for business-to-consumer customers include:

- personal disposable income;
- product mix purchased;
- propensity to purchase products.

Once the revenue drivers have been identified, the next step is to examine the effect of each driver on each segment (Table 7.2).

Table 7.2 illustrates how revenue drivers can help support revenue forecasts. It illustrates two segments of CD and DVD buyers. The young parents in Segment X have high propensity to buy but they buy mainly value line products and have smaller disposable incomes. Segment Y represents professional males in the 25–45 age bracket, the highest-spending group on these products.

Table 7.2 Using customer revenue drivers

	Segment X (young parents)	Segment Y (professional males)
Size of segment	100 000 customers	50 000 customers
Personal disposable income	Average	Well above average
Product mix purchased	Predominantly value line	20% value line, 80% premium
Propensity to buy	High	Moderate and static

Although segment Y is half the size of segment X, customers in this segment have high disposable incomes and prefer fashionable and high-priced items, and so the segment generates large amounts of revenues at present. However, propensity to buy is moderate because these customers are influenced by new technology and are tending to download more and more of their music.

The customer equity forecasts for these two segments can be compiled by identifying the amounts of money involved; the trend in revenues should also follow the 'shape' predicted by the revenue drivers. Thus, the forecast year-by-year revenues for segment X should remain fairly steady for the next three years because the revenue drivers are unlikely to change much. The forecast year-by-year revenues for segment Y, by contrast, are likely to show a sharp decline as the customers migrate from high-price premium products to competing offerings.

[1] Managers often debate whether discounts should be treated as a revenue reduction or a cost increase. Although accountants take the latter view, treating discounts as a price reduction is more appropriate for sales and marketing purposes and for calculating customer equity.

As well as forecast revenues based on extending current forecasts forward, customer equity also takes additional potential into account.

Evaluating additional potential

When forecasting both customer lifetime value and customer equity, additional potential is an important issue. 'Additional potential' is not just an extrapolation of the current relationship; it is about extending the relationship with the customer into new areas. Therefore, supermarkets such as Tesco and Morrisons were able to extrapolate the lifetime value of customers buying food but they identified additional potential

> 'Additional potential' is not just an extrapolation of the current relationship; it is about extending the relationship with the customer into new areas, such as supermarkets moving into clothing, consumer durables, insurance, etc.

through sales of non-food items such as clothing, petrol, insurance, mobile phone services, etc.

As the supermarket example indicates, the ability to identify additional potential involves thinking afresh about market definition. If Tesco had defined its market purely as 'food retailing', it would not have expanded its product range into petrol and clothing. Thinking creatively about its market in terms of its customers' discretionary spending suggested a wide range of additional products that it could offer.

So, rule 1 for identifying additional potential is: think creatively about market definition.

> **Evaluating potential: Rule 1**
>
> **Define your market carefully – but creatively**

The other reason why additional potential plays an important role in customer equity calculations in particular is that identifying and developing potential is in many ways easier with a group of customers than with a single customer. When forecasting the

> When forecasting the potential of a *group* of customers, data analysis and statistical tools can be used.

lifetime value of a single customer, the question of whether they might start to buy very different kinds of products or do business from new business units or geographies is largely a judgement call on the part of the relationship manager. When forecasting the potential of a *group* of customers, data analysis and statistical tools can be used. Many companies are able to forecast that a certain percentage of customers in a segment will behave in a particular way, although it may be next to impossible to identify which individuals will change their behaviours.

The second rule for evaluating potential is therefore to analyse patterns of behaviour and other data that may reveal unexpected potential in the relationship.

> **Evaluating potential: Rule 2**
>
> **Analyse customer patterns to seek out areas of potential**

Examples of pattern analysis and data mining to identify areas of potential include the retail banks, who use lifecycle analysis combined with an evaluation of existing product holdings to help them identify the products and services that customers are buying elsewhere (or may not yet buy, but would have a strong propensity to buy). Similarly, the supermarkets and other loyalty card providers use their analysis of spending patterns, combined with other data inputs such as postcode databases, to identify gaps in their customers' purchasing patterns. The postcode databases provide surprisingly detailed information about income bracket, marital status, lifestyle, and even tastes. This information is also used to tailor the offerings that appear in different stores, even within the same chain.

A very visible manifestation of this phenomenon is the 'localization' of products at chains such as McDonalds, which offers croissants in Paris and noodles in Shanghai, but the effect is still more subtle. Supermarkets, for example, may offer different products or allocate different amounts of shelf space to the same products depending on local differences in purchasing patterns. Amazon has turned pattern matching on its enormous database into an art form: by telling customers 'people who bought X also bought Y', they not only present customers with additional offers at checkout, but they also use the technique to personalize their web pages to returning customers.

Forecasting costs

Forecasting costs for customer equity purposes is analogous to the process of forecasting costs for customer lifetime value (Chapter 6). The same categories of costs apply: product or service costs (Cost of Goods and Services, or COGS) and costs to serve (CTS). The third category of costs that are relevant to customer lifetime value calculations (customer-specific overheads) is unlikely to be relevant where groups of customers or segments are considered, as for customer equity. Instead, it may be relevant to consider channel costs. This issue was touched on briefly in Chapter 4 in relation to calculating the historic profitability of customers top-down.

The *cost of goods and services* will depend on the forecasts for revenue and potential – that is, on the product mix and numbers of products that the customers in each segment buy. The *costs to serve* relate to the sales and marketing costs in each segment, and to other costs such as logistics costs if relevant. *Customer-specific overheads* relate to dedicated overheads such as customer-specific warehousing or stock, any overheads relating to dedicated customer teams, and in the case of customer equity calculations, channel costs if relevant.

Just as forecast revenues can be understood using revenue drivers, so too can forecast costs use cost drivers. Organizations with CRM systems can use these to establish the time costs (so, for example, the sales force automation system records which customers the salespeople spend time with, and call centre software packages enable call monitoring of how much time is spend on the telephone with which customers). Where this information is not available, sales and marketing managers can obtain a better understanding of the cost drivers of customers or segments by comparing high-cost and low-cost customers or customer groups and trying to identify what makes them more, or less, costly to service.

Understanding cost drivers

When companies understand what drives the cost of servicing customers, they are in a much better position to manage those costs. They can also identify the likely cost profile of new incoming customers. One retail bank in the UK, for example, identified the cost drivers for customers of its online banking service. By creating appropriately-worded questions at the beginning of the application process for opening an online account, the bank is able to identify which customers are likely to have unattractively high costs or a profile that would lead to the rejection of their application. This quickly gives the bank the option to stop the application before more time and money is wasted on both sides (bank and applicant).

> Where companies understand what drives the cost of servicing customers, they are in a much better position to manage those costs.

Identifying cost drivers

A useful exercise in developing customer equity models is to identify the cost drivers. The cost drivers for a customer or segment are based on current and future product costs, costs to serve, and any customer-specific overheads. The process is analogous to that used to identify revenue drivers. The sales and marketing managers identify individual customers or customer groups that are high cost and low cost. It is not necessary to know the precise details of the costs, as long as the group agrees that the customers are at opposite ends of the cost spectrum.

Then, the brainstorming group compares pairs of one high and one low cost customer and examines why they are different (the cost drivers). The comparison of the high/low pairs continues until no new cost factors are driven out. Usually, there will be a longer list of cost drivers than revenue drivers, because most companies have a wide variety of different service elements and packages.

It is difficult to generalize the cost drivers for business-to-business customers because they vary from firm to firm and from industry to industry. They might include:

- product mix;
- delivery arrangements;
- customization;
- technical support;
- special packaging;
- quality assurance/testing;
- vendor-managed inventory.

Again, for business-to-consumer customers, the cost drivers may vary considerably, but might include:

- channel;
- average order or purchase size;
- need for information/customer service support.

As with the revenue drivers, once the cost drivers have been identified, the next step is to examine the effect of each driver on each segment (Table 7.3).

Table 7.3 Using customer cost drivers

	Segment X (young parents)	Segment Y (professional males)
Size of segment	100 000 customers	50 000 customers
Channel	Mainly in-store, some Internet	Mainly Internet
Average order or purchase size	Large (but infrequent)	Moderate (but frequent)
Need for support	Moderate to high – advice seekers	Very low – cash and dash

The table continues the analysis of two segments of CD and DVD buyers that began in Table 7.2 (for revenue drivers). Table 7.3 shows the cost drivers for young parents in Segment X and professional males in the 25–45 age bracket in Segment Y.

The analysis reveals that, although Segment X is very large, it tends to be a higher-cost segment because it makes a high proportion of its purchases in-store, which is an expensive channel, and Segment X customers tend to ask for a lot of advice when they are in store, so using up a lot of staff time. This is only partially offset by the larger order quantities because the parents will buy several products for themselves and their children.

Segment Y is a smaller segment but has comparatively low costs, buying through the Internet and using little service time (in fact, this group buys on impulse and on the basis of word of mouth from friends, so they tend to make fast decisions). Even though the average purchase is smaller, the costs overall are lower because of the cheaper channel and low support costs.

Based on Table 7.2, the revenue forecasts for Segment X were steady although for Segment Y they were declining sharply. Combining this with the cost drivers enables the identification of customer equity forecasts for these two segments. The costs of Segment X are likely to rise faster than revenues, so that the year-on-year profits from Segment X will tend to decline. Segment Y will remain profitable year-on-year despite the rapid decline in revenues because of its low costs, but customer equity will depend on the company's ability to generate new products or services that will entice Segment Y customers away from free downloads.

The process for identifying revenue and cost drivers is illustrated in Figure 7.4.

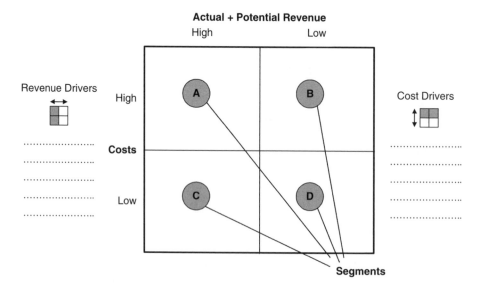

Figure 7.4 Identifying revenue and cost drivers for customer equity

The sales and marketing team has brainstormed four segments, shown in Figure 7.4 as A, B, C, and D. To identify revenue drivers, they compare the high revenue segments A and C to the left of the diagram with the low revenue segments B and D on the right. To identify cost drivers, they compare the high cost segments A and B in the top half of the customer portfolio with the lower cost segments C and D in the bottom half.

In practice, the future revenues from these segments are affected not only by the revenue drivers but also by the retention of customers. Clearly, if the customer is lost then so, too, are the revenues. For this reason, retention is the fourth component of customer equity calculations.

Note
Now use your own version of Figure 7.4 as a creative thinking tool to help you and your team identify revenue and cost drivers and to think about how you manage different customers.

Customer acquisition and retention

The discussion so far has not addressed the problem that a certain proportion of customers is lost each year. If the company takes no action to acquire new customers, forecast revenues will inevitably trend downwards as customers leave. Customer acquisition and retention plans are needed to offset this inexorable attrition.

It can be useful to itemize the forecast customer acquisition and retention separately, rather than lumping it all into a single forecast revenues figure. Listing acquisition and retention assumptions separately enables the firm to carry out sensitivity analyses on these assumptions and also to examine how realistic the acquisition and retention targets are.

> If the company takes no action to acquire new customers, forecast revenues will inevitably trend downwards as customers leave. Customer acquisition and retention plans are needed to offset this inexorable attrition.

Defining customer retention

Customer retention plays an important role in the calculation of customer equity. However, the question of customer retention immediately raises one issue, which is how it is defined. If customer retention simply means 'keeping a customer on the books', retention would look very high for most firms. Unfortunately, that definition would include many non-active customers who are still listed as customers but who had defected to other suppliers or ceased buying for other reasons.

A second definition of retained customers is therefore the proportion of customers
that are retained and active, or retained
and expected to be active, in the period
over which customer equity is to be calculated. Although this is taken as the most
usual and convenient measure of customer

> A useful definition of retained
> customers is the proportion
> that are retained and active in
> the period over which customer
> equity is to be calculated.

retention, and it is the one that we use here, it can conceal an unpalatable truth,
which is the phenomenon of migration. Migration is the partial loss of a customer,
where he or she has migrated some of their purchasing to an alternative supplier.
Migration indicates some deterioration in the relationship and may also signal a
risk of complete defection at some future point. Despite the gradual erosion of the
customer's business, he or she is still technically retained. Thus, customer retention
is a blunt measure.

For more accurate measurement of the
quality of the relationship, it is advis-
able to measure not just retention but
share of spend (also sometimes called
share of wallet). The supplier's share of
spend (whether business-to-business or

> For more accurate measure-
> ment of the quality of the rela-
> tionship, it is advisable to meas-
> ure share of spend.

business-to-consumer) is the percentage of the customer's total spend on goods and
services of a particular type that it gives to the supplier. The share of spend metric
and, in particular, changes in the share of spend, are very good indicators of the
strength of the relationship. This topic is discussed in more detail in Chapter 13. For
the moment, the definition of customer retention used to calculate customer equity
will be as follows:

> **Customer retention = % of customers in that group or segment that are active**

For a full and detailed customer equity calculation, it is necessary to think about
the retention probability segment by segment, compared to the retention spend, as
well as the number of customers that are likely to be acquired, segment by segment,
and the acquisition spend (Table 7.4).

An analysis such as that shown in
Table 7.4 reveals some interesting differences between the segments. Thus, it costs
a lot to acquire a Segment A customer, yet all
that resource has resulted in a segment that
is no bigger than it was at the start of the

> Retention analysis can be com-
> bined with customer equity to
> help the firm set its policies
> for customer acquisition and
> retention.

year. The situation is still worse in Segment
B, where the number of customers has declined despite relatively high retention
and acquisition spending. In Segment C, there is relatively high retention spending

Table 7.4 Calculating customer acquisition and retention within four segments A, B, C, and D

Segment	A	B	C	D
No of customers at start of year	500	700	1000	2000
Probability of retention	80%	75%	95%	30%
No of customers retained*	400	525	950	600
Total retention spend on this segment	£250	£500	£1000	£250
Retention cost per customer**	62.5p	95.2p	105p	41.7p
No of potential customers	300	300	400	1000
Probability of acquisition	30%	30%	30%	50%
No of customers likely to be acquired	100	100	120	500
Total acquisition spend on this segment	£1,000	£500	£250	£500
Acquisition cost per customer acquired+	£10	£5	£2.08	£1.00
Total customers in segment at end of period++	500	625	1070	1100

* Number of customers at start multiplied by probability of retention for this segment
**Retention spend divided by number of customers retained (a measure of relative success for each segment's retention programme)
+ Acquisition spend divided by number of customers acquired
++ Retained customers plus customers acquired during the period

per customer and also the highest retention rates, and so the strategies used here seem to be successful. Segment D is a danger area – this is a big segment of not very loyal customers (only a 30% chance of retention year on year). Although the firm has not spent much on acquiring them, Segment D customers seem to be easy to get. Their average cost of acquisition is a mere £1 per customer. The large size of Segment D and the ease of acquiring customers might mislead managers into targeting this segment, but increasing the proportion of customers from Segment D would result in a decline in average customer loyalty. Comparing the amount spent on customer retention and the amount spent on acquisition, this firm should probably rebalance its spending so that it spends more on retaining the customers in the more attractive segments. The retention analysis could be combined with the customer equity figures for each segment to help the firm to set its policies with regard to customer retention and customer acquisition more effectively.

Improving forecasting using the Delphi Panel technique

In classical Greek mythology, the oracle at Delphi was able to foretell the future, although her forecasts were often couched in language that was difficult to understand! The modern Delphi Panel method has little in common with the original oracle, being much easier to understand. Its interest for sales and marketing managers lies in the fact that research shows that the Delphi Panel tends to produce *more accurate* forecasts than conventional extrapolation methods. Conventional forecasting methods tend to examine trends and try to extrapolate the future from them, often on a 'straight line' basis. But, in fact, this conventional forecasting method has great drawbacks in a changing environment, because the past may be no guide at all to the future. Actions such as industry restructuring, fashion trends, technological developments, or takeover activity, could rapidly change the firm's business environment in ways that are difficult to predict. Hence the development of the Delphi Panel method.

The Delphi Panel works as follows. The firm first identifies a panel of experts who will form the Delphi Panel. This may include managers from within the firm but would typically also involve externals who have a useful view on the issues that are to be examined by the panel. External participants might include academics, journalists, members of trade bodies, or consultants. Members of the Delphi Panel would not necessarily know who else was on the panel.

The second stage is for the co-ordinator of the Delphi Panel to develop a series of fairly specific questions for the panel to consider. Many Delphi Panels, for example, will be asked for specific forecasts for exchange rates, interest rates, etc. There may also be some non-numeric questions that the panel is asked to consider but, again, the questions should be as specific as possible so that the results of the panel can be compared.

In the third stage, the Delphi Panel members are each asked to complete the questionnaire and to submit it anonymously (that is, the panel co-ordinator knows what each panel member has submitted, but no panel members see the results of other panel members). The co-ordinator prepares the results from this first round and sends them back to the members for a second round of comments. In the case of numeric data such as an interest rate forecast, the panel members may receive the lowest forecast, the highest forecasts, and an indication of where their own forecast was.

There is then a second round in which each panel member is asked to submit a revised forecast, and sometimes a third round as well. Some panel members will not change their forecasts but others will, as they see the results from others. The purpose of anonymity is to allow the panel members to change their forecasts, even quite radically, without feeling embarrassed to do so, since they have not publicly committed themselves to any particular position.

How to run a Delphi Panel

1. Assemble a panel of experts, including people from outside the company.
2. Develop a Delphi questionnaire with specific questions, generally numerical (Round 1).
3. Collect responses from all participants and produce an anonymous summary of the range of forecasts.
4. Repeat for Rounds 2 and 3, looking for convergence rather than unanimity.

5. The panel should close at the end of Round 3 even if convergence has not been reached.
6. Thank the panel members and, if commercially feasible, provide them with a summary of the results.

Studies of Delphi Panels have found that the forecasts do tend to converge during the second or third rounds (a third round may be needed if there is high disagreement; the co-ordinator is not looking for perfect agreement, but general convergence). Interestingly, many users of Delphi Panels find that the convergence is not necessarily around the average or mid-point of the scale; rather, it seems as though the panel members start to take the views of others into account and are prompted to think 'outside the box'. As discussed, this seems to produce effective forecasts.

There are many elements of the customer equity calculation into which the Delphi Panel could provide useful input, perhaps through predicting the size of customer segments, the growth rate of certain markets, the trend in customer acquisition or retention, or forecasting propensity to spend.

Once the firm has developed an understanding of the four elements of customer equity (forecast revenues, additional potential, costs, and customer acquisition/retention), the final stage is to pull together these four elements and complete the customer equity calculation.

Completing the customer equity calculation

A standard approach to calculating customer equity is described in this section. There may be minor variations from firm to firm, depending on particular industry or company circumstances.

First, the revenues from each segment or customer group need to be forecast. This may be based on projections derived from the CRM system; the accuracy of any assumptions may be tested using the Delphi Panel technique outlined in the preceding section. The forecast revenues from each segment should be multiplied by the expected retention rate each year. Thus, the forecast revenues will tend to decline, year on year, for the core product or service sales, simply because customer retention is less than 100%. This point is illustrated in Figure 7.5.

Next, the impact of any future marketing or sales campaigns to cross- or up-sell, or the impact of new product launches in the future, need to be factored into the additional potential for existing customers.

Then, the firm has to forecast the number of customers it will acquire, segment by segment, and what their core revenues and additional potential might be. As Figure 7.5 illustrates, the overall revenues from a customer segment are made up of these four items (see Table 7.4).

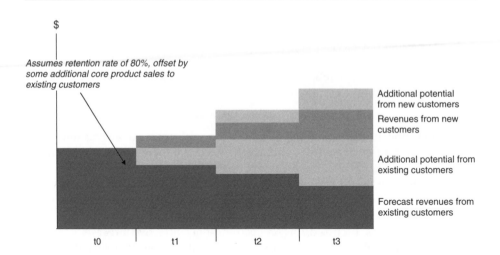

Figure 7.5 The impact of customer retention and acquisition on customer equity (one segment)

To arrive at the customer equity figure, the year-by-year costs need to be deducted from these overall revenue figures, and then the results discounted to express the net present value in today's money (Table 7.5). This process is described in Chapter 6. The difference here is that these results show the customer equity for that segment, rather than the customer lifetime value for an individual customer.

Table 7.5 Calculating customer equity for Segment A (4 year view)

Segment A:	T_0	T_1	T_2	T_3
Revenues from existing customers	10 000	12 000	13 000	13 000
Additional potential from existing customers	50	500	1000	1500
Revenues *and additional potential* from new customers	1100	2000	3000	2000
Forecast revenue before defections	**11 150**	**14 500**	**17 000**	**16 500**
Assumed retention rate in segment A	80%	80%	80%	80%
Forecast revenues net of defections*	**8920**	**11600**	**13 600**	**13 200**
Product costs	1500	1600	1800	2000
Costs to serve	3500	4000	4500	5000
Yearly profits**	**3920**	**6000**	**7300**	**6200**
Discount factor+	0.952	0.907	0.864	0.823
Discounted yearly profits++	**3732**	**5442**	**6307**	**5103**
Customer equity for segment A				**20 584**

* Total revenues multiplied by retention rate
** Forecast net revenues less costs
+ Assuming a discount rate of 5%. See Chapter 6
++ Yearly profits multiplied by discount factor

The use of customer equity

Customer equity, like customer lifetime value, looks forward and takes a view about what may happen in the future. Customer equity looks at the investment in, and the returns from, groups of customers or customer segments. This makes it an essential measure for firms that want to manage their customers as assets, in order to:

- decide on appropriate customer management strategies;
- develop a differentiated strategy for different groups of customers;
- measure the impact of sales and marketing strategies.

These applications of customer equity are about managing customers for value to the firm (rather than purely for value to the customer). Thus, there will be trade-offs between what customers want and what the firm can make money from. There will be times when it is right to say 'no' to customers. There are interesting and insightful discussions that firms should have about what the appropriate level of customer satisfaction is (more customer satisfaction might well mean lower profits for shareholders, for example). There are also challenging questions about what is the right level of spending on customer retention, and on customer acquisition. All of these questions can and should be treated as questions about the impact on customer equity of the sales and marketing strategies that the firm adopts.

This brief discussion indicates that lifetime value measures (customer lifetime value and customer equity) are increasingly regarded as vital tools for marketers and relationship managers to manage their customer relationships profitably.

> **Note**
>
> Use the worksheet on the following page to summarize your customer equity calculations.

Worksheet: calculating customer equity

Segment: ....

	Yr 1	Yr 2	Yr 3	Yr 4
Revenues from existing customers				
Additional potential from existing customers				
Revenues *and additional potential* from new customers				
Forecast revenue before defections				
Assumed retention rate in segment A				
Forecast revenues net of defections				
Product costs				
Costs to serve				
Yearly profits				
Discount factor				
Discounted yearly profits				

Customer equity for this segment:

Where to find out more

Blattberg, R.C., Getz, G. and Thomas, J.S. (2001) *Customer Equity: Building and Managing Relationships as Valuable Assets*, Harvard Business School Press. *A classic book from the originators of the concept, including considerable detail about the components of customer equity.*

Gupta, S. and Lehmann, D.R. (2006) 'Customer lifetime value and firm valuation', *Journal of Relationship Marketing*, **5** (2/3), pp. 87–110. *Argues that valuing customers is a useful approach when calculating the value of the firm.*

8 The relational value of a customer

What's in this chapter

- Four sources of relational value (reference; referral; learning; and innovation)
- Valuing relational benefits
- Relational value index
- Using relational value for marketing decisions
- Getting maximum value from customers: financial plus relational value

Key concepts discussed in this chapter

Relational value	Ways in which customers create values that lie outside the usual measurement of customer profitability or customer lifetime value. There are four types of relational value: Reference; Referral; Learning; and Innovation. The latter may include process as well as product innovation.
Relational value index	Index based on weighting and scoring system (WSS). Built by identifying specific relational value factors, then weighting their importance to the supplier, and then scoring each customer against each weighted factor. The resulting total weighted score identifies the relational attractiveness of one customer against another. Cumbersome method if a large number of customers are to be compared.

True or total value of customer	Financial PLUS relational value. Explains why companies may decide to continue to supply a customer with a negative lifetime value, because they may be obtaining positive relational value.

Key tools explained in this chapter

- Financial impact of relational value: References and referrals tend to reduce the cost of acquiring new customers (they may also increase the speed with which such customers can be acquired). Learning and innovation may reduce costs, increase revenues, or both.
- Valuing referrals: This can be done by asking customers whether they would be likely to refer and comparing the results with the customers who claim to have come to the supplier through a referral. Although this is not a perfect method, the results may indicate useful data about patterns of referrals and their impact.
- Financial value of referrals: Some evidence suggests that referred customers may have a similar financial value to the referring customer. The same may also be true of their risk profiles. If so, a company would be advised to encourage referrals from its more profitable (or lower risk) customers.

Two-minute chapter summary

Some researchers have suggested that customers can add value to companies in ways other than the financial value they bring through their customer lifetime value. This additional source of value is termed 'relational value' because it is value that the supplier obtains from its relationship with the customer.

There are four sources of relational value: References; Referrals; Learning; and Innovation. Reference value is the value that the supplier gets through its association with a customer. This might be the ability to use the customer for a reference or site visit, or to mention its name as a customer; it may also include case studies, links from/to the customer's website, endorsements, etc. Referral value is the value of advocacy or word of mouth, when an existing customer recommends the supplier or brand to a potential customer. References and referrals make it easier for the supplier to win new customers, and so reduce customer acquisition costs. Referrals, in particular, have a measurable impact on the value of the firm.

Learning and innovation include shared planning and market information, process innovation, product testing (concept, prototype, or beta testing), and benchmarking.

Learning and innovation can reduce overall supplier costs, increase turnover, or make the business more efficient. These benefits can be powerful influences on the value of the supplier's business, although their value is difficult to measure precisely.

The existence of relational value explains why suppliers might want to continue a relationship with a customer who has negative lifetime value. The supplier may well feel that it benefits from the relationship in other ways. However, it is important that there is a definite exchange of value; if the customer has a negative lifetime value, value is passing from the supplier to the customer. Enough relational value needs to be captured from the customer to compensate the supplier for the financial cost.

Therefore, it is important to try to measure and manage relational value, even if the measurement of relational value is based on qualitative indicators such as 'power of customer's brand', 'visibility', etc. Better still is to monitor cases in which the customer has created value for the supplier, for example, by asking new customers where they heard about the supplier and noting when new customers come to the supplier as a result of a referral.

The true value of a customer is, in fact, the financial value PLUS the relational value.

How a customer relationship can create additional value for a supplier

So far, we have considered the value of a customer from an accounting perspective, examining customer profitability analysis, customer lifetime value, and customer equity. All three financial methods of valuing customers, particularly the net present value approaches of customer lifetime value and customer equity, are considered useful by marketers. However, some researchers have suggested that the financial approach to valuing customers does not give the full picture and that customers may create value for companies in other ways. These researchers claim that the relationship with certain customers has a value over and above the directly financial. This chapter therefore considers the value of customer assets from a relational, rather than from an accounting, perspective.

> Researchers claim that the relationship with certain customers has a value over and above the directly financial.

Although the relational value of a customer may not affect the financial value of that customer, it may still be valuable to the company. Thus, for example, being associated with a famous name or brand may add value to a supplier by attracting other customers, strengthening the brand, providing valuable press coverage, etc., even if the relationship with the high-profile brand actually costs them money.

Examples of this phenomenon can be seen every day in celebrity endorsements, where celebrities are loaned or given jewellery, clothes, cars, etc. so that they lend their glamour to the brand.

Four sources of relational value

Perhaps the most useful way of thinking about the relational value of customers is to consider the value that is created for the company through its relationships with high-profile customers. The first category of value is the reduced costs of customer acquisition, because other customers are attracted to the supplier as a result of its existing relationships. There are two sources of value creation in this category: reference and referral.

Reference is where the supplier benefits by association with the customer brand (as in the example of celebrity endorsement); referral is actual word of mouth, where customers actively recommend the brand to others. The effect of the association or endorsement is to make it easier and therefore cheaper for the supplier to acquire new customers, and possibly also enable the supplier to acquire customers it would not previously have been able to acquire. This effect does not change the direct financial value of the endorsing customer to the company; they continue to do the same amount of business. However, the effect reduces the cost of customer acquisition and thereby enhances the lifetime value of the new customers acquired through reference or referral.

> Reference is where the supplier benefits by association with the customer brand; referral is recommendation.

The second category of relational value is where the supplier benefits from its relationship with certain customers not through the acquisition of new customers, but in terms of business efficiency. Again, there are two sources of value creation through relationships: learning and innovation. Learning relates to process improvements, benchmarking, etc., such as the way that Toyota 'trains' its suppliers (see Womack, Jones and Roos, 1990, for a highly readable account). Innovation relates particularly to new products, although there can also be process innovation that the supplier gains access to as a result of its association with certain customers. The impact of learning and innovation is to reduce the cost and/or to increase the revenues of the supplier's business; overall these relational benefits are likely to improve the efficiency and performance of the supplier's business. Learning and innovation benefits are more frequently

> Learning and innovation reduce the cost and/or increase the revenues of the supplier's business, improving efficiency and performance.

seen in business-to-business relationships, although they can sometimes be found in business-to-consumer relationships.

The four sources of relational value are illustrated in Figure 8.1 and described in more detail below.

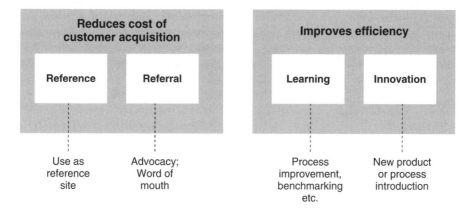

Figure 8.1 Four sources of relational value

Reference value

Reference value includes customer reputation or referenceability. This has been described as 'the kudos of being a supplier to Harrods'. Reference value may take the form of press coverage as a result of association with a high-profile brand. This is most often seen in business-to-consumer, in the form of celebrity endorsement, as noted above. However, reference value is extremely important in business-to-business markets, where it may take the form of case studies, visits to customer sites, inclusion of the customer name or logo on the supplier's website, customer quality awards or certification, etc.

A frequent example of the generation of reference value is the lists of customer names seen on the brochures of professional services firms such as management consultants and architects; the supplier of services gains credibility by association with some major brands. The prospective customer may not have heard of the consultancy, but will have heard of many of its clients. From the point of view of a prospective customer, the risk of selecting this supplier is reduced by its association with companies that are known to be successful.

> From the point of view of a prospective customer, the risk of selecting this supplier is reduced by its association with successful businesses.

Referral value

The relational approach to valuing customer assets is most visible in the substantial interest in customer advocacy or word of mouth. These direct referrals from one customer to another have been identified as an important element of relationship marketing. Referrals are associated not only with satisfaction but also with relationship duration.

Customer-to-customer referrals have repeatedly been shown to have an impact on purchasing behaviour. This seems to be particularly the case in services, where there is no tangible product for customers to examine for themselves. In these circumstances, the opinion of other customers assumes a greater importance. So, customers looking for a new dentist or hairdresser are very likely to seek out referrals.

Not surprisingly, research has shown that prospective customers are far more likely to believe existing customers of the firm than they are to believe the paid sales force of that firm. Referrals (or advocacy levels) are linked to the value of the firm through their role in the delivery of profitable growth. However, it should be noted that customers are likely to refer other customers like themselves, so it is important that any firm aims its referral marketing at profitable customers.

> Prospective customers are far more likely to believe existing customers of the firm than they are to believe salespeople.

Referenceability and referral benefits positively impact firm performance by reducing customer acquisition costs and by increasing sales through the attraction of new customers.

Learning value

Further relational benefits from customer relationships include learning and information benefits. Some of these learning benefits come from the process and quality expertise that the customer passes back to its suppliers. Toyota is well known for 'training' its suppliers, and other customers such as Wal-Mart hold supplier academies at which suppliers are encouraged to exchange best practice. In November 2004, Energis launched a Supplier Academy for all its suppliers. Companies such as Nortel and Marconi participated in the launch, sending their engineers to a course followed by an exam, and committing to six-monthly refresher events. From Energis's point of view, the payoff to them would come in the form of better service to its customers. The suppliers would also benefit from participating in the Academy, because they would be more able to service Energis as a result.

Learning value also includes information benefits. This might take the form of information about new markets, geographical areas, etc. that customers may be prepared to share with their suppliers.

> Information sharing between supplier and customer is usually a sign of a close relationship.

Information from knowledgeable customers may make it easier for the supplier to break into a new customer segment or region. Information sharing between supplier and customer is usually a sign of a close relationship. For example, Wal-Mart has a very close relationship with Procter and Gamble such that P&G have access to till data from within Wal-Mart stores. This information gives P&G a clear lead over its rivals and enables it to act as 'category captain' for a number of products.

Innovation value

Innovation value relates to the value that a firm gains from supplying to innovative customers. Innovative customers are customers that push their suppliers to innovate, or that are willing to collaborate with the supplier in developing new products and services. A clear benefit to the supplier comes in the form of risk reduction on a new product launch; where a customer is willing to trial or beta-test a new product, any flaws can be spotted and ironed out before the product is launched nationally. A customer that contributes to new product success for a supplier creates value indirectly, because a successful new product launch translates into increased sales from both new and existing customers for the supplier. Successful product innovation is demonstrably associated with increases in the value of the firm.

Another form of innovation value relates to process innovation. Process innovation is arguably just as important as product innovation, if not more so, but its value is less widely recognized. Some customers are more willing to adopt process improvements and to integrate with their suppliers than others, and there are substantial benefits to be gained for the supplier's business through the implementation of more efficient ways of doing business.

> Process innovation is arguably just as important as product innovation, if not more so, but its value is less widely recognized.

Thus, learning and innovation value contribute differently to the value of the firm from reference and referral value; rather than reducing the costs of customer acquisition, they enhance the overall competitiveness and revenues and efficiency of the firm. Learning and innovation value can both reduce costs and increase revenues for the supplier firm.

Valuing relational benefits

Probably because of the difficulty of valuing relational benefits, comparatively little has been written about their role in marketing decisions. If the financial returns to relational benefits are uncertain, the return on the investment needed to generate relational benefits is unclear. The most-explored area is advocacy, where it has been found that advocacy is related to company growth and can be influenced by marketing strategies.

From a marketing accounting perspective this raises a question about how the relational aspects of the customer asset can be valued. The relational benefits from a customer do not necessarily accrue to the value of that customer. For example, the impact of advocacy or reference benefits is to reduce the cost of customer acquisition, which increases the profitability of the acquired customer but does not affect the value of the referring customer. The impact of learning and innovation benefits, by contrast, may or may not increase the financial value of that customer through increased sales or reduced costs, but it can increase the overall revenues or improve the overall efficiency of the supplier. Table 8.1 summarizes the financial impact on the supplier firm of the various relational benefits.

> The impact of advocacy or reference benefits is to reduce the cost of customer acquisition, which increases the profitability of the acquired customer but does not affect the value of the referring customer.

Table 8.1   The financial impact of relational benefits

Relational benefit	Financial impact on value of customer	Financial impact on firm
Referrals (Advocacy)	None	Reduced customer acquisition costs; higher lifetime value on acquired customers
Reference	None	Reduced customer acquisition costs; higher lifetime value on acquired customers
Learning	May reduce costs	May reduce overall costs, or increase revenues, e.g., if learning opens up new markets
Innovation	May increase revenues (product innovation) or reduce costs (process innovation)	May increase overall revenues if product innovation is wider than customer-specific innovation[1]; may reduce overall costs through process efficiencies

[1] In some business-to-business relationships, innovation may have to be specific to the key account for which it was developed, as a condition of collaboration between the two companies.

As Table 8.1 illustrates, there are clearly financial pay-offs to the firm through their relationships with certain customers. However, these financial pay-offs may not affect the lifetime value of the customer that provides them. This is particularly the case with referrals and reference value. There is therefore a problem with valuing relational benefits, which is that the customer originating the relational benefit may be undervalued. In other words, a high relational value customer has value to the firm over and above the value that is conventionally measured through customer lifetime value. Similarly, high relational value groups of customers have value that is not measured using a typical customer equity calculation.

Putting a value on relational benefits is a topic that is not well-understood in marketing. In this section, three different approaches will be considered and two case studies presented that illustrate two very different methods for valuing relational benefits. The three methods are:

- simple additive;
- relational value index;
- overall relational value of the customer portfolio.

The method that a firm adopts will depend on its particular circumstances. Method 1, the simple additive method, is suitable where there are relatively few customers that have relational value and where the relational value of individual customers is likely to be very large. Method 2, the relational value index, is useful where there are relatively small numbers (fewer than 20) of individual customers or segments and where it is difficult to attribute financial values to relational benefits. Method 3, the overall relational value in certain segments or in the portfolio, is useful where the number of customers is larger, and where a CRM system or other customer information system is in use.

Method #1: Simple additive approach

A possible, but unsatisfactory, solution to the problem of valuing relational benefits is to calculate the value of the revenues generated from relational benefits and then add this figure to the calculation of the value of the customer. If the relational benefit takes the form of cost savings, these would be deducted from the costs of the customer. Thus, this first method is described as the 'simple additive' method. Of course, it may not be entirely simple in that putting a financial value on some of the benefits set out in Table 8.1 might well be a very demanding exercise!

The reason that this approach is unsatisfactory is that it leads to a problem of double counting. Take the example of referrals. If Customer A refers one of its friends, how can this value be reflected in the value of Customer A? Assuming the company now has two customers, A and B, each with a lifetime value of £100, the customer lifetime value for A now understates A's true value because A has generated a referral.

The simple additive method would argue that A has customer lifetime value of £100, plus has generated referral value of a further £100 (the lifetime value of

Table 8.2 Simple additive method

	Lifetime value	Referral value (lifetime value)	Portfolio value
Customer A	£100	£100	
Customer B	£100	–	
Total	£200	£100	£300

Customer B). However, this creates double counting when the company comes to try and value its total customer base, as illustrated in Table 8.2. Because the referral value of Customer A is also the lifetime value of Customer B, it is counted twice.

In addition to the double-counting problem, there is also a conceptual problem with the simple additive method. This is that attributing all the lifetime value of Customer B to Customer A suggests that Customer A is solely responsible for generating it. This is manifestly not the case: the referral certainly opens the door for the supplier company, but there is still sales and marketing effort, product or service delivery, and relationship management that will all be important in securing the lifetime value of Customer B. For example, if the supplier's account management team is particularly successful with Customer B and manages to double its forecast customer lifetime value to £200, this does not mean that Customer A's value should increase.

One way to get round many of these problems, while still using a simple additive method, is to think of the value of the referral as being a reduction in the cost of acquiring Customer B. If the cost of acquiring Customer B was reduced by the cost of one sales call that saved the company £10 in costs, this cost saving could be attributed to Customer A (Table 8.3).

Table 8.3 Simple additive method using reduction in customer acquisition cost

	Lifetime value	Referral value (cost reduction)	Portfolio value
Customer A	£100	£10	
Customer B	£100	–	
Total	£200	£10	£210

The cost savings approach has removed the double-counting problem, because the referral value is expressed in terms of a cost saving to the business. However, as Table 8.3 illustrates, the referral value attributed to Customer A is quite low. This is a feature of using cost savings that makes it counterintuitive to many marketing managers, who would argue that the referral value created through the acquisition of a major customer is far greater than simply the reduction in acquisition costs. Moreover, the financial value of the cost saving, etc., might be difficult to identify.

For these reasons, marketing and sales managers wanting to incorporate strategies to generate relational value may prefer to use a weighting and scoring method to develop a relational value index that gives them a non-financial picture of the sources of relational value in the customer portfolio and enables them to compare the relational value of one customer with another, without having to carry out multiple complex financial calculations.

Method #2: Developing a relational value index

The relational value index uses a weighting and scoring method to evaluate the relational value of customers. It is useful where financial data are not available and where the number of customers or segments to be considered is not large.

The process for developing a relational value index is that the marketing or account managers brainstorm the types of relational value from their customer portfolio and then weight each type according to their perception of its importance to the firm. Each customer or segment is then scored according to how much of each type of value they are perceived likely to generate.

Case Study: Business-to-business insurance

This evaluation exercise at a leading global insurance company focused on a small number of the organization's major customers where the relational value was believed to be considerable. Eight customers who accounted for 47% of the portfolio were selected for study. The process for calculating relational value used a weighted scored[2] (WSS) approach to provide a degree of objectivity to subjective impressions (see worksheet at end of chapter).

The WSS approach began with an unprompted discussion about relational attractiveness. During this discussion the managers discussed Profile (Referenceability) but also the warmth of the relationship, the time and people resources required, and the skill demands that customers made on the supplier. The latter three (Relationship, Resources, and Skill Demands) were issues that related to the costs to serve the customer, and so would already have been taken into account in the calculation of customer lifetime value. These initial results suggest that relational value is not well understood, even for more important customers.

The workshop was repeated with a focus on relational value only, and all eight customers were scored against the new weighted factors

---

[2] The weighting and scoring method is demonstrated in detail in Chapter 9 on portfolio management.

(Referenceability, Referrals, and Learning; there were not considered to be specific Innovation benefits in this portfolio).

The results were plotted against the financial attractiveness of the eight customers (their lifetime value), as shown in Figure 8.2.

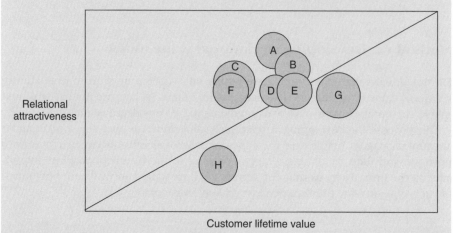

Relational attractiveness

Customer lifetime value

Figure 8.2 Financial versus relational attractiveness

Each circle in Figure 8.2 represents one of eight major customers and the size of the circle indicates the size of the customer. The results suggested that there was some relationship between financial and relational attractiveness; that is, the managers generally perceived that the financially more valuable customers also had higher relational value. This might well have been true, because larger customers would tend to have higher financial value and a higher industry profile, but it might also be a weakness of the weighting and scoring method that relies on managers' perceptions. Managers might simply have a tendency to believe that financially valuable customers must also have higher relational attractiveness.

Thinking of their customers in terms of both lifetime value and relational attractiveness helped the managers at the insurance company to resolve a current business issue, which was how to identify key accounts. There had been some discussion internally about the inclusion within the key account portfolio of three customers that actually had negative lifetime value. Some of the key account managers thought that these customers should not have key account status, because they had low financial attractiveness; other key account managers argued that these customers did have relational attractiveness that compensated for their lack of financial appeal.

The managers used the results of the weighting and scoring exercise to create a simple 2 × 2 matrix to help them position their key accounts. The matrix they developed is shown as Figure 8.3. They applied this matrix to their key account portfolio of 18 customers and found 15 that were 'definitely' or 'probably' key accounts, one that was probably not a key account, and two that were evaluated on a case-by-case basis and remained in the portfolio. The 'probably not' customer was removed from the key account portfolio and handed over to an industry sector team that managed major, but not key, accounts.

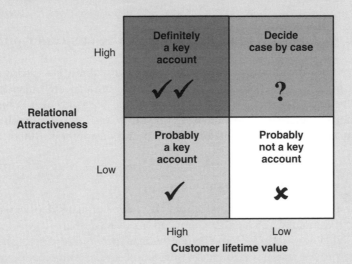

Figure 8.3 Key customer matrix

The case study and Figure 8.3 suggest that the identification of a key account in the insurance company depended more on its customer lifetime value than on relational benefits, which is what might be expected. Customers with high lifetime value (the left side of the matrix) were very likely to be identified as key accounts, even if they had low relational attractiveness. However, two large customers with low lifetime value were retained in the key account portfolio on a case-by-case basis because of their relational value.

The relational value index using a weighing and scoring method had the advantage of producing useful results relatively quickly and did not require complex financial analysis. A concern about the method was whether managers found it difficult to separate financial and relational attractiveness. This was certainly a drawback in the initial phase and may have influenced the results shown in Figure 8.2, where the customers with higher lifetime value were also perceived as having higher relational value.

The weighting and scoring method is not very user-friendly where there are large numbers of customers, as in most consumer markets. Moreover, business-to-consumer companies often have large quantities of data that can be used to analyse and forecast not just customer equity but also the overall relational activity in a customer portfolio. The third method returns to the notion of attributing a financial amount to the relational value, but does it at the level of the customer portfolio or for a group of customers. In this way, it is analogous to the customer equity approach to valuing customers discussed in Chapter 7. Firms that take a customer equity approach to valuing their customer portfolio are likely to prefer method #3.

Method #3: Overall relational value of the customer portfolio

The third method for valuing relational value uses a probability forecasting approach top down on the customer portfolio, and aims to attribute an overall financial value to relational benefits. The process used in the following case study uses a combination of workshops, re-analysis of existing market research, and interviews with managers to develop an estimate of the relational value of this customer portfolio.

Case Study: Personal loans provider

This case study was carried out within the personal loans department of a bank and examined 123 442 loan applications by customers.

The initial workshop with the marketing managers quickly established that the WSS process was not viable with this sample size and moreover that there were no referenceability benefits, because the bank did not identify its customers publicly for commercial sensitivity reasons; nor were there any learning or innovation benefits. Thus the project rapidly focused on the financial value of referrals.

Data on referrals were collected from several sources. The bank already had an extensive rolling programme of market research and the market research department were asked to re-analyse some of its current data and also to modify its monthly market research questionnaire to collect ongoing data. This data source was supplemented with a series of interviews with loan managers who worked in branch offices and signed off the loans to the customers. The loan managers were the people who had first contact with loan applicants; they also carried out detailed interviews with applicants as part of the process of recommending or refusing a loan. Interestingly, the marketing managers who initiated the project were initially sceptical about whether advocacy was a powerful influence in their business. These marketing managers did not have day-to-day contact with customers. The loans managers, on the other hand, who interviewed loan applicants daily, reported regular instances of referrals.

Because the bank had no system for recording the cases where customers had been referred to it, the marketing department perceived that this rarely or never happened. The project was to prove marketing quite wrong and was able to demonstrate that the customer portfolio had considerable referral value that was not recorded and was therefore under-exploited.

Re-analysis of market research data from the previous three months provided 900 customer responses in total and showed that a high proportion of customers declared themselves very or quite likely to refer (Table 8.4).

Table 8.4 Satisfaction, advocacy, and complaints

	Satisfaction*	Very likely to refer	Quite likely to refer	Complaints**
Loans dept (%)	55	39	39	16
Bank overall (%)	53	33	42	<10

*Percentage of respondents describing themselves as 'delighted' or 'completely satisfied'
** Percentage of respondents who had complained within the previous year

The re-analysis of the market research data separated out the results for the loans department and allowed comparison with the bank as a whole (Table 8.4). The analysis showed that customer satisfaction within the loans department was higher than for the bank as a whole, although complaints were also substantially higher. This curious phenomenon illustrates a known problem with customer satisfaction as a business measure, which is that customer satisfaction may not be strongly linked to behaviour. Referrals are a more useful performance measure.

As the company had no data on the actual rate of referrals, the marketing and database managers made estimates of the value of advocacy based on analysis of customer records and behaviour. These estimates were then tested through interviews with loan managers.

First, the marketing and database managers identified those customers most likely to refer. Then the managers assumed that a proportion (in this case, about one-third) of those saying that they were 'very likely' to refer would actually do so. This yielded a figure of 8500 customers per month who were predicted to be advocates. If only one in 10 recommendations had resulted in an application, and given that the company rejected 46% of loan applications, this would still have represented 457 customers per month. Multiplied by the average value of a customer, this would represent £188 100 in revenue per quarter (0.75% of total) and an additional £81 140 in profits per quarter (just over 0.7%).

The final phase of the research was to test the estimates of the value of advocacy that the marketing managers had made through a series of interviews with loan managers and branch managers in four typical branches. The interviewees all reported that they believed that advocacy accounted for 2–3% of actual customers. This translates into 440–660 customers per month, slightly above the estimates of the marketing managers.

However, in financial services it is not just revenues but risk that is important, and the branch office interviews produced some intriguing observations about the profiles of the customers arriving as a result of recommendation (Table 8.5).

Table 8.5 Advocacy sources and risk profile

Relationship to advocate	Source of referral	Risk profile and application behaviour
Family	Usually, parents referring children*	Same. Children's risk profile was felt to be the same as that of parents. This was also felt to be the most likely type of referral.
Peer	Friends (tended to be younger customers)	Similar. Friends may even accompany one another into the branch to apply for loans at the same time.
Colleague	Workmates	Similar. Can result in multiple customers – several customers from same workplace may follow shortly after one customer recommends. Loans may be for same purpose (e.g., car buying).

* 'Children' here merely indicates the relationship to the referrer, as all the customers under discussion are adults.

As Table 8.5 shows, three categories of referral were identified: Family, Peer, and Colleague. Family referrals were usually parents referring children. Peer groups were friends, usually younger customers. It was not unknown for the referring friend to accompany the applicant to the bank for his or her interview. Colleague groups were workmates; the bank had noticed patterns of applicants coming from the same company and had recently created a campaign to appeal to this market without ever recording it as referral activity.

On the subject of risk, the loans managers commented that they perceived that the risk profile of the customer being referred was similar to, or the same as, that of the advocate. Thus, where the loan manager had lent money to a parent whose child was now applying, the repayment history of the parent would colour the loan manager's view of the likely repayment performance of the child. The loan managers had some discretion as to whether the loan was awarded or not, and they definitely preferred to lend to the relatives, friends, and colleagues of customers with a good repayment track record.

When the marketing managers were asked about implications for marketing strategy, several points emerged. The first was that the firm should start to collect data about which customers had come through referral by including a specific question to that effect on the loan application form. The second was that the risk profile of the family, not just of the applicant, might be taken into account when making a loan to the relative of an existing customer. Third, the firm could analyse its database to identify clusters of customers all working for the same company; this would be indicative of advocacy by a business colleague. Finally, if the firm wanted to encourage referrals, it would have to ensure that its pricing strategy was consistent with an advocacy strategy. The branch managers commented that sometimes they became aware that a customer was there as a result of advocacy only when the customer queried the rate (price) for the loan and complained that his or her relatives, friends, or colleagues had received better deals.

Putting an overall financial value on the referral value of this portfolio involved further analysis of the bank's existing market research data, plus additional data collection. It was, however, a useful exercise that established that there was a measurable value-creating effect from referrals and also provided some intriguing hints about the risk profile of those referred. As the case study shows, there were a number of implications for marketing strategy and decision making.

Using relational value for marketing decisions

The cases described in this chapter provide some evidence of the role of relational value in marketing decisions. Relational value can be a substantial source of benefit to the supplier, particularly in business-to-business markets. It can also vary considerably between customers or segments. Therefore, it should be taken into account when making marketing decisions.

However, it is difficult to put a value on relational benefits, which means that it is hard to measure the impact of marketing strategies designed to foster relational effects. One of the case studies suggests that companies that do not record when relational benefits occur may have the erroneous impression that there are no relational effects or that they have no value. This chapter has described three methods of evaluating relational benefits that may be adopted in different organizational circumstances.

For those organizations that measure relational value, even if they only do so using a
weighting and scoring method, the information is of value. The first case study showed
how the relational value information was

> Managing relational value can
> be an important activity for key
> account managers.

used to confirm which of the insurer's larger customers should be included in the
key account portfolio. This case study also raised the possibility that bigger and more
valuable customers also tend to have higher relational value, suggesting that a key
account management programme could pay off for the organization as a whole. So,
managing relational value can be an important activity for key account managers.

The second case study demonstrated how existing data, supplemented by some
additional interviews, revealed a valuable pattern of referrals among customers of
which the loan provider had been unaware. Not understanding the relationships
between its different customers had actually caused problems for this bank when it
had offered different prices to customers who talked to one another. The marketing
strategy implications are that referrals can be valuable and that pricing and special
deals need special handling where there are referrals taking place in the market. The
discovery of a steady stream of completely unprompted referrals opened the door to
some positive strategies to promote referrals. Some companies reward customers for
referrals; this is a useful strategy both business-to-business and business-to-consumer.

The second case raises the intriguing possibility that the risk/return profiles
of referred and referring customers might be similar, in which case companies
need to think carefully about which customers they target for referrals. It seems
likely that financially valuable customers attract financially valuable customers;
possibly, unprofitable customers might refer other unprofitable customers. The marketing strategy implications are to encourage and reward referrals from profitable
customers, not necessarily from the customer base as a whole.

This case study also suggests that the main relational value in business-to-consumer
services might be advocacy. Other researchers have found a similar pattern in
consumer services but with a markedly higher impact of advocacy in other service industries. It seems that the absence of a tangible product makes word of
mouth more valuable. Therefore, service businesses should pay particular attention
to stimulating positive advocacy. Conversely, negative advocacy can have a disproportionately damaging effect on service businesses and processes, and so complaints
handling should take this into account.

Summary: financial plus relational value

In recent years there has been considerable exploration of the financial value of
customer assets and it is now widely accepted that net present value approaches to
the financial value of customers (customer

> The total value of a customer
> relationship is a combination of
> financial and relational value.

lifetime value and customer equity) are to be preferred in developing profitable customer management strategies. However, research shows that customers can also create value through relational benefits. Therefore, the total value of a customer relationship is a combination of financial and relational value (Figure 8.4).

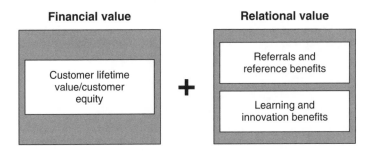

Figure 8.4 The total value of a customer

Customer lifetime value or customer equity is the main measure that marketers use to support the development of customer management strategies, because this is the direct way in which the value of customers flows into the organization. However, some customers create value in indirect ways through the relationship. There can be cases where a customer with negative lifetime value is not only retained, but also valued, because of the relational value generated.

Note
Now use the worksheet on the following page to evaluate the relational value of your customers.

Worksheet: creating a relational value index

	Importance to our company	Customer score	Weight x score	Customer score	Weight x score
Reference					
Referrals (advocacy)					
Learning					
Innovation					
Total:	100%				

First, create a list of relational values or use the generic list provided. Then identify which are more/less important, so that the total importance weighting is 100% (some may have zero importance). Score each customer or segment on a scale of 0 to 10, according to the likely amount of relational value in each category. Multiply the weight by the score and add up all the weighted scores for each customer or segment, to give a total weighted score for each.

Where to find out more

Stahl, H.K., Matzler, K. and Hinterhuber, H.H. (2003) 'Linking customer lifetime value with shareholder value', *Industrial Marketing Management*, **32**(4), pp. 267–279. *Discusses financial and relational value.*

Womack, J.P., Jones, D.T. and Roos, D. (1990) *The Machine that Changed the World.* Rawson Associates, New York. *A classic description of Toyota's relationships with its suppliers, showing how suppliers benefit from learning and process innovation.*

Section Two

How to manage a customer portfolio

The four chapters in this second section provide strategic and practical guidance about customer portfolio management. The notion of managing customers as a portfolio is increasingly central in marketing and sales. The fundamental issue about portfolio management is that some customers are more attractive than others, because their returns are higher or their risks are lower.

Chapter 9 shows how the straightforward customer equity tool explained in Chapter 7 can be quickly developed into a powerful method for managing customers. Based on customer returns, this chapter helps you identify which customers you need to defend from competitors, which customers you need to manage more effectively, and which customers you may not want at all.

One of the most important components of customer risk is the risk that customers will defect (leave you and go to a competitor). Chapter 10 sets out some practical methods for incorporating the customer's perspective into your portfolio analysis, and Chapter 11 gives you some advanced tools for evaluating customer risk more broadly, and developing customer-specific strategies for managing these risks.

However, portfolio analysis can only deliver profitable growth if it is applied in the real world. Segmentation is the process of dividing up a customer base into different groups of customers that can be targeted with specific marketing and sales messages. Chapter 12 reviews different approaches to segmentation and suggests a service-based technique for the profitable management of customers. This is a highly effective technique for implementing customer portfolio management. It identifies when to say 'no' to customers, and helps to prevent 'service creep', the tendency of managers to offer increasing levels of service to customers even when their profitability does not warrant it.

When you have read this section, you will be able to:

- apply a customer portfolio analysis to your customers, using it to identify your most and least valuable customers;
- develop strategies for managing customers so as to maximize their customer equity;
- analyse your customer portfolio in terms of your firm's appeal to the customer as well as the customer's attractiveness to the firm;
- use critical success factor analysis to determine your company's performance relative to the competition on the factors that are most important to customers;
- analyse and manage the risks in your customer relationships;
- apply service-based segmentation, creating service packages that reflect the value of the customers and preventing 'service creep'.

Managing a customer portfolio using customer equity

What's in this chapter

- Why companies should manage customers as assets
- Introduction to portfolio management
- Customer portfolio management using customer equity
- How to maximize customer equity in the portfolio
- Using customer equity with other forms of segmentation

Key concepts discussed in this chapter

Customer asset management	Managing customer relationships as valuable assets, recognizing that the company needs to invest sales and marketing effort in them.
Portfolio management	Thinking of, and managing, a group of assets as a whole portfolio rather than managing them singly. Portfolio management involves decisions about investment (both increases and reductions). These investment decisions are designed to optimize risk and return in the portfolio; meaning that, as well as the level of profits generated by the portfolio, the level of risk (volatility) in those profits would also be considered and managed.
Highly profitable customers	Customers with high actual plus potential revenue but lower costs. Highly profitable customers are also attractive to competitors, and therefore need defending from the competition.

Demanding customers	High revenue but high cost customers. Some key accounts may fall into this category. Should be retained for the high revenues, but costs need to be managed.
Commodity customers	Low revenue, low cost customers with little incremental value opportunities. Manage and contain costs.
Uncommitted customers	Low revenue, low cost customers but low share of spend, suggesting that there could be opportunities to develop the relationship as long as the supplier changes its customer management strategy.
Less profitable customers	Low revenue, high cost customers. These customers should be positively managed to reduce costs and, where possible, to increase revenues.

Key tools explained in this chapter

- Customer equity portfolio management: Plotting a portfolio matrix of revenues (actual plus potential) against costs. This produces a general guide to where the most and least profitable customers are (that is, those with the lowest and highest customer lifetime value). This matrix is then used to develop appropriate management strategies for customers in each quadrant. The success of these strategies can be measured in terms of its impact on customer equity in that quadrant. Successful strategies will increase customer equity.

Two-minute chapter summary

Customer portfolio management is about managing the entire customer base as a group of assets that need investment to maximize their value. Thus, customer portfolio management is closely associated with the idea of customers as assets or, perhaps more accurately, with the notion that customer *relationships* are assets of a business.

To make decisions about the type and amount of investment in different customer assets, managers need to think about the customer equity in the portfolio. A simple tool that indicates customer equity is to plot customers or segments on to a matrix of high/low lifetime revenues versus high/low costs.

The customer equity portfolio matrix reveals five different types of customer, which need different management strategies to optimize their customer equity.

Customer equity portfolio management can be combined with existing segmentation.

Why companies should manage customers as assets

The essential principle underlying the profitable management of customers is customer asset management.

Customer asset management means that the firm considers its customers as assets, in the same way that products, brands, machines, etc. are assets. Assets are things that the company can use to create value. An asset has perceptible and measurable value even if it is intangible, as brands and customer relationships are. However, assets also need investment in them to retain their value. Machine and building assets need servicing and maintenance to keep them in a condition to produce value. Brands need investment in the form of advertising, promotion, etc., or customers forget about them and the value of the brand begins to deteriorate. Customer assets need investment in the relationship, or customers begin to feel neglected and may move their business elsewhere, which would reduce the value of the relationship asset.

> Customer assets need investment in the relationship, or customers begin to feel neglected and may move their business elsewhere, reducing the value of the asset.

Most managers are used to the idea that their company has assets and that the totality of these assets forms a portfolio – of brands, of machines, of properties, etc. This chapter introduces the notion of customers as assets in a customer portfolio, and shows how these assets can be managed using customer equity.

Introduction to portfolio management

Customer portfolio management is about the way that the firm perceives its whole customer base as a portfolio. Portfolio management implies that some customers are seen as more attractive than others, in the same way that some shares in a financial portfolio are more attractive than others.

In a financial portfolio that consists of a number of different stocks and shares, there will be some shares that perform unusually well over a period of time and other shares that underperform. The overall performance of the portfolio is determined by the weighted average of the performance of the individual shares

> The overall performance of the portfolio is determined by the weighted average of the performance of the individual shares (assets) within the portfolio.

(assets) within the portfolio. However, it is difficult for financial portfolio managers to predict *which* shares will perform better and which will perform worse. In other periods, the previously underperforming shares may outperform. Conversely, some apparently sound investments may decline or even go bankrupt. To deal with the risk that they might over-invest in poorly performing shares and under-invest in better-performing shares, fund managers always hold a variety of shares in their portfolio. This process is known as diversification.

There are many parallels between financial and customer portfolios. It can be difficult to predict the performance of different customers in the portfolio (performance in the sense of how much of which products they might purchase, and when). Also, there is a need for diversification in the customer portfolio, because over-dependence on a very small number of customers could be risky. The main difference is that financial portfolio managers have a much greater degree of control over the assets in their portfolios than customer managers do. Stocks and shares cannot choose to end their relationship with the company and just walk away, as customers can decide to do. However, the concept of portfolio management is an essential one for companies that want to manage their customer base profitably.

Customer assets and customer portfolio management

Customer asset management – managing customer relationships as assets, recognizing that these assets are valuable to the company and that they need investment in sales and marketing effort to ensure that they remain in the best possible state.

Customer portfolio management – managing the customer assets of a firm as a portfolio, recognizing that some customers are more valuable to the company than others and that there are risks as well as returns in the portfolio. Also implies the importance of forecasting the future value of customers using customer lifetime value or customer equity measures.

Customer portfolio management

Portfolio management is about taking the firm's list of current customers (and, often, potential customers) and considering this as a portfolio of assets. In any portfolio, some assets are more valuable than others, and they also have different characteristics. The portfolio manager needs to find the most useful way (to the firm) of representing the portfolio, and so the first task of the portfolio manager is to decide which variables will be considered.

The most common variable in customer portfolio management is obviously the value of each customer to the company. A second variable that is often considered in portfolio management is the warmth of the relationship or, in other words, some measure of the value of the *firm* to the customer. A third variable that may be important is risk. An important point here is that risk may be affected by the warmth of the relationship, and so warmth and risk are not fully independent variables. Risk is such an important topic in customer portfolio management that it will be considered separately in Chapter 11.

> **Variables used in constructing the customer portfolio**
>
> - value of the customer to the company (financial and other value);
> - warmth of the relationship;
> - risk.

In this chapter, the first variable will be examined: how to create a customer portfolio model that incorporates the value of the customer to the firm. This approach uses customer equity as the basis for constructing and managing the portfolio. This kind of approach can be very useful. It is also the thinking that underlies service-based segmentation (see Chapter 12), which is a profitable method for managing customer service levels.

Managing a customer portfolio based simply on customer equity is a sensible approach where:

- the market is growing fast or the company has just been launched, and so the focus is on customer acquisition;
- the market is largely transactional (as in very price-sensitive or commoditized markets), and so the value of customer relationships is less;
- the firm's business consists of a series of individual projects, where the value of relationships is low.

Portfolio management using customer equity

As discussed in Chapter 7, customer equity is the most useful measure when considering the value of groups of customers to the firm.

The customer equity model provides a detailed basis for managing the customer according to their value to the firm. However, it is important that not only current value to the company is taken into account, but also potential value. The reason for this is that the future potential value of a customer may be very different from historic value. The future potential value is measured in today's money using customer lifetime value (for a single customer) or customer equity (for a group of customers or for customer segments).

The drivers of customer equity are lifetime revenues and lifetime costs (Chapter 7). It is usual to divide these two dimensions into high revenue, low revenue, high costs, low costs, giving what appears to be four different categories of customer equity. However, when firms apply this analysis to their customer portfolios, an important distinction emerges in the low/low category. There are in fact two types of customer there – customers where the firm's share of spend is already high, and customers where it is low (Figure 9.1). The difference is that some customers are already giving the supplier most of their business and there is little more to be gained by managing these customers differently or developing new products for them. These are 'commodity customers'. However, there may be some customers that are low/low but where the share of spend is low. These are 'uncommitted customers', because they take most of their business elsewhere. Something about their current needs or about the offer currently made by the supplier means that the share of their spend is low.

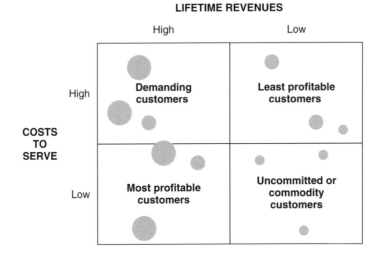

Figure 9.1   Five types of customers in the customer equity portfolio

Figure 9.1 demonstrates that there are five different types of customer when categorized in terms of their lifetime revenues and costs:

- highly profitable customers (high lifetime revenues, low costs);
- demanding customers (high lifetime revenues, high costs);
- commodity customers (low revenues, low costs, medium to high share of spend);

- uncommitted customers (low revenues and costs, low share of spend);
- less profitable customers (low lifetime revenues, high costs).

Considered purely from the perspective of customer equity and managing the financial value of the customer portfolio, there are particular strategies that should be used for each of these five groups. Each of these will now be discussed.

> **Note**
>
> Plot customers or customer segments on to your own version of Figure 9.1 for a 'quick and dirty' analysis of customer equity. Consider whether the customer management strategies you currently use are appropriate (see Figure 9.2, and worksheet at end of chapter).

Customer type 1: Highly profitable customers

For highly profitable customers, the dominant strategy is to defend the relationship and the value in that relationship. Highly profitable customers are very valuable to the company but are also likely to be attractive to competitors. They will therefore be the main target of attempts by competitors to acquire them or to increase the competitor's share of business with these desirable customers.

> Highly profitable customers are very valuable to the company but are also likely to be attractive to competitors.

Companies use numerous strategies that are designed to defend their relationships with their most profitable customers, but the most important ones relate to relationship management rather than to products. It may be useful to note, however, that there is one product strategy that is associated with increased customer retention, and that is *cross-selling*. The more products or service lines that a customer buys from a supplier, the less likely that customer is to defect to a competitor. One reason for this is the 'hassle factor' – it is more hassle for a customer to find replacement suppliers for a number of products or services than to replace a supplier of a single product. Of course, there is also a question of cause and effect in the observed correlation between the number of products held and customer retention. Holding a number of products from a single supplier may lead to retention, but it may also

> The more products or service lines that a customer buys from a supplier, the less likely they are to defect to a competitor.

signal a good relationship as a result of which the customer would be less likely to defect in any case.

The relationship strategies that help companies to defend their relationship with these highly profitable customers include *communication and information sharing*. These relationships are worth investing in, and they should be nurtured to the best of the supplier's capability. For major business-to-business relationships of this type, there may be electronic data exchange. Wal-Mart, for example, shares data from its tills with suppliers such as Procter and Gamble, which enables the supplier to manage an entire category of products, including those supplied by P&G's competitors. In return, the supplier may provide information about delivery performance, market trends, etc. In very close collaborative relationships this information exchange may have become formalized into a shared planning system that involves the supplier and the customer working together to forecast future demand patterns and then to plan together how the supplier will manufacture and deliver the product to meet that demand. This process is known as CPFR – Collaborative Planning, Forecasting, and Replenishment.

Business-to-consumer relationships with profitable customers can also incorporate closer relationships that may involve information sharing. Some banks, for example, provide additional information to their most valuable customers for free for which other, less valuable, customers may have to pay. At many banks, the more valuable customers are provided with named account managers that they can talk to, as compared to less valuable customers who have to take their chance with an anonymous call centre. The costs of providing these additional information or services can be comparatively low, but the relationship value is considerable.

Another interesting strategy to defend relationships with highly profitable customers is to *change the relationship terms* on which the two companies do business. This can be an important strategy in contractual relationships of all types, whether business-to-business or business-to-consumer. Contractual relationships (such as insurance) typically involve an annual renewal. This is as good as an invitation to the customer to look elsewhere for a supplier. Moreover, the annual renewal process has contributed to customers becoming highly price-sensitive in markets such as consumer motor insurance in the UK. In other countries, consumer insurance is sold on a 'menu pricing' basis, in which the customer may be offered a menu of products and the contract might run for several years. The menu approach offers a combination of a multiple product purchase with a longer-term contract.

Similarly, a leading global facilities management company had a standard contract of three years across its customer portfolio. However, it noticed that there were a number of customers that were particularly valuable. It began to manage these customers through a series of carefully-planned *seminars* and *corporate entertainment* events. More importantly, it used these opportunities to improve its relationships with its most profitable customers and to persuade them to change over to longer-term contracts. Soon, almost all these very valuable customers were on contracts ranging in duration from five to eight years. *Extending the contract duration* reduced the chances of losing these customers in any particular year, because a smaller proportion of contracts came up for renewal. It also sent a strong signal to the customer about the importance of the relationship. Moreover, service to these customers tended to improve as the longer duration enabled the account managers to learn more about the customers and to plan for and invest in systems and processes that would improve the management of the relationship.

In summary, the core strategies for defending relationships with highly profitable customers are as shown in the following box.

Core 'defend' strategies for highly profitable customers:

- cross-selling;
- communication and information sharing;
- integrated processes;
- corporate events/entertainment;
- longer-term contracts.

Customer type 2: Demanding customers

Demanding customers are large customers in terms of revenues/potential revenues, but are expensive to look after. Some key accounts may fall into this category – large customers that use their buying power to demand unusually high service levels. The costs may also relate to their demands for customized products or services, or their usage of technical or support services. There may also be particular logistics or stockholding costs associated with servicing large customers.

> Key accounts may be demanding customers that use their buying power to demand unusually high service levels.

The headline strategy for managing demanding customers is retention, combined with managing customer costs. The company wants to retain these customers and secure the large revenues and potential that they bring, but also manage the costs so that the relationships are profitable. This can be a particular issue in key account management, where there is a danger that the supplier may over-service a high-profile customer without properly appreciating that this can result in an unprofitable relationship.

> There is a danger that the supplier may over-service a high-profile customer, resulting in an unprofitable relationship.

Retention strategies have already been discussed above, but account managers need to pay attention to the trade-off between the costs of the retention strategy and the additional income. So, there needs to be considerable attention to the high costs in these relationships. One way that this may be managed is by encouraging customers like these to buy through *cheaper channels* or to *buy in a more efficient way*: for example, providing on-line ordering services for customers. An automotive supplier did this with some of its largest and most demanding customers, the major car manufacturers. It developed an on-line ordering and process tracking system and offered this system to its demanding customers. The customers were delighted, because their service levels improved and it was also cheaper and more convenient for them to buy on-line; the supplier benefited from lower order processing and customer service costs. Other companies manage customers to buy in a more efficient way, such as setting minimum order quantities, or imposing restrictions on the visits that account managers can make to more costly customers. This has the effect of reducing customer costs.

In addition to changing the customer's behaviour through channel management and managing the way that customers buy or interact with the company, there are also pricing strategies that suppliers can use to help them manage the costs of demanding customers. One of these pricing strategies is *price unbundling*. Price unbundling is the process of breaking down product/service packages into their constituent parts and establishing which of these components the customer actually wants and needs. In many cases, customers are receiving service offers that they do not want or use, but that incur a cost for the supplier. Price unbundling can help a supplier to understand where this might be happening and to match the service they provide to the specific needs of the customer. Once the precise service package and price is agreed with the customer, any additional service elements that the customer wants must be paid for separately or the supplier is back in the original position of over-servicing the demanding customer for the amount they are paying. Price unbundling may slightly reduce revenues, because the benefits of no longer providing unwanted services may be shared with the customer in the form of a price reduction. However, it is a strategy worth considering where there is any suspicion that the company is over-servicing a customer.

A third strategy for managing a demanding customer is *cost transparency*. This can take many forms, but in major business-to-business relationships there can be open book accounting, in which the supplier gives the business customer insight into how much it is costing the supplier to look after the customer and even into how profitable the customer is. Although suppliers tend to be wary of open book, because of the high degree of commercial sensitivity, it can be beneficial to a relationship for both sides to agree what is a fair return for the supplier. It may be the case that the customer is simply unaware that the supplier is struggling to make a reasonable return on the relationship.

> Although suppliers tend to be wary of open book, it can be beneficial to a relationship for both sides to agree on a fair return. Most customers are worried about being overcharged by their suppliers.

Most customers are worried about being overcharged by their suppliers, and so open book can reduce risk on both sides. It does, however, imply considerable closeness and trust between the two sides. In other cases, where open book is not an appropriate strategy, the supplier may elect to renegotiate with the customer. This strategy might well follow from a customer lifetime value exercise in which the company discovered that some particularly demanding customers deliver little or no profit, or are even loss-making.

The successful and profitable management of demanding customers is largely about finding creative ways to manage the costs of the relationship, as summarized in the following box.

> **Core 'retain but manage' strategies for demanding customers:**
> - cheaper channels/buying efficiency;
> - price unbundling;
> - cost transparency;
> - renegotiation.

Customer type 3: Commodity customers

Commodity customers have low revenues and low costs, but give a medium to high share of spend to this supplier. The high share of spend indicates that there is not much additional business that the customer could give to the supplier, and so these customers have low additional potential.

In a business-to-business context, the commodity customer might be a small retailer or distributor, a 'mom and pop' store. In a consumer marketing context, these might be low income or low need customers. Commodity customers can be surprisingly prevalent; the customer portfolio of many companies contains a very long tail of only marginally profitable customers.

The key issue with commodity customers is recognizing that they have little additional potential. It is all too easy for a company to offer products and services to these customers that involve inappropriate levels of resources. This might happen simply because the company makes a general offer to its entire customer base, to which these low-potential customers are disproportionately attracted. This was the case with a Scottish insurance company that launched a new life insurance policy a few years ago. The product was bought

> It is all too easy for a company to offer products and services to 'commodity customers' that involve inappropriate levels of service, reducing its ability to service more valuable customers.

largely by commodity customers and the consequences were that the company signed up a lot of poor-quality business while at the same time running short of the resources it needed to service its more valuable customers.

So, the dominant strategy for commodity customers is to *contain the costs*. This strategy might include improving their buying efficiency (for example, reducing the number of sales visits or encouraging them to collect their orders). It might involve setting minimum order quantities or minimum invoice amounts, setting up direct debits, etc. Most importantly, strategies for commodity customers should include limitations on the goods and services they get 'for free'. This includes strategies to limit offerings to them that would increase the cost to serve them.

Core 'cost containment' strategies for commodity customers:

- cheaper channels/buying efficiency;
- minimum order quantities;
- payment for additional services;
- do not offer complex products.

Customer type 4: Uncommitted customers

Uncommitted customers exhibit low revenues and low costs. They are differentiated from the other category of low/low customers (commodity customers) by the supplier's low share of spend. This indicates that they are buying most of their product elsewhere. These customers cannot be categorized as having high *potential* revenues, because clearly the supplier is failing to appeal to the customer. The customer may have a low level of commitment to the relationship, implying low loyalty. Such customers may easily be persuaded by competitors (or by a minor service failure on the part of the supplier) to switch their business elsewhere.

> Uncommitted customers cannot be said to have high *potential* revenues, because the customer has a low level of commitment to the relationship.

Diagnosing an uncommitted customer can be tricky. Uncommitted customers in a business-to-business environment may be identified by an analysis of their turnover and comparing this to the current purchases from the supplier, if they are not prepared to disclose share of spend (in fact, many business-to-business customers are prepared to disclose this).

In a business-to-consumer marketplace, purchase data may be used to identify share of spend by combining it with lifecycle or other similar data. So, for example, a supermarket may examine the loyalty card data of a customer segment that appears to be affluent (based on postcode or income data) but that is spending little in-store. Then, the loyalty card can be used to promote particular products or services to increase share of spend. An example would be fine wines – some affluent customers may prefer to buy their wines from a wine merchant rather than the supermarket. Special vouchers or promotions might encourage these customers to switch to the supermarket.

Because there could be many causes of lack of commitment in a customer, the dominant strategy for uncommitted customers is to *investigate* the reasons for lack of commitment. The investigation should reveal what can be done about it. Some-times, for example, the problem may be a lack of chemistry between the customer and account manager. It is unlikely that an account manager or salesperson will volunteer the information that a customer simply does not like them or feel com-fortable with them, but changing the account manager might have a real effect on the share of spend. In the case of the supermarket failing to persuade its wealthiest customers that it can supply wines that are as good as they can buy from a wine merchant, it may be necessary to promote the better wines that the supermarket can provide.

The core strategy for uncommitted customers is easier to say than to do: to develop new strategies or offers to these customers that might attract additional profitable business. This inevitably means that the supplier needs to better understand the attractions of the competing supplier. To some extent, this involves thinking about the warmth of the relationship with the customer, which is discussed later.

> **Core 'develop' strategies for uncommitted customers:**
>
> - investigate reasons for lack of commitment;
> - understand relative competitive position;
> - develop switching strategies (where it would be profitable to do so).

Customer type 5: Less profitable customers (low lifetime revenues, high costs)

Less profitable customers can be a problem. They have low revenues and high costs to serve. This situation might have arisen for historical reasons – customers that have been with the firm for longer tend to be able to 'find their way around' and know how to secure additional services for themselves. Or, they may be very vocal customers, perhaps keen complainers who have managed to cajole their account manager into giving them more services than can really be justified by the level of their business. Sometimes, the fault lies with the supplier: poor negotiation may have resulted in a contract in which the service provided by the supplier is not justified by the level of business that materializes.

There are cases in which less profitable customers create value in other ways, as discussed in Chapter 8. The discussion here about how to manage customer equity for less profitable customers does not fully apply to customers that might have high relational value (so-called 'flagship customers'), although some of the principles may be useful in reducing the cost of such relationships.

The first problem with less profitable customers is that they may actually be loss-making. A second problem is that, even if they are not actually loss-making and manage to make a contribution to overheads or even a small profit, they are tying up resources that could be diverted to serving other, more valuable customers. Thus, customers in this quadrant need some positive management to improve their value. At the end of the day, these strategies fall into three categories: increase revenues, reduce costs, or (and only if all else fails), divest. The dominant strategy needs to be *positive management* of the situation, rather than ignoring the problem and hoping it will go away, as happens all too often.

> One problem with less profitable customers is that they may be tying up resources that could be diverted to serving other, more valuable customers.

The first general strategy that should be considered in the case of less profitable customers is to increase revenues. One obvious way to do this is to *increase prices* to these customers. Managers are always being told that customers are extremely price sensitive and that price increases are impossible but this is by no means always true. The situation that the supplier is in at the moment is that the customer is being over-supplied or over-serviced for their level of business: in other words, they are getting a really good deal. So, it may be possible to charge them more for it[1]. Organizations who try putting up their prices are often astonished that they lose fewer customers than they expected. If this strategy is being contemplated, the marketing manager should set up a spreadsheet model of the likely reaction among these customers, factoring in the increase in customer equity caused by higher prices less the reduction in customer equity caused by the customers who leave. This model can be run for multiple price levels and customer defection rates. An economist would advise the manager to keep on increasing prices until the marginal additional customer equity was just balanced by the loss of customer equity through customer defection, but it is difficult to predict this precisely. A linked method to

> Organizations who try putting up their prices are often astonished that they lose fewer customers than they expected.

---

[1] Some markets (such as utilities) are regulated so that suppliers are not allowed to price differentially to certain groups of customers, or to withdraw their services; this section does not apply where this is the case.

increase revenues from less profitable customers is to try *price bundling*. Price bundling is where the customer is sold a package of goods or services in a 'bundle', where the bundle has an overall price. In this way, customers are not able to see the prices of the individual elements in the bundle. Moreover, the bundle itself may have value – it might be useful to the customer to have a package of goods or services that saves them having to select and pay for each item separately.

Price bundling has become very common in telephone markets. Mobile phone line rental is typically sold in 'bundles' of text and telephone time; the bundle also includes certain types of phone. Providers such as British Telecom or Virgin also offer packages that combine elements such as land lines, broadband, a mobile phone, etc. These packages are attractive to customers who perhaps do not know what their usage of the individual elements might be, or who are short of time so that buying the package is convenient.

If the option to increase revenues is not available or is unsuccessful, the second option is to seek to cut the costs of serving these customers. There are a number of strategies that companies have deployed here. One is to *switch these customers to cheaper channels*. This might be achieved in a business-to-business context by reducing the number of sales calls made by the field sales force on these types of customer, or even preventing visits altogether. Business-to-consumer, the strategy might be to channel these customers through the call centre or Internet rather than through stores or branches. The problem may be that these customers like the levels of service they get, face to face, and so some companies have even resorted to relocating branches away from areas where they service high proportions of less profitable customers.

Another strategy that reduces the cost to serve is to cut down on logistics/delivery costs. There are many options here, from persuading customers to *collect*, rather than have their goods delivered, right through to *consolidating deliveries* so that fewer drops are made. It may also be possible to *reduce or refuse* emergency delivery, unless the customer agrees to pay extra for this, or to *increase the minimum drop size for free delivery*. As discussed earlier, logistics and delivery costs are an important element in customer profitability and lifetime value, and so they should be a focus for attention where customers are less profitable.

An interesting question where less profitable customers are concerned is whether the organization can profitably look after them directly or whether these customers should be *referred to distributors* or other third parties. Some companies have achieved considerable success in increasing their overall customer equity by deciding that certain categories of customer should be dealt with indirectly, through resellers, dealers, or distributors. A decision to pass a number of customers over to a dealer

> Some companies have increased their customer equity by deciding that certain categories of customer should be dealt with indirectly, through resellers, dealers, or distributors.

can have unexpected positive repercussions, because the dealer is likely to become a friend and the customers may even prefer a relationship with a local outlet.

Finally, if all else fails and if the customer is loss-making (and not creating value in other ways), the company may make a decision to *end the relationship* with the customer. This is also known as 'firing the customer', and is a strategy that should be used only as a last resort and with extreme caution. The success of the strategy depends crucially on how it is carried out, because bad publicity can easily result from clumsy or ill-managed decisions to withdraw services. A small engineering company proudly recounted how it disengaged successfully from a number of troublesome customers: having expressed its sorrow at being unable to continue the relationship, it referred the customer to one of their local competitors. As the sales director commented, not only did they solve a problem for themselves, they also succeeded in creating a problem for the competition!

Core 'positive management' strategies for less profitable customers:

- increase prices;
- introduce price bundling;
- switch to cheaper channels;
- reduce delivery costs;
- pass customer to a distributor/refuse to deal direct;
- withdraw from the relationship.

How to maximize customer equity in the portfolio

The purpose of customer portfolio management using the customer equity approach is to maximize overall customer equity from the customer portfolio. Figure 9.2 sets out the dominant strategies for each quadrant and suggests some specific strategies that could be used to achieve that aim. More detail on these strategies is set out earlier in this chapter, and Chapter 7 describes how to construct the customer equity portfolio.

The dominant strategy for the most profitable customers is to retain them, so that their value can be captured. For demanding customers, the issue is how to retain them while managing costs. For the customers that are low/low, the supplier should first examine this quadrant in some detail to see whether there are uncommitted customers that might be won over with some product or service modification (uncommitted customers usually have a low share of spend with the supplier). If not, these customers should be classed as commodity customers and their costs should be contained. Finally, there are the less profitable customers: here, the core

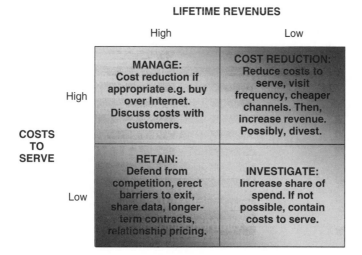

Figure 9.2 Overview of customer equity management strategies

strategy is positive management of the problem, unless the customer is valuable to the company in other ways.

There is a straightforward test that will measure the success of the various strategies recommended here, which is to monitor the effect on customer equity in that quadrant. For example, successful 'defend' strategies with profitable customers should reduce customer defections and therefore increase the customer equity in that quadrant. Successful positive management of less profitable customers should reduce costs and may also increase revenues in this quadrant, again leading to increases in customer equity even after the costs of implementing the new strategies are taken into account.

> The straightforward test of the success of sales and marketing strategies is to measure their impact on customer equity.

The maximization of customer equity is such an important topic that it merits a chapter of its own. Chapter 13 deals in detail with how to acquire, retain, and manage customer relationships so as to maximize the customer equity of the portfolio.

Using customer equity with other forms of segmentation

One final note about the customer equity approach to portfolio management is that it may not map on to the firm's pre-existing approach to segmentation. In some cases it will, because the current segmentation is based on dimensions that affect customer equity, even if indirectly. For example, demographic segmentation using tools such as ACORN (postcode data) or Financial ACORN (propensity to buy) may map quite well to customer equity because wealthier customers tend to live in better houses and to buy more things. Some types of behavioural segmentation will also correspond quite well to customer equity. Other approaches to segmentation may not. In particular, it is notoriously difficult to match attitudinal segmentation to actual buying behaviour.

Marketing managers planning to implement customer equity portfolio management need to be aware that it can be applied to existing segments but the result might be that there is high heterogeneity within the segment (some very valuable and some much less valuable customers). Inevitably, having segments that are heterogeneous in this way may reduce the impact of the customer equity management strategies. This does not make customer equity portfolio management any less valuable a tool; in fact, it may lead to a reappraisal of current segmentation.

Summary

The simple principle of customer equity portfolio management, and of categorizing customers in terms of high or low potential revenues and high or low costs, yields a powerful tool for the profitable management of customers.

Many companies have pre-existing approaches to segmentation that may be valuable to them. In such cases, they may prefer to manage their customer portfolios not only by customer equity but also by taking the customer's view into account, perhaps incorporating some measure of the warmth of the relationship or of the importance of the relationship to the customer, not just to the supplier. This dual supplier/customer perspective is another approach to customer portfolio management that will be considered in the next chapter.

> **Note**
>
> Now use the worksheet on the following page to create your own customer equity portfolio management matrix.

Worksheet: customer equity portfolio management matrix

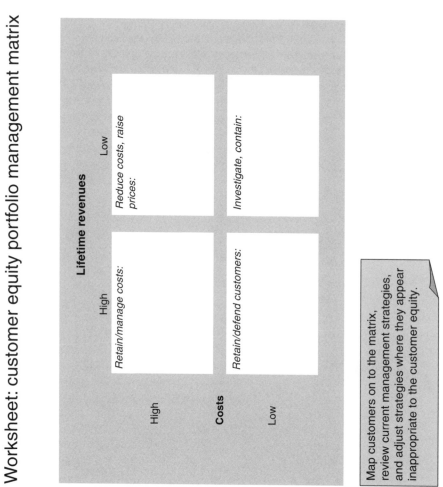

Lifetime revenues

	High	Low
Costs High	*Retain/manage costs:*	*Reduce costs, raise prices:*
Costs Low	*Retain/defend customers:*	*Investigate, contain:*

Map customers on to the matrix, review current management strategies, and adjust strategies where they appear inappropriate to the customer equity.

Where to find out more

Berger, P.D. and Bechwati, N.N. (2001) 'The allocation of promotion budget to maximise customer equity', *Omega*, **29**(1), pp. 49-61. *Very specific application of customer equity, but written in an accessible manner.*

Rust, R.T., Lemon, K.N. and Zeithaml, V.A. (2001) 'Where should the next marketing dollar go?', *Marketing Management*, **10**(3), pp. 24-28. *This is one of a series of excellent papers by these authors on various aspects of customer equity.*

Bowman, D. and Narayandas, D. (2004) 'Linking customer management effort to customer profitability in business markets', *Journal of Marketing Research*, **41**(4), pp. 433-447. *A useful reminder that the way in which relationships are managed has a profound impact on their value.*

The customer portfolio using both supplier and customer perspectives

10

What's in this chapter

- Why including the customer perspective in portfolio management is vital
- The customer equity/relationship warmth portfolio
- How to construct a customer portfolio using the Directional Policy Matrix

Key concepts discussed in this chapter

Attitudinal metrics	Measure attitudes. Customer satisfaction is an attitudinal metric. Problematic, because customers may not behave in ways that reflect their stated attitudes.
Behavioural metrics	Measure behaviours. Often thought more reliable than attitudinal metrics, because 'actions speak louder than words'. However, the accuracy of behavioural metrics as a guide to relationship warmth is affected by the degree to which customers genuinely feel there is a real alternative available; if not, the customers are actually 'hostages'. In the latter situation, there could be high dissatisfaction but high retention.
Customer or segment attractiveness	Measures the attractiveness of a portfolio of customers, or groups of customers such as segment, relative to one another and from the point of view of the supplier. To do this, the supplier constructs an index of attractiveness factors and their importance weightings and scores each customer or segment against this index. Customer attractiveness should include measures of customer equity and of relational attractiveness.

DPM	Directional policy matrix: a method of constructing a customer portfolio that plots customer or segment attractiveness against the relative business strength of the supplier. Relative business strength is measured from the customer's or segment's point of view, relative to the competition in that customer or segment. The DPM is a useful tool for portfolio management and strategy development.

Key tools explained in this chapter

- Directional policy matrix: A widely-used approach to mapping a customer portfolio and developing marketing strategies. The portfolio is usually constructed with customer attractiveness on the vertical axis and relative business strength on the horizontal axis. Customer (or segment) attractiveness is viewed from the supplier's perspective, so it measures the attractiveness of the customer to that supplier. This can be influenced by the customer lifetime value or customer equity of different customers, plus their relational value to the supplier. Relative business strength is plotted from the customer's point of view and relative to the best competitor for that customer or segment. Thus, the supplier's relative business performance can be better or worse than the best competitor. In the DPM, this is reflected in whether the customer or segment is plotted to the left or to the right of the centre line. Customers or segments plotting in the top half of the matrix are strategic or investment customers; customers or segments plotting in the lower half of the matrix should be managed and are not targeted for strategic development.

Two-minute chapter summary

This chapter extends the customer portfolio model to include the customer's perspective on the relationship. The customer equity approach focuses purely on the financial value of the customer to the company. However, customers are unlike other forms of assets in that they can choose to exit from the relationship. Losing a customer affects customer retention which, in turn, reduces customer equity. That is why the inclusion of the customer perspective is important.

Two ways to include the customer perspective in the portfolio model are discussed in this chapter. The first is to include the perceived warmth of the relationship as one of the dimensions of the portfolio, and plot this against customer equity. The warmth of the relationship might be mapped based on stated customer satisfaction, or based on a behavioural metric such as share of spend. Customer satisfaction measures attitude, and there can be a gap between the stated level of satisfaction and the actual resulting behaviour. So, much previous research has found that customers who say they are satisfied may still exit from the relationship.

Because of this known problem with relying on customer satisfaction as a measure of the warmth of the relationship, it may be preferable to measure relationship warmth in terms of behavioural metrics that measure purchasing behaviour such as share of spend. A high share of spend probably indicates a good relationship (unless the supplier has an effective monopoly). However, measuring share of spend is not a completely reliable guide to the warmth of the relationship because there may be no effective competition. If the customer is a 'hostage', there could be low satisfaction yet high share of spend.

A more widely-used approach to constructing a dual-perspective customer portfolio is to use the directional policy matrix (DPM). The DPM measures the attractiveness of customers or segments against the relative business strength of the supplier from the point of view of that customer or segment. Thus, the DPM plots the supplier's point of view (the attractiveness of customers, measured in terms of customer lifetime value and/or relational value) against the customer's point of view, measured as the performance of the supplier on the factors that are most important to the customers, compared with the competition.

Why the customer perspective is vital

The customer equity portfolio management approach demonstrated in Chapter 9 focuses purely on the lifetime revenues and lifetime costs of customers and how the net customer equity can be maximized. However, there could be other issues that might be important in managing a customer portfolio. One of these is customers that give only a small share of their spend to the supplier. Low share of spend may be one symptom of a weak relationship, or indicate that the supplier is of low importance to the customer.

In this chapter, the portfolio is extended to incorporate the customer perspective. Two techniques are demonstrated for doing this. Including the customer perspective is useful because customer relationships are unlike any of the other assets of the firm: customers can choose to walk away. Including a customer view in the portfolio helps to give a supplier insight into whether or not this is likely to happen.

There are two main methods of incorporating the customer perspective into customer portfolio analysis. The first method is to compare the value of the relationship (the customer equity) with the warmth of the relationship. The second method is to compare the value of the relationship (the customer equity) with the relative performance of the supplier from the customer's point of view.

An interesting technical point to note here is that both customer perspectives (warmth of the relationship, and relative performance) are likely to affect customer retention. The warmer the relationship, and/or the better the performance, the more likely the customer is to stay with

> Customer retention is one of the drivers of customer equity, and so customer equity and the customer perspective are inter-related.

the supplier. Customer retention is one of the drivers of customer equity, as shown in Chapter 7, and so customer equity and the customer perspective are inter-related. Clearly, the status of the relationship may affect the level of risk, and this issue will be discussed in greater detail in Chapter 11.

The first approach to including the customer perspective is to look at the warmth of the relationship. This can be as simple as categorizing each customer segment into three categories: friendly, neutral, and unfriendly. This simple categorization can be done based on the subjective experiences that account managers have when they encounter customers face-to-face or over the phone.

Alternatively, and for greater objectivity, metrics such as share of customer spend or customer satisfaction can be used as a measure of the warmth of the relationship. Share of customer spend is a behavioural metric; it reflects what customers actually do. Customer satisfaction is an attitudinal metric; it measures what customers think (or what they say they think, which is not quite the same thing!).

Extended portfolio approach #1

Plot the customer portfolio using customer equity (or total value to the supplier, if relational benefits are to be included) against the warmth of the relationship (measured subjectively, or using share of spend or customer satisfaction).

The first extended method of portfolio analysis in this chapter will create a portfolio based on customer equity and relationship warmth. This approach to customer portfolio analysis is particularly useful in sales management, because it provides guidelines for sales resource allocation[1].

The second method of extending the portfolio is to include the customer perspective, which looks at customer equity versus the relative performance of the supplier. To do this, the supplier has to analyse the customer's specific needs and then compare its own performance against that of key competitors. This method gives a more detailed picture of the supplier's position, but is more costly and

---

[1] I am indebted to my colleague Richard Yallop for the original suggestion, which I have adapted.

difficult to do. However, this form of portfolio analysis has achieved wide accept-
ance in business. In particular, it is used in business-to-business contexts where
the number of competitors is limited and customers are more open about the
supplier's relative performance. Some customers even use relative supplier performance as the framework within which they provide benchmarking and other detailed
feedback.

> **Extended portfolio approach #2**
>
> Plot the customer portfolio using customer equity (or total value to the
> supplier) against the supplier's relative competitive position.

The second extended method of portfolio analysis shown in this chapter will demonstrate the creation of a customer portfolio using customer equity and relative
competitive strength. Taking its relative competitive position into account enables
a supplier to develop specific strategies that will improve its position.

Each portfolio approach will now be considered. For each method, the following
will be shown:

- how to construct the customer portfolio using the extended method;
- its uses and applications;
- advantages and limitations.

The customer equity/relationship warmth portfolio

A popular way of developing a customer portfolio, which looks at more than just
customer equity or the value of the customer, is to add an additional dimension
that reflects the warmth of the relationship. The underlying reason why this can be
useful is that some customers are locked in to their suppliers unwillingly, perhaps
for lack of an alternative, whereas others are happy to give a lot of their business
to the supplier. The implications are very different. The customers that are locked
in are sometimes known as 'hostages', because they will try to escape the first
opportunity they get, such as when a competing supplier makes an offer to them.
The second type are known as 'supporters', and they are more likely to stay with
their supplier even when competitors enter the market. This is a useful distinction
because it is widely recognized that there is a difference between behavioural loyalty (customers that stay because they believe there is no effective alternative for
them) and attitudinal loyalty (customers that stay because they genuinely like their
supplier).

The classic case that highlights the difference between these two types of loyalty is UK retail banking. For decades, the Big Four retail banks in the UK (Barclays, Lloyds, Midland, and NatWest) had experienced very low levels of customer churn. In the 1980s and 1990s, however, the sector opened up to competition and suddenly customers started leaving in droves, attracted by new offers such as First Direct. It turned out that many customers had stayed with their Big Four provider because they thought that there was no real difference between it and its competitors. Although this might have looked like loyalty, it was in fact dissatisfaction but with no outlet. When a genuine alternative came along in the form of First Direct, not only did many customers leave but First Direct also received an unprecedented level of endorsement from its customers, reflecting their satisfaction with a perceived better service level.

> It is widely recognized that there is a difference between behavioural loyalty (customers who stay because they believe there is no effective alternative for them) and attitudinal loyalty (customers who stay because they genuinely like their supplier).

This example illustrates why a company might want to use the customer equity/relationship warmth method of portfolio analysis.

How to construct the customer equity/relationship warmth portfolio

When considering relationship warmth, it is natural to think about it in three categories – friendly, neutral, and unfriendly. To match this, it makes sense to categorize customers into three bands: high, medium, and low customer equity. Therefore, the basic framework for the customer equity/relationship warmth portfolio is as shown in Figure 10.1.

The method for calculating customer equity was described in Chapter 7.

The customer portfolio might consist of individual customers (where the numbers of individual customers are quite small; if this is the case, customer lifetime value is used), or of customer segments or groups of customers. Whatever level of granularity is used (see Chapter 7 for more detail about granularity in customer equity calculations), there should be a number of different customer groups for which the customer equity is known. These customer groups are then plotted on to a customer equity scale that can then be divided into three parts, as shown in Figure 10.2.

This example shows five segments, A to E, plotted vertically according to the amount of customer equity in each segment. In this customer portfolio, there are three segments (A to C) that have more than £2m customer equity and are regarded as high value. One segment, D, has customer equity of £1.5m and so is

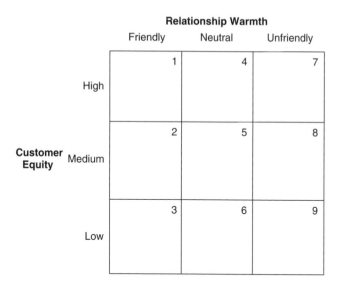

Figure 10.1 Basic framework for customer equity/relationship warmth portfolio

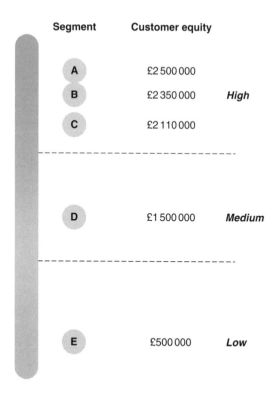

Figure 10.2 Customer equity scale

moderately valuable. The fifth segment, E, has customer equity of £500k and is therefore categorized as low value within this portfolio.

The next step is to decide what measure of relationship warmth will be used to complete the portfolio. The simplest way to define relationship warmth is to ask the account managers dealing with that group

> It is best to use an objective measure of relationship warmth when constructing the portfolio.

of customers how warm the relationship is. There are two problems with this approach: the first is that the notion of relationship warmth can mean different things to different account managers; and the other is that the account manager may not be motivated to give a completely truthful answer if the relationship is not particularly good. Therefore, it would be better to use an objective measure of relationship warmth when constructing the portfolio.

One such measure is recorded customer satisfaction levels.

Using customer satisfaction to measure warmth of relationship

To use customer satisfaction data as a measure of the warmth of the relationship, the marketing manager takes the average satisfaction for each customer group and plots each group on a three-point scale ranging from unsatisfied to neutral to satisfied. A word of caution here: customer satisfac-

> There is a tendency for customers to bias their responses towards more favourable responses, even if they are not particularly happy with the relationship.

tion scales are notorious for being a blunt instrument to measure what people really think about the relationship. There is a tendency for customers to bias their responses towards the more favourable (fairly satisfied, very satisfied), even if they are not particularly happy with the relationship. Thus, when plotting the portfolio, it might be necessary to rescale the customer satisfaction data so that 'neutral' satisfaction responses are taken to represent unfriendly customers, 'satisfied' is taken to represent neutral customers, and 'very satisfied' is taken to represent friendly customers.

Because of the known difficulty with customer satisfaction surveys, other measures such as proportion of complaints or proportion of returns could be taken into account. Attitudinal measures such as customer satisfaction are useful where attitudes strongly affect customer behaviour (as in high-involvement purchases such as hobby and sports equipment) or where share of spend data is difficult to obtain or not very helpful (as in the banking sector example earlier, where customers would unwillingly give 100% of their personal banking to a supplier with whom they weren't actually very happy).

Using share of spend to measure warmth of relationship

Customer satisfaction measures attitude rather than behaviour, and behaviour may be very different from attitude. Therefore, relationship warmth could be measured by behaviour rather than attitude. An important behavioural measure is share of spend. This measure is increasingly used both business-to-business and business-to-consumer, where it is often referred to as share of wallet.

> An important behavioural measure is share of spend or share of wallet, which is increasingly used in both business-to-business and business-to-consumer markets.

To use share of spend to create the customer equity/relationship warmth portfolio, the company could identify three categories (high, medium, and low share of spend). The actual percentage share of spend associated with each category will vary according to the industry sector. In business-to-consumer markets such as food retailing, a high share of spend might be close to 100%. However, in many business-to-business markets, high shares of spend might be only 30% and business-to-business customers might have explicit policies to use multiple suppliers. In such cases, the status of the supplier might be a useful indicator of the warmth of the relationship: a lead supplier would have a relatively high share of spend, for example.

> **Categorizing relationship warmth using share of spend in business-to-business markets**
>
> Friendly = lead supplier, high share of spend
>
> Neutral = one of several suppliers, share of spend near that of main
>
> competitors
>
> Unfriendly = minor supplier, share of spend lower than competing suppliers

Share of spend is a very useful indicator of relationship quality and can also signal changes in relationship warmth. A falling share of spend should be taken very seriously as an indication that something is not right in the relationship. Sometimes, however, customers are effectively 'hostages', either because there is no effective competitor or because the customer does not perceive that there is an effective competitor. In these admittedly increasingly rare cases, the marketing analyst or manager building the portfolio needs to use an alternative behavioural measure.

> Share of spend is a very useful indicator of relationship quality and can also signal changes in relationship warmth.

There are two other behavioural measures that could also be used as proxies for relationship warmth. One of these is churn; the other is advocacy.

Churn rates are the reverse side of customer retention, discussed in Chapter 7. The churn rate of a customer segment is the percentage of customers each year that leave. The absolute percentage will vary by industry and by company, but a low churn rate indicates a warm relationship in which most customers stay with the supplier. A moderate churn rate indicates a neutral relationship and higher churn rates indicate a cool relationship. Churn rates are a useful indicator of relationship warmth where the segments are large, because the churn data are likely to be more reliable where there are large numbers of customers to study. This might be the case with mobile phone companies, which typically have a small number of very big customer segments.

Advocacy, otherwise known as word-of-mouth or referral, is where one customer recommends the supplier to another. Advocacy is one of the most difficult aspects of customer behaviour on which to collect data, but it is one of the most powerful indicators of relationship warmth. Where advocacy is high, this strongly indicates a warm relationship. Where advocacy is moderate or low, this strongly indicates a neutral relationship. Where advocacy is absent altogether or is negative (customers tell others *not* to use the supplier), this is strongly indicative of a cool relationship.

There are three ways to measure advocacy: intention; actual advocacy; and the results of advocacy.

Measuring advocacy

Intention to advocate: 'Would you recommend company X to a friend?'

Actual advocacy: 'Have you recommended company X to a friend

within the last year?'

Results of advocacy: 'How did you come to use company X?'

Advocacy, particularly actual advocacy, has often been considered to be a more powerful measure of what customers actually think and feel than customer satisfaction, to the extent that one guru (Frederick Reichheld) has recommended replacing customer satisfaction measurement with advocacy measurement (see the 'Where to find out more' section at the end of this chapter for more information).

Clearly, actual advocacy is more powerful than the intent to advocate, but both are important. Measuring the results of advocacy is not only interesting in its own right, to see whether customers acted on the recommendations of their friends and relatives, but it can also be an indicator of the amount of advocacy that is taking place within a customer segment if this cannot be measured directly. Customers tend to recommend suppliers to their friends and family, and their friends and family will most likely be in the same segment as they are. Thus, if many customers say they first heard about the supplier from a friend, it is likely that the recommendation came from within that segment.

Building the relationship warmth portfolio

The portfolio has two dimensions, customer equity and warmth of relationship, as shown in Figure 10.1. To build the portfolio using these dimensions, the marketing analyst or manager has to define each dimension as described above and then plot all the customer segments or groups on it. It is important that all customer segments are plotted; otherwise, this will not be a complete portfolio. Some companies operate both business-to-business and business-to-consumer; in these cases, the marketing manager will probably have to plot two separate portfolios, because the scales for each dimension are likely to be different between business-to-business and business-to-consumer. Figure 10.3 illustrates the completed portfolio.

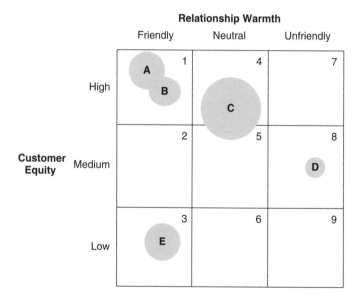

Figure 10.3 The customer equity/relationship warmth portfolio

The company illustrated in Figure 10.3 has plotted all its customer segments on the portfolio matrix. Using three categories of customer equity (high/medium/low) and three categories of relationship warmth (friendly/neutral/unfriendly) means that the portfolio grid contains 9 (3×3) boxes, which are numbered 1 to 9 in

Figure 10.3. There are some clear differences in positioning between the segments, both in customer equity (vertical axis) and in relationship warmth (horizontal axis).

Each segment is represented by a circle but an additional piece of information has been included as the portfolio has been developed, because the size of the circle now gives an indication of how many customers are in each segment. Larger circles indicate more customers in a particular segment (e.g., segment C) and smaller circles indicate there are fewer customers (e.g., segment D). This information can be useful when the company considers how to use the customer equity/relationship warmth portfolio.

Using customer equity/relationship warmth portfolios

This approach to the customer portfolio is useful for planning sales and customer management resource allocation. In fact, potential customer equity and potential relationship warmth could also be used to position prospective customers on the matrix.

The way in which this matrix can be used for sales and marketing resource allocation depends on which box the customer or segment is in.

Boxes 1 and 2 contain important, friendly customers (medium to high customer equity and a friendly/warm relationship). In this portfolio, segments A and B are in this position. It is tempting to conclude that these customers should be a priority for sales and marketing effort but, in fact, the strategy here should be to maintain the relationship. There may be some possibilities for additional business but, by and large, these customers are already giving the supplier most or all of their spend. So, there is an important customer management role here, but sales effort can reasonably be directed elsewhere: specifically, to boxes 4 and 5.

Boxes 4 and 5 contain neutral customers or segments where there is a lot of customer equity but not much warmth in the relationship. These relationships should be a focus for sales and marketing, as there may be additional potential by winning business from competing suppliers, and there could also be a positive payoff from marketing effort aimed at improving the relationship warmth, because that would reduce the risk of defection. Any customer segments in boxes 4 and 5 should be considered a top priority. In the completed portfolio example shown in Figure 10.3, segment C is in this position, being valuable in terms of customer equity but neutral in its attitude to the supplier.

> Neutral customers or segments should be a focus for sales and marketing, because there may be additional potential by winning business from competing suppliers and a reduced risk of defection.

Interestingly, the size of the circle for segment C indicates that there are many customers in this segment. This also explains how it can produce substantial customer equity while having customers that are only lukewarm towards the supplier. Investing more sales and marketing resource in segment C makes good financial sense.

Boxes 7 and 8 are under threat, because these are valuable customers but where the relationship is unfriendly/cool. This is the case with segment D in Figure 10.3. The important issue here is to change the strategy, because whatever the supplier is doing is not particularly appealing to these customers. One option is to change the salesperson or account manager; sometimes this simple action will be enough to improve the relationship. More generally, it would be worth investing some time and resource in understanding the customer segments in boxes 7 and 8, because this valuable income could be under threat from the competition and new offers or value propositions might need to be developed.

Customers in box 3 have relatively low customer equity but a friendly/warm relationship with the supplier. Salespeople sometimes refer to these types of customers as 'tea and biscuits' customers, because they are likely to welcome the salesperson warmly and offer them something to drink and eat. The problem is that the warmth of the welcome that salespeople get from these types of customers can easily encourage them to spend disproportionate amounts of time there. Given that these customers are small and are already friendly, there is little chance that there will be much incremental business from them. The company shown in Figure 10.3 unfortunately has a substantial number of customers of this type, as shown by the size of the circle for segment E. The sales force may be tempted to spend too much time – proportionately – with segment E customers.

> The sales force may be tempted to spend too much time with low value 'tea and biscuits' customers.

Boxes 6 and 9 represent low equity customers that are neutral or cool towards the supplier. In terms of sales force time, there are serious questions about whether salespeople should actually be visiting these customers at all. Luckily, the portfolio shown in Figure 10.3 does not contain any segments of this type but, if they did, a sensible strategy would be to try to replace sales visits with desk-based account management in these boxes.

These strategies are summarized in Figure 10.4.

In summary, sales effort should be focused on boxes 4 and 5, which is the zone of greatest potential. Maintenance effort should go into boxes 1 and 2, to manage the valuable ongoing relationship and seek opportunities selectively. Boxes 7 and 8 require a change of strategy and/or a change of account manager. Box 3 ('tea and biscuits customers'), and more particularly boxes 6 and 9, are prime targets for the use of cheaper sales channels and customer management methods, such as telephone or Internet-based.

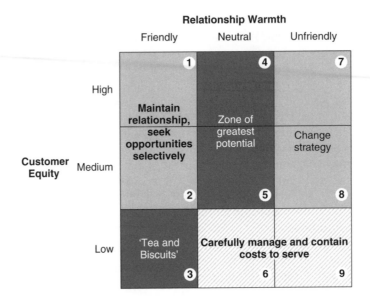

Figure 10.4 Strategies using the equity/warmth portfolio matrix

Advantages and limitations of the equity/warmth method

Constructing a customer portfolio based on customer equity and relationship warmth has a number of advantages. First, it is straightforward to construct and can be based on existing measures of relationship warmth, such as the account manager's reports of the customer relationship or actual metrics such as customer satisfaction or share of spend. This makes the equity/warmth method a relatively fast and low cost way of implementing customer portfolio management.

However, there is a potentially important limitation to the equity/warmth portfolio approach, which is that it fails to take into account the relational benefits from a customer relationship. Generally, it is financial value that is used (customer equity) and, because there are almost no companies that are able to put a financial value on the other benefits they can get from a customer relationship, this is not taken into account. For example, a customer might be comparatively cool towards a supplier and give them little business (box 9), but still have value because the supplier is associated with their powerful brand. Chapter 8 discusses the interesting area of how to evaluate relational benefits and also shows how a financial value could be assigned to these benefits. Thus, a more general measure of the value of the customer to the firm might be preferable.

Another limitation of the equity/warmth method lies in its very simplicity. Some firms would argue that the notion of relationship warmth is not the right dimension to measure and that, in fact, it is the importance of the customer to the supplier and its relative competitive position that is important.

The equity/warmth method is a useful tool, particularly when a firm is just starting out in portfolio management. It also has practical applications in sales resource allocation and has been widely adopted by sales managers. However, for strategic decision making about customers and segments, many marketing managers prefer a version of the directional policy matrix (DPM), because of the greater richness of analysis that goes into building a DPM.

How to construct a customer portfolio using the DPM

The directional policy matrix (DPM) is such a widely-accepted tool in the field of marketing and key account management that it is difficult to trace its exact origins, although it seems to have been developed by GE, McKinsey, and Shell during the 1970s. Since then, it has been adopted by many companies as a core planning tool, used as the basis for a number of commercial marketing planning software tools, and adapted for use specifically with key accounts and in sales management (see the 'Where to find out more' section at the end of this chapter).

The essential idea that underlies the DPM is that the customer portfolio is constructed along two dimensions: the attractiveness of the customer to the supplier; and the relative attractiveness of the supplier to the customer. Both dimensions are built in the form of indices, using a weighing and scoring technique. The tool is attractive because of the amount of detailed information that can be incorporated into these indices.

Measuring customer attractiveness

Customer attractiveness to the supplier can be measured in terms of financial and relational attractiveness. The financial attractiveness is measured using customer lifetime value for individual customers or customer equity for customer segments. Relational attractiveness also has to be defined and measured (see Chapter 8).

The first stage in measuring overall customer attractiveness is to decide on the relative importance of customer equity and other attractiveness criteria to the firm. The second step is to define specifically what would constitute high, medium, and low attractiveness for each element. An example of these two steps is shown in Table 10.1.

Table 10.1 shows that customer equity accounts for 70% of the overall attractiveness of a customer segment to this firm, but that advocacy and participation in new product trials are also important. The importance weighting always sums to 100%.

For this company, a highly-attractive segment (that is, one that would score 8 to 10 for attractiveness on a scale of 1 to 10) would have customer equity of over €1 million. A segment with customer equity of between €500 000 and €1 million

Table 10.1 Importance weighting and defining customer attractiveness criteria

Attractiveness criteria	Importance weighting to the firm (%)	Scoring criteria		
		High: 8–10	Medium: 4–7	Low: 0–3
Customer equity	70	Over €1m	€ 500 000 to €1m	Up to €500 000
Advocacy	20	More than 5% of customers recruited this way	0–5% of customers recruited this way	Very few or no customers recruited this way; some signs of negative advocacy
Willingness to participate in new product trials	10	High	Medium	Low
	100			

would be seen as moderately attractive, scoring somewhere between 4 and 7 on a 10-point scale. A segment with customer equity of less than €500 000 would be regarded as less attractive by this company.

This company measures the proportion of its customers coming to it through advocacy and regards word of mouth as the second most important determinant of customer attractiveness, scoring 20%. Because it measures referred customers, it is able to define what level of advocacy would make a segment attractive (in this case, more than 5% of customers being recruited through advocacy).

Wherever possible, precise definitions of each attractiveness criterion should be given. This makes the portfolio exercise more objective. Even achieving the first two steps – agreeing what makes a customer segment attractive and how this is defined – can be a struggle for many companies. Sometimes, however, it is just not possible to define an attractiveness criterion and in this case the definition would typically be simply high/medium/low, as is the case for the participation in new product trials shown in Table 10.1.

Once the attractiveness criteria, importance weightings, and definitions have all been completed, the third step is to score each segment against the factors and then multiply the weight by the score to give a total weighted score for each segment (Table 10.2).

As Table 10.2 shows, this firm would view segments X and Y as considerably more attractive than segment Z. X's total weighted score is 6.1 and Y's is 5.5, compared to Z's total weighted score of just 3.0. The reason that X and Y are more attractive is primarily customer equity; looking up the scoring criteria in Table 10.1 suggests that both X and Y have customer equity approaching €1 million, whereas segment Z has customer equity of less than €500 000.

Table 10.2 Scoring the segments and calculating the weighted score

Attractiveness criteria	Weight (%)	Segment					
		X		Y		Z	
		Score	WxS	Score	WxS	Score	WxS
Customer equity	70	7	4.9	6	4.2	2	1.4
Advocacy	20	2	0.4	6	1.2	5	1.0
Willingness to participate in new product trials	10	8	0.8	1	0.1	6	0.6
	100		6.1		5.5		3.0

WxS = Weight × Score

However, there are some interesting differences between segments X and Y, the more valuable segments. Customers in segment X are considerably less likely to recommend the supplier than are customers in segment Y. However, they are far more likely to participate in new product trials. It might pay this supplier to try and increase advocacy rates within segment X, perhaps offering a reward to customers if they recruit another customer.

Once the weighted scores for customer attractiveness have been calculated, the company can create a 'thermometer' showing the relative attractiveness of each of its segments (Figure 10.5). The principle of the customer attractiveness thermometer is similar to that of the customer equity scale shown in Figure 10.2, but the thermometer reflects additional aspects of the relationship that are attractive to the supplier. For more information on relational attractiveness of customers, see Chapter 8.

The customers or segments towards the top of the thermometer are the 'hottest', or most attractive; the customers or segments towards the lower end of the thermometer are less attractive. In this case, segments X and Y from Table 10.2 are relatively attractive and positioned in the upper half of the thermometer. Segment Z is less attractive, and so is lower down the thermometer.

The criteria that make customers attractive to companies may change over time, or their importance may vary. For example, at certain points of a company's life-cycle, advocacy might be very important (perhaps in a growing but fast-changing and competitive market). At other times, the ability of customers to help the supplier to enter new markets might be much more important. This can be the case in business-to-business, when the supplier is looking to expand geographically and therefore finds customers that can help it into new markets more attractive. The important point about customer attractiveness is that there is a single index against which each segment or individual

> The important point about customer attractiveness is that there is a single index against which each segment or individual customer is evaluated.

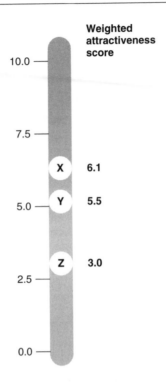

Figure 10.5 Customer attractiveness thermometer

customer is evaluated. This can be politically tricky in some firms, where some segment managers can become indignant if their segments are deemed less attractive than others. Clearly, this would have implications for the allocation of sales and marketing resource.

> **Note**
>
> Remember that the firm should have a single scale of customer attractiveness so that it can compare one customer against another (and it can also compare the attractiveness of potential customers against the attractiveness of actual customers).

Measuring the relative attractiveness of the supplier

Once customer attractiveness has been defined, the next stage in building the DPM is to understand what the relative competitive position of the supplier is, in each segment. A 'quick and dirty' method of doing this is to divide the supplier's market share by the market share of the closest competitor. This does not have to be the largest player in the market, simply the one that customers would most often consider in the same purchase context.

However, comparing market shares can be tricky where companies operate in many slightly different marketplaces. In addition, simply looking at market share, even if it can be determined accurately, does not give the supplier any useful information about *why* it has the market share it does.

Therefore, for its horizontal axis measuring the relative attractiveness of the supplier to the customer, the DPM uses a tool called Critical Success Factors (CSFs) to try to understand not just *what* the supplier's relative competitive position is, but *why.*

The CSFs are the few vital things that determine the customer's choice at the point of decision. In other words, they are not the general factors that get the supplier on to the customer's radar, such as having more or less the right product at more

> The critical success factors are the few vital things that determine the customer's choice *at the point of decision.*

or less the right price, because these are survival factors without which the supplier is not taken seriously by that customer or segment. Instead, the CSFs are the factors that swing the customer's decision either for or against the supplier. They may be factors that seem to be of little importance to the supplier but that are clearly of great importance to the customer. The CSFs will be different for different customers or segments.

The process for locating a customer or segment's position along the horizontal axis is as follows:

1. Identify the CSFs for that segment, remembering that these must really be the critical ones. They should be few in number – if more than six have been identified, some are probably not critical.
2. Identify the importance weights that customers in that segment would attach to each CSF, summing to 100%.
3. Identify the closest one or two competitors. The closest competitors are defined as the other suppliers that customers in that segment seriously consider using.
4. For each CSF, score the supplier and each competitor.
5. Calculate the weighted score.
6. Repeat for each segment.

An example of a completed CSF table is shown as Table 10.3.

It is important that the analysis is done from the customer's point of view and is not based on what the supplier knows, or thinks it knows, about its competitors. The point of this analysis is to gain an understanding about why customers make the buying choices they do, and to help the supplier develop some strategies to improve its relative position.

Table 10.3 Using CSFs to analyse relative performance

Segment:......X..... Critical Success Factors	Importance weighting to customer (%)	Relative performance					
		Supplier		Competitor 1		Competitor 2	
		Score	WxS	Score	WxS	Score	WxS
24/7 availability of technical support	30	6	1.8	6	1.8	6	1.8
Quality of installation advice and training	25	7	1.75	5	1.25	6	1.50
Technological differentiation of product	20	5	1.0	6	1.2	2	0.4
Product scalability	15	6	0.9	5	0.75	5	0.75
Corporate brand	10	8	0.8	7	0.7	3	0.3
	100		6.25		5.70		4.75

Table 10.3 shows a fairly tough competitive position within that segment, because the scores are fairly close, although the supplier just has an edge over competitor 1 and both do rather better in this segment than competitor 2. If this analysis has been carried out by the supplier, rather than by asking the customer, it is particularly important to carry out a 'sanity check' on the total weighted scores. The company with the highest total weighted score should have the highest share of business in that segment, or should be winning more new business than others in that segment, because it is better at the things that are important to customers at the point of decision.

Looking across the scores for each CSF gives some insight into why this is a competitive segment. From the customer's point of view, there is no difference between the competitors in terms of technical support and virtually none for product scalability. Whether this is correct or not is not the issue; the point is that the customers in this segment believe it to be correct. The supplier and its closest competitor are both seen to have good brands and competitor 1 is seen as having a slightly superior product, but the supplier in this instance just takes the edge in this segment through the quality of its installation advice and training.

The CSF analysis can suggest strategies that companies could use to improve their competitive position. In the example given here, the company would sub-stantially improve its position in this

> The CSF analysis can suggest strategies to improve competitive position.

segment if it could persuade customers that its product was technologically better, or by differentiating its technical support or installation advice still further. Additional brand building, however, would not be a good investment of marketing effort in this segment as the brand already scores better than the competition and, moreover, corporate brand is not particularly important for customers in this segment.

> **Note**
>
> Remember that each customer segment should have distinct CSFs. If the CSFs are the same, the segments can be combined and treated as a single segment for marketing planning and customer management purposes.

Building the DPM

To build the DPM, the customer attractiveness 'thermometer' has to be combined with the segment-by-segment CSF analysis. The weighted attractiveness score gives the position of the segment or customer on the vertical axis. The relative CSF score gives the position on the horizontal axis.

To calculate the relative CSF score, the total weighted score for the supplier doing the analysis is divided by the total weighted score for the closest competitor in that segment. This number, multiplied by 100, gives the supplier's position relative to the best competitor in that segment. So, in the example shown in Table 10.3, the supplier's total weighted score is 6.25 and the best competitor scored 5.70. Therefore, the supplier's relative CSF score is calculated as shown in the following box.

> **Calculating the relative CSF score to plot the DPM**
>
> $$\frac{\text{Supplier total weighted score}}{\text{Best competitor total weighted score}} = \frac{6.25}{5.70} \times 100 = 110\%$$

The supplier shown in Table 10.3 has a total weighted score equivalent to 110% of the best competitor's score. Of course, in the other segments there may be very different competitors and CSFs and the relative competitive positions might be completely different.

It is important to note that the supplier may not be the best competitor in the segment. Imagine, for example, that the above analysis was actually carried out by competitor 1, which scored 5.70. For competitor 1, its relative competitive position is the reverse:

$$\frac{5.70}{6.25} \times 100 = 91\% \text{ of best competitor}$$

Figure 10.6 shows how each segment is located on the DPM.

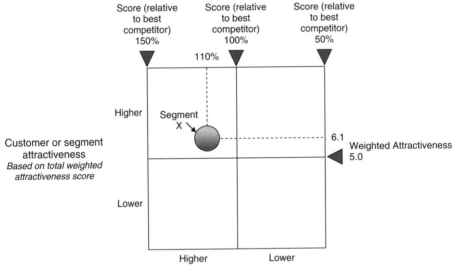

Figure 10.6 The DPM

Circles are used to represent each segment, and the size of the circle can be scaled to represent the number of customers in a segment or the amount of revenue generated by that segment. Only one segment (segment X) is shown in Figure 10.6, although in the completed customer portfolio there would be one circle per segment (or per key account if the portfolio being considered was a key account portfolio). If the DPM has been constructed for a number of individual key accounts, the circles can be proportional to the revenue from each customer.

To locate segment X on the vertical axis is a matter of positioning it relative to the centre line. Since the attractiveness scale runs from 1.0 to 10.0, 5.0 is the centre point. Table 10.2 shows that the attractiveness score of segment X is 6.1, and so it is located in the upper half of the matrix.

In the DPM, the more attractive segments or customers are in the top half of the portfolio matrix and the less attractive segments or customers are in the lower half. This does not mean that these segments are necessarily unattractive, simply that they are relatively less attractive than other customers or segments included in the analysis.

The location of segment X on the horizontal axis depends on the supplier's performance relative to the best competitor. Where the supplier has a total weighted score that is *higher* than the best competitor in a particular segment, the supplier's relative score will be more than 100% of the competition and that segment will be positioned to the left of the centre line. Where the supplier has a total weighted score that is *lower* than the best competitor, the supplier's relative score will be less than 100% of the competition and the circle for that segment will lie to the right of the centre line.

From Table 10.3 and expressed as a percentage, the firm's relative performance against competitor 1 in segment X is 110%. Thus, segment X lies to the left of the centre line. The problem is: how far to the left of the line? A useful general rule for plotting the DPM is that it is unusual for there to be a disparity of more than plus or minus 50% in the relative competitive performance. So, the horizontal scale in Figure 10.6 is scaled from 50 to 150% of best competitor. If the differences between competitors are greater, this axis may have to be re-scaled to 25/125%, or even 0/200%.

Taken together, segment X is located somewhere in the top left quadrant of the matrix. The dotted lines in Figure 10.6 show how the scores on each dimension are used to locate the centre point of the circle representing segment X.

The detailed analysis that goes into the construction of the DPM makes it a very useful tool for developing strategies for managing the customer portfolio. How to use the DPM to develop customer management strategies is the subject of the next section.

Uses and applications of the DPM

The DPM can help in customer portfolio management through the recognition of the position of each segment and also the development of appropriate strategies to manage each segment based on the desired CSF scores.

Each quadrant of the DPM has a generic approach associated with it that should be adopted for each of the segments in that quadrant (although the specific strategies will vary by segment). The generic approaches and their associated strategies are shown in Table 10.4[2]. Which of these strategies is selected and the investment that is made in each segment depends to some extent on the way in which the circles may move over time. The circles can move *up* or *down* in attractiveness, because certain segments or customers may become more influential in the market, or their customer equity might even change because of changes in buying patterns or regulatory changes. Alternatively, the firm itself might go through changes that make them view the attractiveness of their customers differently, perhaps because advocacy in certain markets was no longer important to them.

---

[2] This table draws on work by my colleague Professor Malcolm McDonald.

Table 10.4 Strategies using the DPM

Quadrant	Generic approach	Strategies
Upper left	Invest	Product differentiation; relationship pricing; substantial promotion; broaden distribution; invest in R&D and production; invest in high-quality management
Upper right	Build selectively	Range or product line expansion; pricing for market share; targeted but intensive promotion; fund growth and invest in people
Lower left	Maintain	Maintain or slightly rationalize product range with some differentiation for segments; consider raising prices; limit new promotions but keep broad distribution base; utilize capacity effectively; reward efficiency
Lower right	Manage	Prune the product portfolio; raise prices if possible; reduce promotions and distribution; free up capacity and resources for other uses; very tight cost control; consider divestment

In addition to upwards and downwards movements, the segment position on the DPM can move to the *left* or *right*, depending upon the action of the firm or of its competitors. For example, the entry of a strong competitor might tend to reduce the relative performance of the firm, moving the circle to the right. The exit of a strong competitor might improve the firm's relative competitive position, moving the segment circle to the left. The firm itself can, of course, also cause the circles to move right or left relative to the competition through the decisions that it makes about strategies, investment, and resources.

Figure 10.7 illustrates a completed customer portfolio with all the firm's customer segments plotted on the DPM. The generic approaches for each quadrant are shown. On the right hand side of Figure 10.7 there are two small segments where the firm might/should definitely consider divesting itself of its interests, because its relative competitive position is so weak.

For four segments in Figure 10.7, the future position (hatched circle) as well as the current position (solid circle) is shown. This future position is taken to be the position of the segment circle at the end of the planning horizon, which would typically be in three years. The direction of each future position movement is shown with an arrow. Four different possible directions are shown:

- up and left;
- down and right;
- up and right;
- down and left.

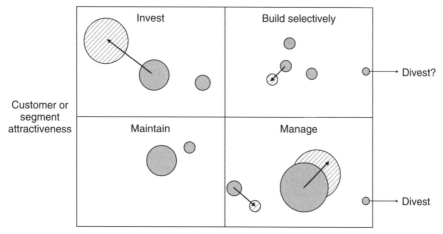

Figure 10.7 Using the DPM

The 'up and left' directional movement can be seen in this example in a segment in the top left 'Invest' quadrant. A movement up and left means that the firm aims to improve its relative competitive position in an increasingly attractive segment, which is a consistent objective. In this case, the future circle is larger than the current circle, indicating that the firm expects to receive more business from this segment as a result of its improved competitive position.

The 'down and right' directional movement can be found in the lower right quadrant of the DPM ('Manage'). Again, this represents a consistent situation in which the firm expects to reduce its competitive position in a declining segment; thus, its business from this segment will fall and the future circle is smaller than the current one.

There is an 'up and right' movement in the same 'Manage' quadrant, indicating a situation where the firm's relative competitive position is declining in a segment that is nevertheless getting more attractive. This is an anomalous situation that needs further analysis. If a new competitor is entering, it may be that the firm needs to increase its investment in the segment. Alternatively, the firm may have chosen to allow its competitive position to reduce slightly for reasons of efficiency; the size of the circle remains unchanged, indicating that the reduction in competitive position is predicted not to harm the level of business.

Finally, this DPM contains a 'down and left' movement that, in this portfolio, happens to be in the upper right ('Build selectively') quadrant. This is again a case that requires investigation, because a down and left movement indicates an improvement in competitive position in a segment that is becoming less attractive. It could be the case that the firm is over-investing here, and should really be assigning some of these resources elsewhere, where there are more attractive opportunities. A second reason could be that a strong competitor has exited, resulting in an automatic improvement in relative competitive position. This could also be an opportunity for the firm to review its resource levels in this segment and make sure that they are appropriate.

The above analysis of the customer portfolio using the DPM illustrates how it can be used to review the overall portfolio and to ensure that there are appropriate levels of sales and marketing resource allocated to each segment (or customer, if the DPM is used to look at a key account portfolio). The directional element of the DPM is particularly useful in resource allocation decisions.

The DPM is also a powerful tool for developing the strategies that are to be used for each segment. Not only does the segment's position in a particular quadrant suggest certain strategies (see Table 10.4), but also the CSF analysis indicates specific areas of

> The DPM is a powerful tool for developing strategies and identifying specific areas for improvement.

improvement that a firm needs to make in particular areas of its segment offering, in order to overtake or stay ahead of its competition. Repeating the CSF analysis in Table 10.3 for the future period will indicate the impact of the proposed strategies on the firm's relative competitive position.

Advantages and limitations of the DPM

The DPM, in various guises, is a powerful and widely-used tool in strategy formulation. It has the advantage of asking the user to make comparatively detailed estimates and forecasts about the firm, the marketplace, and the actions of competitors. This detail, as well as being an advantage of the DPM, is also a limitation, because it can be that numbers that are an approximation or best guess come to be believed simply because they are presented as numbers and appear scientific.

One way to increase the validity of the DPM is to collect genuine data. Thus, the CSF table (see Table 10.3 on page 216) should really be used as a market research tool and completed by representative customers from each segment. Still better is if this is done through a market research agency or consultancy, so that the customers do not know which supplier has commissioned the research. The anonymous approach reduces possible bias.

The DPM is a more complex tool than the customer equity/relationship warmth approach demonstrated earlier in this chapter. This makes it suitable for organizations that have some experience in customer portfolio management, or where there is good market and competitor data that enable the DPM to be completed accurately.

Summary

The dual perspective approach to the customer portfolio is a useful tool for developing strategies. One perspective is the customer attractiveness to the supplier, which includes customer equity and perhaps also other aspects such as relational attractiveness. The other perspective is the customer's perspective, which might be measured in terms of customer satisfaction or share of spend, or by using CSFs.

Including the customer perspective helps to give the supplier some indication of the likelihood that the customer will be retained, because there is some link between the warmth of relationship and customer retention, which is in turn a component of customer equity.

The inverse of customer retention is the loss of the customer. Clearly, this is a risk that the supplier experiences in a relationship. Customer relationship risk is the subject of the next chapter.

Note
Now use the worksheets on the following pages to create a DPM. Once the worksheets have been completed, follow the guidelines in Figure 10.6 to locate each customer segment on the DPM.

Worksheet A: customer attractiveness factors

Attractiveness criteria	% importance to our company	Segment............		Segment............		Segment............	
		Score	WxS	Score	WxS	Score	WxS
	100%	Total:		Total:		Total:	

Worksheet B: Critical Success Factors

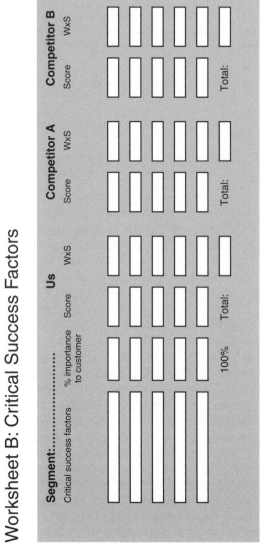

Where to find out more

Reichheld, F.F. (2003) 'The one number you need to grow'. *Harvard Business Review*, **81**(12), pp. 46–54. *Discusses the importance and measurement of advocacy.*

Ryals, L.J. and McDonald, M. (2008) *Key Account Plans: the Practitioners' Guide to Profitable Planning*, Butterworth Heinemann, Oxford. *Describes key account planning, including the use of a DPM-style customer portfolio matrix (chapter 2, pp. 21–52).*

Rogers, B. (2007) *Rethinking Sales Management*. John Wiley & Sons, Ltd, Chichester. *Another version of a DPM-type approach, this time in the business-to-business sales arena.*

11 Risk

What's in this chapter

- Analysing the risk of individual customers
- How to identify risk drivers
- Risks that reduce revenue
- Risks that increase costs
- Risks affecting both revenues and costs
- What causes customers to defect?
- Strategies to reduce customer risk
- How to analyse the risk of a customer portfolio

Key concepts discussed in this chapter

Optimization	Making a choice that has the highest return for a given level of risk; or the lowest risk for a given level of return. Optimization choices are made not only in respect of required returns, but also reflect the investor's appetite for (or aversion to) risk.
Risk	Risk is usually defined as 'quantified uncertainty'. Thus, risk is something that might or might not happen, and the likelihood is quantified in some way. Thus, risk may be expressed in terms of probability. Note: risk is not always about downside; there can be upside risk, too, which might include higher than expected sales of a new product.
Volatility	The degree of variation from the norm, or from forecast values. Thus, volatility is a form of risk.

Key tools explained in this chapter

- Portfolio risk analysis: Analysing the risk of the customer portfolio by detailing the risks of each customer or each segment. Can be analysed by identifying the risk drivers, then analysing the best and the worst cases in the portfolio. The analysis is then used to manage the overall risk of the portfolio, implementing strategies to improve the worst case risks.
- The efficient frontier of marketing portfolios: For a given level of sales and marketing spend, there are potentially a large number of different combinations (portfolios) that the manager could choose. The choice of portfolio is determined by the risk preferences of the company. If marketing spend increases, more different portfolios become available to the manager. Managers should ensure that whatever portfolio they select lies on the efficient frontier. This means that there should be no alternative portfolio available that would provide the same level of return for lower risk.

Two-minute chapter summary

The risks incurred by suppliers in their relationships with customers are neither well-understood nor effectively managed. In most companies, risk management in customer relationships takes the form of obtaining a credit reference when the customer in acquired. This may or may not be updated adequately.

Credit ratings measure the customer's ability to pay, and are therefore used to set, and later to adjust, credit limits. However, in many business situations, the customer's ability to afford the product or service is not the main risk; instead, the main risk is the potential loss of the customer. This risk is particularly high where a company has high customer dependency, meaning a portfolio that is skewed towards a small number of high-value customers (Chapter 2 discussed how to measure customer dependency).

Total or partial loss of the customer affects revenues, but other forms of customer risk also affect costs. These risks include volatile buying patterns, slow payment, and litigation. Other risks affect both revenues and costs: these risks include customer default (non-payment) and negative word of mouth. This chapter discusses the measurement and reduction of these different types of risk.

The existence of risk may also affect the way in which the customer portfolio is managed. The risk of individual customers affects the riskiness of the overall portfolio. There are therefore decisions to be made about the trade-off between risk and returns. It may be better to invest in customers with slightly lower returns but which are lower risk and therefore more certain, rather than investing in too many customers with high potential returns but with a high potential risk that these returns may not be realized.

Managing a customer portfolio properly involves making decisions about both the risk and the returns of the portfolio. There are, in fact, many different combinations of decisions that could be made about how much sales and marketing time to invest in different groups of customers. Another way of thinking about these options is that there are many *possible* portfolios that marketing and salespeople could select. The decision about which combination of marketing strategies (which portfolio) to choose will be affected by the risk preference or risk aversion of the organization. The final section of this chapter considers a portfolio theory approach to making an optimization decision.

Optimization is about selecting the best returns for a given level of risk; this is different from maximizing returns, which seeks the highest returns irrespective of risk.

How risk affects sales and marketing decisions

An important notion in the concept of the management of any portfolio is that of risk. Risk has been defined as 'quantified uncertainty'. The uncertainty, in portfolio management terms, is whether the performance of the portfolio will overshoot or undershoot the target that the portfolio manager has set. The purpose of a risk analysis is to try to put some objective measure on to that uncertainty about performance. Once the risk is properly understood, it is possible to make logical decisions about whether there is a need for risk management strategies and how much resource should be allocated to these.

If this is translated into customer portfolio terms, the application to sales and marketing is immediately clear. The performance of the portfolio, as discussed in earlier chapters, is measured in terms of customer equity and the achievement of other relational benefits. A performance undershoot (lower customer equity than planned) might mean that the company as a whole misses its short-term profit targets. However, an overshoot may also be a problem. Customer equity growing faster than forecast may mean that the company becomes overstretched, or that resources are in the wrong places, so that service to customers suffers. Although a performance overshoot (achieving higher than target portfolio returns) is not usually thought of as a risk, it can be.

> A sales overshoot might be a risk. It might mean that the company becomes overstretched, or that service to customers suffers.

Risk is also an important concept in the management of individual customer relationships, particularly business-to-business key accounts, where these exceptionally large and often demanding customers can have a considerable impact on the overall performance of the business. The same may be true for some key segments in a business-to-consumer context. Sadly, far too few marketing managers or account managers are aware of the risk issue or know about the portfolio management tools that they could use to examine risk.

This chapter demonstrates two risk analysis tools. The first is a straightforward tool that can be used to analyse the risk of individual customers in a portfolio. This tool helps managers to find strategies that will reduce the risk of those customers.

The second tool is about how to analyse the risk of the portfolio as a whole. This is a rather more technical approach, but it does help to give marketing managers information about whether they have chosen an efficient portfolio. An efficient portfolio is one in which there are no alternative options that could give the firm the same level of returns but with less risk. The concept of portfolio risk will be discussed in more detail in the second half of the chapter.

> **Note**
>
> Think about the possible upside risks that your business faces: what would happen if sales were much higher than expected? Could you continue to manage your customer relationships? Is there a contingency plan for success, as well as for failure?

Analysing the risk of individual customers

It is easy to forget that customers can be a source of risk as well as of value. In fact, companies do routinely check their customers for one source of risk, which is the risk of default. They do this using credit scoring. A credit score or credit rating gives an indication of the risk that the customer might not pay their bills; the higher the credit score, the lower the risk. Where customers are going to be provided with goods or services on credit, it is common for both business-to-business and business-to-consumer firms to consult a credit rating agency such as Experian or Dun and Bradstreet. From electricity supply to financial services, credit rating is becoming essential. A customer's credit score is based on known risk factors. Thus, 'length of time at current address' is one factor that a credit referencing agency will take into account, because people who default on their payments tend to change address often.

> It is easy to forget that customers can be a source of risk as well as of value.

The importance of credit scores is indicated by the credit referencing agencies that are bowing to pressure and now allow customers to check the details of their credit status. If these details are incorrect, the customer may find they are unable to obtain a mortgage, for example, because the bank will certainly run a credit check on the customer as part of any loan approval process. Business-to-business firms use credit scoring to help them set specific credit limits for individual customers or for segments. When the customer approaches or reaches their credit limit, the supplier's accounts department will contact the customer and ask for some invoices to be settled before any more goods or services are supplied. In this way, the supplier limits its bad debt risk.

Credit scoring measures one very specific type of risk, which is the risk of default (bad debt). Although bad debts can be very damaging, particularly to small firms that can themselves be made bankrupt as a result of a customer defaulting, the absolute risk of bad debt is relatively small. In most markets, the proportion of customers who actually default is very small, although this risk still needs to be managed. Credit scoring is a very effective tool for measuring and monitoring default risk, but there are very few tools indeed for managing other sources of risk from customers.

How to identify risk drivers

The first task in managing the risk of individual customers is to understand precisely what those risks are. A brainstorming session or a risk workshop is a useful way to start thinking about customer risk. It may be helpful at this stage to define what 'risk' is, in the context of an individual customer or segment.

> **The risk of the customer**
>
> The risk of the customer to the supplier is the risk that the supplier will not achieve the forecast customer lifetime value for that customer.
>
> This overall risk is made up of a number of risk drivers. One of these risk drivers is the risk of default. However, other risks (such as the risk of losing the customer) may actually be more important, particularly in major business-to-business relationships.

The risk workshop should consider the following question: what risk drivers might threaten the customer lifetime value forecast for this customer, either by reducing customer lifetime revenues or by increasing costs, or both?

Typical answers to this question, drawn from a series of interviews with key account managers, are as follows:

- loss of the customer;
- customer migrates towards other suppliers (declining share of spend);
- volatility;
- slow payment;

- litigation;
- default;
- negative word of mouth.

The first two risk drivers – loss or migration of the customer – affect revenues. The next three risk drivers – volatility, slow payment, and litigation – affect costs. The final two risk factors – default and negative word of mouth – affect both revenues and costs.

Each of these three classes of risk drivers will now be considered in turn.

Risks that reduce revenue

There are two risk drivers that directly impact customer revenues. These are total loss of the customer, and partial loss of the customer through migration to another supplier.

Total loss of the customer

Total loss of the customer is also known as customer defection where the loss is to another supplier. This is probably the most frequent reason for a firm failing to secure the forecast customer lifetime value. At some point in the relationship, the customer takes their business elsewhere. This is a substantial risk that requires more analysis and will be considered in more detail later in the section 'What causes customers to defect?'.

Customers can be completely lost for two other reasons. The first, particularly in business-to-consumer, is that the customer no longer needs the particular products or services that the firm provides. The reason might be a change in lifestyle or a different lifecycle stage. Thus, customers stop buying Pampers when their children are potty trained. Private school fees stop when the pupils graduate. Hospital fees end when a customer comes to the end of a course of treatment. All of these are in the normal course of business and should be forecast by the marketing department, which should also have in place a customer acquisition strategy to replace the departing customers.

A second reason why a customer might stop buying completely is prevalent in business-to-business markets. This is the risk that a customer switches supplier because it (the customer) has been taken over. There has been a substantial level of mergers and acquisitions activity over the past few years and one of the first things that happens when a company is acquired is that there is a review of suppliers to try and reduce costs.

> One of the first things that happens when a company is acquired is that there is a review of suppliers to try and reduce costs.

Professional services firms, such as lawyers and accountants, are familiar with this phenomenon. When one of their clients is taken over, it is expected that legal and accounting services for the combined group will be provided by the suppliers to the acquirer. Alternatively, what had been a Tier 1 supplier may become a Tier 2, losing its direct access to the customer and having to supply instead through a Tier 1 supplier. The risk that a customer might get taken over is a real one, but it is intrinsic to the business process and outside the ability of the supplier firm to manage that risk. All that can be done is for the supplier to maintain a portfolio of customers so that it has others who continue to provide business even if one or two are taken over. This is known as 'portfolio diversification'.

Partial loss of the customer

The risk of partial loss of the customer is often described as 'customer migration'. The customer migrates to another supplier but may then return to the original supplier from time to time. It can be difficult to see that customer migration is taking place, because the transactions continue (albeit probably at a reduced level) and so the customer appears to be a live account. The main symptom of customer migration is a reduced share of spend. The phenomenon of customer migration is why measuring share of spend is such an important notion in key account management.

Customer migration is becoming an increasing feature of business life. In most markets, customers have so much choice and there is so much proliferation that loyalty has substantially decreased. From breakfast cereals to cookies and colas, customers buy from a wider selection of offerings, giving a smaller proportion of their purchasing to each.

> Customer migration is becoming an increasing feature of business life.

In business-to-business markets, customer migration may be driven by procurement practices such as e-auctions and multiple sourcing policies.

Like the total loss of the customer, the important phenomenon of customer migration is not well-understood by most marketing and sales managers. Although the initial impact is on revenues both phenomena also affect costs, though indirectly, because the supplier will need to find more customers to replace defecting ones (sales costs) and will want to try to persuade migrating customers to switch back (marketing costs).

Risks that increase costs

Although this is not intended to be a comprehensive list of the risks that affect costs, there are some factors that account managers perceive as particular risks or threats to the achievement of customer equity. They are volatility, slow payment, and litigation.

Volatility

Volatility refers to irregular ordering patterns. The more irregular the ordering (high
volatility), the more risk the supplier is
exposed to. Take the example of a packaging company that had a major client that
decided to review its inventory holding

> Where volatility is high, the sup-
> plier is both at more risk of hold-
> ing too much stock and at risk of
> running out of stock.

policy. This customer bought nothing for several months and then suddenly placed
orders for eight container-loads of packaging! Where volatility is high, the supplier is
both at more risk of holding too much stock *and* at risk of running out of stock. This
phenomenon is a headache for retailers, who experience weather-related problems
in deciding how much ice cream and sun lotion to stock. A few days' rain means
that the retailer sells out of umbrellas but is sitting on a stock pile of ice cream; a
sudden warm spell can mean the opposite.

The impact on costs is that when the customer does not place the anticipated
order, the supplier may have to carry the cost of stock holding. This includes the
cost of storage, handling, spoilage, shrinkage, the cost of capital tied up, and the risk
of obsolescence. Some logistics experts suggest that the true annual cost of carry
for stock is 25–30% of the value of the stock per year. In service businesses, the
cost of a downswing in the business is the cost of having to pay the salaries and
additional costs of people who are 'on the beach' (consultant speak for employees
that are not on holiday but for whom there is no work).

Conversely, when the volatile customer suddenly starts ordering again, perhaps
in large quantities, the supplier is at risk of running out of stock or of having to hire
in temporary staff or pay workers overtime to work additional shifts.

Volatility is considered by portfolio managers to be the prime measure of risk
and its impact on the portfolio will be discussed in the second half of this
chapter.

Slow payment

Slow payment is a risk with some customers because the supplier then has to
wait a long time for its money, meaning that the supplier has to finance the gap
between the supply of goods and the receipt of money. This sometimes means
that suppliers will in turn delay payments to their suppliers, and so the effects
are passed back along the supply chain. This problem is particularly acute for
suppliers that have to pay up-front for their raw materials, because they will
have a very long cash-to-cash cycle. The cash-to-cash cycle measures the length
of time from cash going out on raw materials to cash coming in as actual payments for those finished goods. The cash-to-cash cycle explains why companies
can run out of cash and have to go bankrupt despite showing healthy trading
volumes.

Some customers are prone to slow payment and suppliers need to manage this risk, either through incentivizing early payment or through avoiding any triggers that might cause the customer to delay payment. An example of delaying tactics has been reported widely by account managers who look after large distributors who place huge and complex orders. If even one item on the delivery is incorrect, there is a tendency for the distributor to delay payment on the entire invoice. It would pay the supplier to be particularly careful with deliveries to such customers, aiming for OTIFNIE:

> The cash-to-cash cycle measures the length of time from cash going out on raw materials to cash coming in as payments for finished goods. Companies can run out of cash and go bankrupt despite healthy trading volumes.

OTIFNIE: On Time, In Full, No Invoice Errors

Note

Try using the OTIFNIE concept to analyse your own organization's delivery performance. Does the paperwork ever let other parts of the business down?

Litigation

Sadly, some customers are more prone to be litigious than others. This is partly a cultural phenomenon and partly related to industry sector. In business-to-business relationships where there are many formal contractual arrangements, such as construction, there are also likely to be high levels of litigation. This can be extremely costly to the supplier, with spiralling legal fees and insurance costs.

One way to reduce litigation risk is to avoid litigious customers, but this approach may not be practical. An alternative is to try to work on the cultural aspect. Where relational contracts exist between two parties, the risk of litigation may be lower. Relational contracts are informal contracts or agreements about how the relationship will work, a commitment to communication, service, responsiveness, etc. on both sides. Relational contracts are not legally binding, but they may have a moral persuasion effect that discourages opportunistic behaviours.

Risk drivers affecting both revenue and costs

Some risks may affect both revenues and costs directly. These include, for example, default and negative word of mouth.

Default

The actual default of a customer, although thankfully comparatively rare, can be very damaging. Not only is the future revenue lost, but also the supplier is often involved in costly recovery litigation or refinancing arrangements.

Credit scoring is the most powerful tool available to companies to manage default risk. In industries where default risk is more extensive, such as in the banking and loans industry, it is common practice to use behavioural risk analysis techniques in which the ongoing behaviour of customers is analysed for clues to changes in their likelihood of default. Other businesses could learn from this practice, perhaps using their CRM system to look for changes in customer behaviours that might signal impending default.

Negative word of mouth

Negative word of mouth is a difficult source of risk to measure. It is the opposite of advocacy, where customers say positive things about the company to other potential customers. Negative word of mouth may be occurring without the firm being aware of it, but it can cause severe loss of business because bad news spreads fast.

> Negative word of mouth can cause severe loss of business: bad news spreads fast. The firm may need to increase its marketing spend to counteract the negative effect.

Negative word of mouth may also affect costs directly, because the firm may need to increase its marketing spend to counteract the effect of the negative word of mouth. Moreover, the cost of acquiring new customers will tend to rise as potential customers become harder to convince and conversion rates fall.

Some interesting examples of the risks of negative word of mouth can be seen where customers set up websites that complain about a particular company. A number of major corporations have had to engage either in litigation or have had to buy out the negative website in order to shut it down.

What causes customers to defect?

Identifying the main risk drivers may not give enough understanding of the underlying problem to enable the account manager to develop risk management strategies. This is particularly true of risk factors such as customer defection or migration, and may also be true of volatility (unexplained fluctuations in demand). For this reason, it is useful to consider the specific risk factors that underlie these issues. The technique presented in this section is based on work carried out with a major

international business-to-business insurer, where the customer management team were interested in understanding more about one risk driver – customer defection.
To examine this issue, a simple question was devised:

What factors might cause major customers to defect?

This question was used as the basis for a series of discussions with key account managers, senior managers, and other executives who had extensive customer contact. The responses were analysed and a list of nine factors identified. Then, working with the finance department, the entire portfolio of key accounts was analysed to see what the status was of each key account against each risk factor. This enabled the identification of the best case and worst case in that portfolio (Table 11.1).

Table 11.1 Portfolio risk analysis for defection risk

No	Defection risk factor	Worst case in portfolio	Best case in portfolio
Overall relationship			
1	Number of relationships customer has with other parts of supplier	0	3
2	Number of business lines customer buys	3	10
3	Longevity of relationship in years	0.5	16
Account relationship			
4	Quality of supplier's relationship with broker*	1	5
5	Quality of supplier's relationship with customer*	1	5
6	Number of contacts at customer	2	8
7	Number of contacts customer has at supplier	3	10
Knowledge of customer			
8	Understanding of customer*	1	5
9	Understanding of customer's industry*	1	5

* measured on scale 1 to 5 where 1 was very poor and 5 was excellent

As Table 11.1 illustrates, the nine risk factors were grouped into three categories. The first category was the overall relationship that that customer had with the insurer, and included the customer's relationships with other business units, the number of products (business lines) that the customer bought, and the longevity of the relationship in years (factors 1 to 3). Customers that had relationships with more than one business unit, that bought more business lines, and where the relationship was more mature, were thought to be less likely to defect. In the key account portfolio at that time, some customers bought from up to three parts of the insurer, purchasing up to 10 business lines, and the longest duration relationship was 16 years long whereas the shortest was only 6 months.

There were also risk factors related to the specific relationship that this business unit had with the customer (factors 4 to 7). The better the quality of the relationship with the broker who intermediated the relationship, and the better the quality of the relationship with the customer, the more unlikely they were to defect. Interestingly, the key account managers' self-perception scores on these questions ranged from 1 (very poor) to 5 (excellent) for the different accounts in this portfolio. The number of contacts on both sides was also thought to be influential in reducing defection risk. There were considerable differences in the numbers of contacts. For example, the insurer had only two contacts with certain of these key accounts but eight contacts with others (factor 6).

Finally, there were two factors (factors 8 and 9) that related to the KAM team's self-reported knowledge of the customer and the customer's industry. The self-reported scores ranged, alarmingly, from 1 (very poor) to 5 (excellent).

Strategies to reduce customer risk

The portfolio risk analysis presented in Table 11.1 was for a key account portfolio of the 18 most important customers of the firm. The overall analysis indicates that there are considerable differences in riskiness between the best and worst cases in the portfolio. This analysis enables some specific strategies to be worked out for the individual customers. In some cases, for example, a good strategy would be to cross-sell more business lines to customers who only buy three. Another specific strategy would be to review the number of customer contacts and understand why there are such large differences and whether this represents the most effective way to do business. Finally, the key account managers for some customers need to learn more about the customer and their industry. Even a less tangible factor such as relationship duration could be influenced by persuading customers to switch to longer-term contracts and also be taking special care to manage the relationship in the early months and years if the risk analysis reveals that short-duration customers are more likely to defect.

Analysing the possible risk factors for a single customer or for a group of customers is a powerful but neglected tool that can provide valuable insight into the risk in the customer portfolio. This is particularly so for the risk of total or partial loss of the customer, but a similar analysis could be carried out to examine the root causes of purchasing volatility, for example. This in turn could enable the development of strategies to reduce volatility, once the underlying factors driving that volatility are understood.

A simple scale for each customer will demonstrate whether that customer is more or less risky compared to others in the portfolio. Figure 11.1 shows how this risk comparison might work.

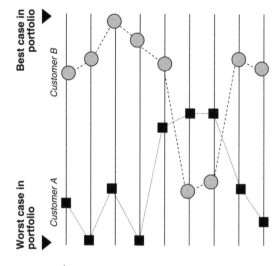

Figure 11.1 Risk comparison of two customers

In Figure 11.1, it is clear that Customer A is a riskier customer than B. Many of the risk factors for Customer A are at, or near to, the worst in the portfolio whereas for Customer B most of the risk factors are towards the best in the portfolio. A simple comparison chart like that in Figure 11.1 is useful to show whether a particular customer is more or less risky than others.

However, it is still difficult to compare the two. If Customer A is more risky than Customer B, the supplier should be looking for higher returns from Customer A to compensate for those higher risks. The question is, how much higher? Or, to put the same question another way, what is the impact on A's customer equity of its higher risk status?

There is a systematic way in which the risk of the customer can be incorporated into the customer equity calculation. This technique will be discussed in the next section.

Incorporating risk into customer equity calculations

Earlier chapters on calculating customer lifetime value (Chapter 6) and customer equity (Chapter 7) have discussed the role that the discount rate plays in discounting future profits back to the present day so that the lifetime value of a customer can be described in terms of today's money. One way to adjust the lifetime value of a customer for risk is to adjust the discount rate that is used.

Adjusting the discount rate

An example would be as follows. Say that the overall discount rate for the company is 10%. A risk comparison between Customers A and B such as that shown in Figure 11.1 might suggest that Customer A is twice as risky as the average customer and Customer B is half as risky. So, if an averagely risky customer was discounted at 10%, Customer A should be discounted at 20% and Customer B at 5%. These figures are, respectively, twice the portfolio average and half the portfolio average. Notice that, the riskier the customer, the higher the discount rate and vice-versa.

The problem with this method is that the absolute values for the lifetime value of the customer do not change much, even for a doubling of the discount rate. This can easily be proved by turning back to Chapter 6 and recalculating customer lifetime value using different discount rates. The discount rates would have to be varied massively – several hundred percent differences – to have much effect on customer lifetime value.

Mathematically, the reason why this is the case is that most calculations of customer lifetime value take place over relatively short time periods. The examples shown in previous chapters are based on time periods of about four years, which is typically the length of time that most key account managers feel they can realistically forecast the revenues and costs of the customer relationship. Over these relatively short time frames, the impact of discounting is quite low. If the forecast were to be extended for 20 years or more, a change in the discount rate would have a substantially greater impact on the lifetime value of the customer. This is because, over a longer lifetime, a greater proportion of the value is accounted for by distant years which are, in turn, more heavily discounted.

Because adjusting the discount rate does not have a great impact on customer lifetime value, an alternative approach to incorporating risk into customer lifetime value is to probability-adjust the lifetime value forecast.

Adjusting customer lifetime value for probability

Probability is a way to measure risk. A customer lifetime value forecast that has low probability is high risk; that is, it is less likely to come true. A customer lifetime value forecast with high probability is low risk; that is, it is more likely to be correct. The probability that is at issue

> Probability is a way to measure risk. A customer lifetime value forecast that has low probability is high risk; that is, it is less likely to come true.

here, therefore, is the probability that the customer lifetime value forecast is correct.

So, how is this probability to be calculated? The starting point is the same risk factor analysis shown in the earlier Table 11.1. This time, however, the objective is to assign a probability to the forecast, based on the risk analysis.

An example is shown in Table 11.2.

Table 11.2 Forecasting probability from risk

No	Defection risk factor	Worst case in portfolio	Best case in portfolio	Value/score for this customer	Probability (%)
Overall relationship					
1	Number of relationships customer has with other parts of supplier	0	3	0	60
2	Number of business lines customer buys	3	10	5	75
3	Longevity of relationship in years	0.5	16	8	80

Table 11.2 *Continued*

Customer:. . . . .

No	Defection risk factor	Worst case in portfolio	Best case in portfolio	Value/score for this customer	Probability (%)
Account relationship					
4	Quality of supplier's relationship with broker*	1	5	5	95
5	Quality of supplier's relationship with customer*	1	5	5	95
6	Number of contacts at customer	2	8	8	90
7	Number of contacts customer has at supplier	3	10	5	80
Knowledge of customer					
8	Understanding of customer*	1	5	4	80
9	Understanding of customer's industry*	1	5	4	80
				Average:	83

* measured on scale 1 to 5 where 1 was very poor and 5 was excellent

The method here is to assign a probability to the actual values against each of the risk factors. So, if this is overall a relatively stable portfolio with high customer retention, there might be an overall portfolio probability of 80% that a typical customer lifetime value forecast will be achieved. The supplier may take the view that there is no 100% probability about any future forecasts, but that 'almost certainty' would be 95%. This can be seen against factors 4 and 5, where both relationship quality indicators are as good as they can be (5 out of 5). Against those risk factors, therefore, the company has assigned a 95% probability. The lowest probability (in this case, 60%) is assigned to risk factor 1, because this customer only buys from a single business division.

The average probability across all nine factors is 83%. To adjust the customer lifetime value for this probability, the two numbers are simply multiplied together (Table 11.3). So, if the unadjusted lifetime value for this customer is £100 000 with a probability of 83%, the probability-adjusted customer lifetime value is £100 000 × 83% or £83 000.

This calculation is conceptually equivalent to saying that the probability of each year's forecast profits is 83%. In fact, this tool can be used more creatively. The year-by-year forecasts could be subject to risk scrutiny and the probability could be different in different years, perhaps because of some future actions that the customer or the supplier might be forecast to take.

Table 11.3   Adjusting customer lifetime value for probability

Customer:. . . . .

Customer lifetime value	Average probability	Probability-adjusted customer lifetime value
£100 000	83%	£83 000

The risk analysis tool can also be adapted to take account of risk factors that have greater or lesser impact on overall risk. The calculation in Table 11.2 uses a straight average of all the probabilities. 83% is the sum of all the probabilities, divided by the number of risk factors (nine). However, it might be the case that one or two of the risk factors were thought to be more important than others. If so, each of the nine risk factors would be weighted such that the importance weights for the nine risk factors summed to 100%. Then, the probabilities for each factor would have to be multiplied by the importance weight for each factor. In this way, the overall probability for each customer would be a weighted average of the probabilities of each factor, rather than a straight average as shown.

Advantages and disadvantages of customer-by-customer risk analysis

The main advantage of carrying out a customer-by-customer risk analysis is that it opens up another set of strategies, which are the strategies discussed above to manage the risk in the relationship. Moreover, a risk analysis is a very useful tool to remind salespeople and marketing managers that customers do not just bring value, they also bring risk. From the perspective of the company and of creating value overall, a supplier may be better off with a customer having moderate customer equity but low risk than with a high equity customer that had high risk. The risk/return trade-off is vital in portfolio management and will be considered in the next section.

> The main advantage of a customer-by-customer risk analysis is that it opens up a set of strategies to manage the relationship risk.

The main disadvantage of the customer risk analysis is the difficulty in assigning values (probabilities) to the risk factors. The risk factors themselves can be identified by interviews or observation and tested through analysis of data on the CRM system or by modelling. However, the assignment of probabilities is a somewhat subjective exercise.

Risk analysis is an unusual and sophisticated tool borrowed from the world of financial portfolio management. It is likely to become increasingly important, particularly in key business-to-business relationships where the individual customers are so large that the continuation of the relationship is essential to the survival and success of the supplier.

As the example in Tables 11.1 and 11.2 illustrates, risk is not just about individual customers; it is also about the overall risk in the portfolio. Financial services companies are very aware of this issue and have risk managers whose job is to manage the overall level of risk in the portfolio. Ideas about how to manage risk come from an approach known as Modern Portfolio Theory. The application of these ideas to a portfolio of customers will now be discussed.

How to analyse the risk of a customer portfolio

The previous discussion has focused on the risk of individual customers and how that can be managed. However, when a number of individual customers are formed into a portfolio, that portfolio will have a certain level of risk. The overall level of risk of the customer portfolio is an important issue that companies should be aware of, as it affects the performance of the business. The concept of portfolio risk is well understood in risk-based businesses such as banking and insurance, both business-to-business and business-to-consumer, but is usually neglected by other businesses.

The overall risk of the customer portfolio is affected by three factors:

- the individual risk of the component customers;
- the weighting (proportion) of each customer in the total portfolio;
- the degree to which the returns of individual customers co-vary.

The first factor, the individual risk of the customer, has already been discussed. The second factor, the weighting of each customer, simply means that the larger customers will have proportionately greater influence on the overall risk of the portfolio.

> If the company acquires a number of larger, riskier customers, the portfolio tends to become riskier.

Thus, if the company acquires a number of larger, riskier customers, the portfolio will tend to become riskier. Note that 'larger' in this context means the amount of business that the customer does, not the absolute size of the customer firm.

The third factor, the degree to which the returns of individual constituents in the portfolio co-vary, is an important concept in portfolio management and deserves a little more explanation. The reason why investors put their money into different kinds of assets to create a portfolio is to benefit from diversification. At certain times some assets in the portfolio may perform poorly, others will perform well; at other times, different assets will perform well. The returns from a diversified portfolio should be less volatile than the returns from an undiversified portfolio. The degree to which returns from one asset will 'cancel out' fluctuations in the returns from another asset will depend on the degree to which the assets co-vary (Figure 11.2).

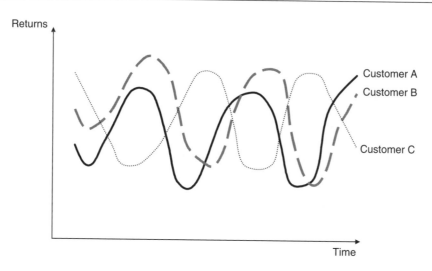

Figure 11.2 How assets in a portfolio co-vary

The returns from Customer A (solid line) and Customer B (dashed line) tend to fluctuate together. This may well be because both customers are in the same business sector, and so their orders are affected by the general industry background in their sector. The returns from Customers A and B have positive covariance. If this customer portfolio consisted only of Customers A and B, the overall risk of the portfolio would be the weighted average of A and B and there would be considerable volatility in portfolio returns over time.

Customer C (dotted line) exhibits negative covariance with A and B. When the returns from A and B are high, those from C are low, and vice versa. With Customer C in the portfolio, the overall portfolio performance is considerably smoother and the risk of the portfolio (measured in terms of its volatility) is lower.

The role of portfolio management in marketing portfolios

The idea that marketing assets can be managed as a portfolio, applying financial portfolio concepts of risk and return, has been of considerable interest to marketers for several decades. The portfolio management approach is about prioritizing the investment of scarce resources while maximizing returns for a given level of risk. Marketing portfolios consist of marketing investments such as products and brands, as

> Marketing portfolios consist of products and brands, as well as customer segments or individual customers. For international companies, marketing portfolio decisions also involve investment optimization between country markets.

well as customer segments or individual customers as described here. For international companies, marketing portfolio decisions also involve investment optimization between country markets. The goal of portfolio management is not maximization, but optimization. Maximization implies trying to obtain maximum returns, whatever the risks, whereas optimization is about managing both risks and returns and achieving the highest possible return *for an acceptable level of risk*.

As this discussion indicates, the measure of risk that is most used in portfolio management is volatility in returns. Volatility is by no means a perfect measure of risk and there may well be other components of risk that are important, as shown earlier in this chapter. Eventually, however, all risks have some impact on returns. Customer defection or migration will reduce returns, as will negative word of mouth, legal actions, etc. Therefore, risk for the portfolio can be measured using volatility.

Marketing spend and the marketing portfolio

Applying portfolio thinking to a marketing portfolio of customers or segments reveals an interesting aspect of marketing management, which is that the decisions that marketing and sales managers make about how to allocate resources and which customers to target are actually decisions *about different portfolios*. In other words, there are numerous marketing portfolios that the firm could invest in. Each portfolio would contain slightly different combinations of customers or segments and there would be slightly different resource and investment allocations.

So, how do managers choose between these different portfolio options? Sadly, many decisions are made on the basis of 'percentage of revenue' or 'last year's budget plus X%'. There are much better ways to make choices like these, not least using the response curves that advertising agencies and marketing consultancies can calculate for their clients. These response curves enable the firm to model the returns on particular marketing campaigns; although it is still uncommon for risk measurement and management to be applied to the customer portfolio as a whole, outside of the financial services industry.

One reason why risk and return based portfolio management techniques are not widely adopted by marketers may be that the technique is rather mathematical. Modelling portfolio risk and returns is complicated in marketing by the fact that marketing decisions have an impact on the returns of the portfolio. For example, deciding to run a promotional campaign targeted at a particular segment will increase the return on that segment. This is not the case in the management of the classical financial portfolio, where a decision to invest in some shares in Wal-Mart or Dell would not affect the financial performance of those companies! This means that the modelling techniques that were originally developed for financial portfolio analysis have to be adapted for use with marketing portfolios.

Finding an optimal marketing portfolio

The optimal marketing portfolio is one in which there are no other portfolio options that give a higher return for a particular level of risk. However, there are many levels of risk; some managers prefer a riskier portfolio that gives higher returns and others prefer a lower-risk portfolio that gives lower returns. For each level of risk, there is an optimal portfolio. If all these optimal portfolios are plotted, they lie along a curve that is known as the efficient frontier (Figure 11.3).

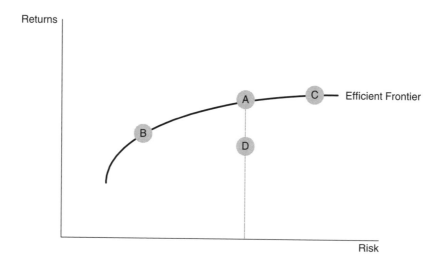

Figure 11.3 The efficient frontier of marketing portfolios

Figure 11.3 shows four marketing portfolios. Portfolio A combines moderate risk with moderate returns. Portfolio B has lower risks but lower returns. Portfolio C has higher risks and higher returns. These three portfolios, A, B, and C, are all optimal because they lie on the efficient frontier; there are no possible alternatives that would give a better return for that level of risk. Portfolio D is a different case. This portfolio does not lie on the efficient frontier. It offers relatively low returns for a moderate level of risk. Portfolio D is sub-optimal; for the same level of risk, portfolio A represents a better investment combination.

Note that the efficient frontier is in fact a frontier: there are no portfolios that lie above the frontier curve. The position of the curve is, however, affected by the overall level of marketing investment that the company makes. If marketing investment went up, returns would also go up and the entire curve would move up. In that case, new portfolio combinations become available to the marketing managers and there would be a new set of optimal portfolios along the new efficient frontier.

There is no right or wrong about the eventual selection of the portfolio, as long as the portfolio selected lies on the efficient frontier. The purpose of calculating the efficient frontier is to ensure that the portfolio that is chosen is one of the optimal options. The final selection between portfolios A, B, and C depends on the risk preferences of the manager and the organization.

Selecting an optimal portfolio

There is a four-step process for optimizing the choice of the marketing portfolio[1]:

1. calculate portfolio returns;
2. calculate portfolio risk;
3. generate the efficient frontier;
4. select the preferred portfolio.

Portfolio returns are usually measured in terms of monthly profits and data for 36 months are considered necessary for portfolio modelling. The risk is calculated in terms of covariance of the assets and the standard deviation of the portfolio. The standard deviation is effectively a measure of the shape of the normal distribution curve that was discussed in Chapter 2. The efficient frontier is then generated by software. Finally, the marketing managers need to make a decision about which combination of risk and return they prefer, ensuring that they select a portfolio that lies on the efficient frontier.

Advantages and disadvantages of customer portfolio risk analysis

Marketing managers should be concerned about risk as well as returns in their customer portfolios. Without an appreciation of the implicit risk in the customer portfolio, there is a real danger that managers may make decisions that reduce the performance of the company below its true potential because they selected a portfolio that lay below the efficient frontier. Such a decision would be suboptimal because there would be other portfolios that gave better returns for that level of risk.

The main disadvantages of the portfolio approach are that it requires a reasonable amount of historic data and it is computationally demanding. It can be difficult to obtain sufficient and comparable data where the company is new, has gone through a major reorganization, or where customer profitability measurement

---

[1] I am indebted to my co-authors Maya Berger and Sam Dias, and to OMD Metrics, London, for the development of the process and tool described here. The original idea was Sam's.

has only recently been introduced. The calculation of the efficient frontier almost certainly requires some technical input and support.

Summary

It is rare for marketing managers to use risk and portfolio management methods such as the ones described in this chapter, and yet the issues that are raised here are important ones for the business as a whole. In particular, considerations of risk as well as returns should influence decisions about investing in customers, especially in terms of the service level that the supplier offers its customers.

The issue of investment in service levels in the customer portfolio will be discussed in the following chapter.

Note

Now use the worksheet on the following page to create your own portfolio risk analysis.

Worksheet: portfolio risk analysis

Risk factor	Best case in portfolio	Worst case in portfolio	Actions/comments

Where to find out more

Ryals, L.J. and Knox, S. (2007) 'Measuring and managing customer relationship risk in business markets', *Industrial Marketing Management*, 36(6), pp. 823–833. *Describes the insurer's approach to creating a relationship risk scorecard in more detail and discusses how this scorecard was used to develop customer risk management strategies.*

Ryals, L.J., Dias, S. and Berger, M. (2007) 'Optimising marketing spend: return maximisation and risk minimisation in the marketing portfolio', *Journal of Marketing Management*, **23** (9), pp. 991–1012. *Moderately technical paper describing risk and portfolio management theory.*

12 Service-based segmentation

What's in this chapter

- Different approaches to segmentation
- Combining two or more segmentation approaches
- How service-based segmentation differs from other approaches
- How to implement service-based segmentation

Key concepts discussed in this chapter

Demographics, socio-demographics	Demographics concern the observable characteristics of a population or group, such as age or geographical location. Socio-demographics include social factors such as social class.
Segmentation	The process of dividing up a market into groups of customers in some way. Usual methods segment customers by similarity of characteristics or needs.
Segment maps	Two-dimensional representation of segments based on some combination of segmentation approaches, thus combining demographics/attitudinal factors/behavioural factors.
Service-based segmentation	Another method of segmentation based on the value of customers and offering them service packages appropriate to their value.

Key tools explained in this chapter

- Service-based segmentation: An approach to segmentation based on offering service packages according to the value of the customers in that segment. May also involve negotiation with customers to increase services in exchange for an increase in revenues. Can be implemented using a six-step process:

  1. list service elements;
  2. map service elements to customers;
  3. identify patterns of service provision;
  4. overlay customer revenues and costs;
  5. design service packages;
  6. roll out to customers.

Two-minute chapter summary

Segmentation is a vitally important business decision. Segmentation is a process for dividing up markets into groups of customers, traditionally having similar characteristics or needs. Recognizing the differences between customers is the first step in differentiating the company's offer.

Traditional approaches to segmentation tend to divide customers up by socio-demographics, attitudes, or behaviours. Socio-demographics are observable characteristics of customers (whether these customers are companies or individuals). Although this is the most straightforward method of segmentation it is unlikely to yield substantial insights or competitive edge, in part because customers of a similar type do not necessarily have the same buying behaviour.

Attitudinal approaches to segmentation give insight into customer motivation, but are difficult to use in practice because customers may not behave in ways that align with their stated attitudes. Segmenting on behaviour is practically useful although offers little insight.

Traditional approaches to segmentation start from an analysis of the customer. Service-based segmentation is about the service offerings of the company, and which of these service offerings it makes to which customers. Service packages can be created that are attractive to the company (because they can provide the services profitably) and to the customer (because they can select a service package that meets their needs, and is convenient).

Service-based segmentation is a useful tool for the implementation of profitable customer management.

Why most approaches to segmentation are incomplete

The way in which an organization segments its market can have a profound impact on its business success. Segmenting markets enables companies to develop differentiated value propositions, appeal to customers, and increase overall market share.

Market segmentation is one of the most powerful tools in the sales and marketing armoury, and yet it is one of the areas with which most companies struggle. Most approaches to segmentation take customer characteristics of some kind as their starting point. This chapter suggests a very different approach to segmentation, which takes the value of the customer as the starting point. This approach to segmentation enables an organization to work out what service levels it should be providing to its customers.

Segmentation is an important and difficult topic for most companies, and there are a number of different approaches to how it should be done. The first section of this chapter briefly compares and contrasts the different approaches, before examining service-based segmentation in more detail.

Different approaches to segmentation

The many and varied approaches to segmentation can be grouped under four headings: demographic, attitudinal, behavioural, and service-based segmentation (Figure 12.1).

As Figure 12.1 suggests, the simplest approach to segmentation is demographic. Demographics describe the visible characteristics of a group of customers or consumers. Attitudinal segmentation groups customers or consumers according to their values, attitudes, or beliefs. Behavioural segmentation, as its name suggests, groups customers or consumers according to how they behave or how they react to particular promotional messages. Finally, service-based segmentation – the main subject of this chapter – groups customers according to their profitability and service packages. This may have nothing to do with any of their attitudes or behaviours, but rather is an internal segmentation specific to the supplier.

Demographic segmentation

Segmentation that uses demographics is a descriptive segmentation based on factual or observable characteristics of the customer. Business-to-business, this might be the customer's industry sector, size of business, geographic location, or structure. Therefore, a simple business-to-business segmentation may be to group customers in terms of their industry sector ('automotive manufacturers', 'biotech', etc.), or to group them in size terms ('SMEs'; 'Large regional distributors', etc.).

In business-to-consumer marketing, demographic segmentation can refer to segmentations of customers based on their age, income, etc. Thus, customers may be grouped according to age band or lifestage ('18–25', 'students', 'retired') or according to employment or income ('city traders').

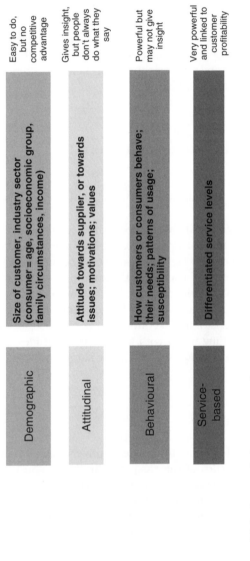

Demographic	Size of customer, industry sector (consumer = age, socioeconomic group, family circumstances, income)	Easy to do, but no competitive advantage
Attitudinal	Attitude towards supplier, or towards issues; motivations; values	Gives insight, but people don't always do what they say
Behavioural	How customers or consumers behave; their needs; patterns of usage; susceptibility	Powerful but may not give insight
Service-based	Differentiated service levels	Very powerful and linked to customer profitability

Figure 12.1 Approaches to segmentation

Demographic segmentation is widely-used, but it is a relatively ineffective form of segmentation that rarely delivers any competitive advantage to the supplier. There are two reasons for this: the first is that these

> Demographic segmentation is widely-used, but it is a relatively ineffective form of segmentation.

characteristics are visible to all suppliers, and so there is no advantage to be gained by segmenting in that way. Second, and more importantly, demographic segmentation is limited in its ability to distinguish between different types of customer. So, for example, a demographic segmentation can tell you the broad picture (for example, customers' income levels or wealth are related to spending), but does not give you useful fine detail about what, precisely, these customers will spend their money on. Some city traders spend their bonuses on property, but others buy luxury holidays, boats, expensive sports gear, fine wines, and works of art (or all those things!).

Another example of the limited usefulness of demographic segmentation is age-based segmentation: although younger consumers are more likely as a group to spend money on hip-hop or Indie music than older customers, not all younger consumers like hip-hop. So, although demographic descriptors of a firm's customers or consumers are interesting and important pieces of information that may help the firm to make broad decisions about appropriate products and services, demographics are a blunt instrument for segmentation purposes. The fine detail that might help a company to develop truly differentiated strategies and value propositions is missing from demographic segmentation.

Note
Check what demographic information your company currently collects. Do you know enough about the basics of your customer base?

Attitudinal segmentation

The idea that customers in the same demographic group will have different tastes and preferences (for example, some teenagers like hip-hop but others prefer classical music) leads to the notion of attitudinal-based segmentation. This second type of segmentation has much greater success in explaining why customers react as they do, and is correspondingly a more useful form of segmentation.

An example of attitudinal segmentation can be found in consumer preferences for fair trade products. Some consumers feel very strongly about these products and are prepared to pay a price premium for them; other consumers, who might be demographically identical, will not. Attitudinal segmentation has been very successfully applied in respect of fair trade and organic products and health foods. Elements of attitudinal segmentation can also be seen in the way that some drinks, high-technology products, motor bikes, and cars are promoted. Thus, mobile phones or high-tech gadgets are promoted to people who want to be seen to have the newest technology, or who might want to be part of a particular set of people. Some cars are promoted based on environmental claims; others are advertised in a way designed to appeal to customers who want to impress their friends.

There are two problems with attitudinal segmentation. The first is that attitudes cannot directly be observed. So, if a customer buys a fair trade product, it is not clear whether he or she is doing so mainly because it is fair trade, just because he or

> Not only can attitudes not be observed directly, but also customers do not always act in ways that match their attitudes.

she likes the taste, because it is convenient, or because the packaging is appealing. The second problem is linked to the first: not only can attitudes not be observed directly, but customers do not always act in ways that match their attitudes. In other words, customers can espouse values that they then do not live up to. In the fair trade example, customers might answer surveys in such a way that they appear to be passionately interested in the issues, but when they are in the supermarket they carry on buying cheaper, non-ethically sourced products. This gap between attitudes and behaviours is why researching and launching new products is so difficult. Customers often say one thing, but do another. For this reason, many companies prefer to use behavioural segmentation.

Behavioural segmentation

Behavioural segmentation observes what customers actually do, and then uses this as the basis for segmentation. So, an airline might segment frequent flyers in business class from infrequent flyers in economy class. An example of behavioural segmentation would be the packages put together by mobile phone providers for their customers, notably the 'animal' segments that reflect the differential usage patterns or needs that mobile phone customers have.

Orange (http://www1.orange.co.uk/service_plans/paymonthly/plans_overview. html) has used a behavioural approach to segmentation to create product/service packages that will attract customers with different patterns of phone usage. Figure 12.2 illustrates four of their segments.

Canaries, for example, use their phones a lot to chat to family and friends, and so their packages have more off-peak minutes; whereas Dolphins are people who are frequent texters, and so their packages have fewer phone minutes but more texts included in them.

Behavioural segmentation is very useful for creating relevant packages that reflect customers' current behaviour. The problem is that this approach does not address unrecognized needs. There may be things that customers would like, if they were offered, that are not reflected in their

> Behavioural segmentation is very useful for creating relevant packages that reflect customers' current behaviour, although it does not address unrecognized needs.

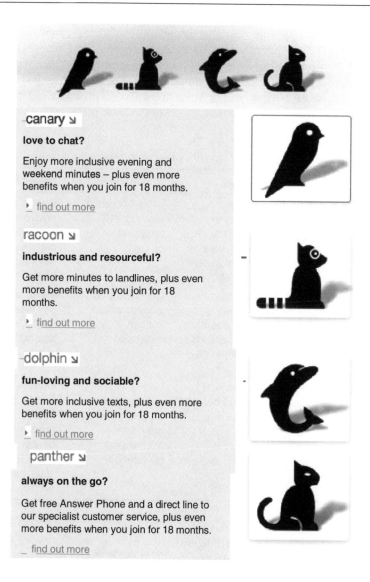

Figure 12.2 Orange mobile phone animal segments (reproduced by permission of Orange PCS)
Source: www.orange.co.uk

behaviours at present. Texting is a good example of this. It was originally developed as a tool for engineers and was included on mobile phones almost as an afterthought; yet, for some customers (such as the Dolphins), it has become a very important part of their mobile phone usage.

Another drawback of behavioural segmentation is that it may not be clear *why* customers behave in the way that they do. So, behavioural segmentation may offer useful information but little insight, whereas attitudinal segmentation offers considerable insight into customer's attitudes and feelings but is less predictive with regard to actual behaviour. The advantages and disadvantages of these three different approaches to segmentation are set out in Table 12.1.

Table 12.1 Advantages and disadvantages of segmentation approaches

Approach	Definition	Advantages	Disadvantages
1 Socio-demographic	Describes customers in terms of factual characteristics such as income, location, etc.	Straightforward method, relatively easy and cheap to do.	Everyone else can do it, so it confers little competitive advantage unless the supplier has better information.
2 Attitudinal	Describes customers' attitudes about products, brands, issues of the day, etc.	Can yield powerful insights about customer motivation.	What customers say they think may not be what they actually think.
3 Behavioural	Describes how customers behave.	Very useful to observe actual behaviour, which may differ from stated preferences.	Does not offer insight into why customers behave this way, so behaviour can seem to change in ways that are not predictable.

As Table 12.1 shows, demographic, attitudinal, and behavioural approaches to segmentation each have drawbacks. Demographics are easy to observe and relatively cheap to collect, but do not offer particular insights. Attitudes are difficult

> Combining different segmentation methods is one way to reduce the shortcomings of using a single method.

to observe and can be expensive to collect information about, and are not always a reliable guide to purchasing behaviour. Behaviours are straightforward to observe but can be inexplicable unless the underlying attitudes are known. Combining different segmentation methods is one way to reduce the shortcomings of using a single method. An example of one organization's combination of segmentation methods is demonstrated in the next section.

Combining two or more segmentation approaches

To improve the usefulness of their segmentation, many companies now experi-
ment with using two or even all three
segment approaches simultaneously. They
draw segment maps in two dimensions or
segment cubes in three or more dimensions. Three-dimensional segment cubes

> To improve the usefulness of
> their segmentation, many com-
> panies now experiment with
> using two or even all three seg-
> ment approaches simultaneously.

are more complex, but they do enable a much more effective segmentation. The
multiple dimensions of the cube might include more than one behavioural aspect,
plus some demographics. Segment cubes have been applied successfully by consumer businesses that have very large numbers of customer records and frequent
interaction with their customers. Organizations who apply these complex segmentation approaches successfully include banks, retail insurance companies, retailers,
and mobile phone service providers. Segmentation in multiple dimensions usually
requires substantial IT support.

How to create segment maps

In business-to-business situations, or for business-to-consumer companies with
fewer customers or with a less diverse customer base, two-dimensional segment
maps that combine just two aspects of demographic, attitudinal or behavioural elements can be very useful. Figure 12.3 illustrates a two-dimensional segment map for

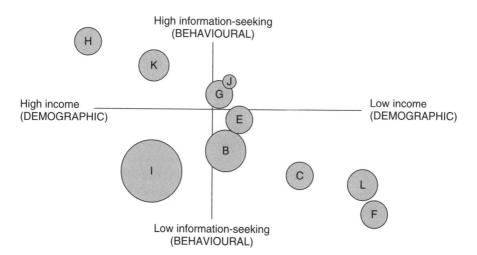

Figure 12.3   Segment map for personal loans provider

a personal loans provider that is in a relatively non-complex business-to-consumer marketplace.

The loans provider has decided to segment its market along income (demographic) and information-seeking (behavioural) lines. On the horizontal axis, the customer's income is an important variable that affects his or her ability to repay a loan and also informs his or her credit rating. On the vertical axis, the company recognizes a substantial difference between customers who are well-informed and seek many alternative quotations and ask for a lot of information before making a decision of which loan provider to go with (more sophisticated behaviour), and customers who are short of time or not interested in the details of the process; they simply want a loan quickly with minimum fuss (less sophisticated behaviour).

Using a segment map

From the loans provider's point of view, its preferred segment is segment I consisting of customers who have a high capability to borrow but also to repay, and who do not shop around or use up a lot of the loan advisors' expensive time. The larger size of the circle for segment I illustrates the greater number of customers in this segment. The loans provider has been actively developing simpler products that are easy to buy for this segment. It also follows up these customers in future months and years to see whether they need a new loan.

The map shows that the loan provider has customers in three of the four quadrants. The upper right quadrant consists of customers with lower incomes who are expensive to sell to. Thus, the loans provider can see from its segment map that it has no customers of this type. However, it is happy with this good strategic decision: lower income but difficult customers are unlikely to be an attractive segment.

The example of the loans provider illustrates a combination approach to developing segments; the actions that the loan provider took to target certain segments and not others show how segmentation should be applied in practice. There should be a specific, slightly different value proposition for each segment (see Chapter 15). In the case of the loans provider, the most attractive segment was segment I and so the company put a lot of effort into targeting this segment with attractive propositions.

However, all three approaches to segmentation discussed so far share a common drawback, which is that they do not consider the profitability of the segments. A rather different way to approach segmentation is to design the service packages according to the profitability of the customer segment (rather than according to the attitudes and preferences of the customers, as in traditional segmentation). This fourth approach is known as service-based segmentation.

Service-based segmentation

In a sense, the first three types of segmentation shown in Figure 12.1 are from the customer's perspective, whereas the fourth type, service-based segmentation, is from the perspective of the supplier. Service-based segmentation is about creating 'packages' of products and services that are differentiated from segment to segment, based on the profitability of that segment. In other words, the level of service that customers receive is related to their profitability. Without service-based segmentation, it is all too easy for a company to provide additional services to the customers who shout the loudest, rather than the customers who deserve them the most.

The starting point for service-based segmentation is to develop a good understanding of costs to serve, which is essential so that appropriate packages can be developed for different groups of customers. This involves setting up a list of all the different service elements that are offered to customers. This in itself is a useful exercise to carry out in conjunction with a customer lifetime value analysis, because the service elements largely determine the cost to serve part of the customer lifetime value calculation. Many firms are astonished to find out just how many different services they unearth when they create a master list of all their different offerings.

The services list is used to create product/service packages (e.g., gold, silver, bronze, etc.). Next, the supplier needs to decide whether the service package that each customer is getting is appropriate. This is a judgement that can be based on customer lifetime value – do the more valuable customers get better service levels, or are there some anomalies where less valuable customers are actually receiving too high a service level?

Implementing service-based segmentation involves managing service levels that customers receive over the relationship lifetime, so as to optimize customer lifetime value. This may involve some 'tough conversations' with customers about the amount of resources they are using compared to the value they give back. Customers in the bronze segments, for example, may be able to access certain services that are provided

> Implementing service-based segmentation may involve some 'tough conversations' with customers about the amount of resources they are using compared to the value they give back.

to gold segment customers for free, but the bronze level customers have to pay. Discussions may be held with customers about whether they are fully satisfied with their service package and what business they would have to give the supplier to migrate up to silver or gold level. These frank conversations can be very useful in making it clear to customers that their service demands come at a substantial cost to the supplier, and as a basis for future business agreements.

How service-based segmentation differs from other segmentations

The notion that customers can move from segment to segment based on discussions with the supplier about the service levels they need, combined with the stratified nature of the service packages in service-based segmentation, tend to differentiate this system from other approaches to segmentation. In other

> Service-based segmentation is characterized by differentiated service packages, and by value exchange discussions with customers about service levels and expected purchases.

segmentations, service levels may not differ between segments (although marketing messages might); or customers may be moved into different segments retrospectively (that is, *after* the change in their business levels has occurred) rather than proactively, based on discussions and agreements about future business levels. Service-based segmentation is characterized by differentiated service packages, and by value exchange discussions with customers about service levels and expected purchases.

How to implement service-based segmentation

A classic service-based segmentation project would be implemented in the following six-step process, as shown in Figure 12.4:

1. list service elements;
2. map service elements to customers;
3. identify patterns of service provision;
4. overlay customer revenues and costs;
5. design service packages;
6. roll out to customers.

Each of these steps will now be discussed.

Step 1: List all service elements available

The first step in service-based segmentation is to understand all the different service offers that the firm currently makes to customers, plus service items that could be offered but are not currently. This may range from named account managers and direct dial telephone numbers, to specialized logistics and inventory management, through joint branding, special packaging, point of sale support, training, and many more.

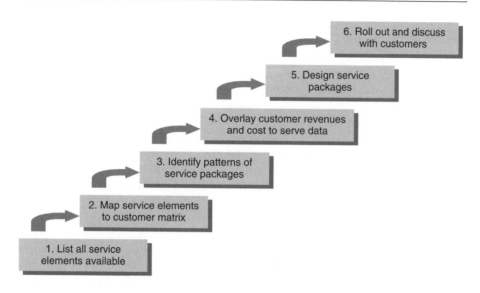

Figure 12.4   Process for implementing service-based segmentation

It is worth interviewing both the sales and the customer services teams to get this information, because many of them will be providing service elements to customers that are not officially offered by the organization. So, for example, business-to-business salespeople will often provide an informal order-tracking service to customers, even if the company itself does not offer this facility. In fact, most companies are surprised by the extent of the service elements that its sales and marketing people offer. One chemicals manufacturer that did not see itself as service-oriented at all discovered that more than 30 service elements were currently being offered to different customers across its customer base.

> Most companies are surprised by the extent of the service elements that its sales and marketing people offer.

Note

Even if you are not planning to implement service-based segmentation, take a few minutes to find out about all the different service offers that your company makes, and consider whether they seem appropriate given what you know about the profitability of that customer or segment.

Step 2: Map service elements to customer matrix

Having identified all the different service elements, the next step is to create a 'map' of the services that are offered to each customer. This is relatively straightforward in a business-to-business context where the number of customers is not large, because it can easily be plotted on a spreadsheet. Where there is a larger number of customers, some data mining may be necessary.

The outcome of this exercise is a matrix showing 'who gets what'. Figure 12.5 illustrates what such a map might look like. This is based on a real example of a manufacturing company, which had 20 regular customers who accounted for more than 80% of its turnover (occasional customers were excluded from the analysis for reasons of simplification).

In a service-based segmentation exercise for this manufacturer, Step 1 resulted in a list of 30 service elements. These were then plotted against each major customer. Where the customer received the service element, this was plotted against that customer. At this point, the customers were listed in descending order of revenues, because that was the way in which they were listed on the company's database. Thus, customer A was the largest customer (that is, it had generated the most revenues in the year to date). Customer T was the smallest revenue-generator in the year to date.

A closer analysis of Figure 12.5 reveals that, although the larger customers tended to receive more service elements, this was not a consistent pattern. Customer Q, for example, was one of the smaller customers but received considerable service elements. At this stage, the cost of providing the different service elements was not taken into account but it is clear that some elements (such as service elements 4 and 6, field sales and technical visits) would be much more costly than others (such as element 27, access to online technical manuals).

Step 3: Identify patterns of service packages

Having identified all service elements and created a map of which customer receives which service, it is possible to look within the data set to identify patterns of service provision. These patterns can form the basis for the development of service packages that are at the heart of service-based segmentation. For example, Figure 12.5 reveals that there are patterns of service provision. One pattern relates to what might be termed 'technologically savvy' customers. These customers tend to use fast telephone access to technical services, plus they will use online order processing and online technical manuals, and they will self-invoice. There is another cluster of customers who use high service levels, often associated with product or packaging customization; and a third cluster is delivery-sensitive, using services such as guaranteed or timed delivery and sometimes also secured delivery.

Service element	A	B	C	D	E	F	G	H	I	J	K	L	M	N	O	P	Q	R	S	T
1. Named account manager	x	x	x		x			x		x	x		x	x		x		x	x	x
2. Online OP	x	x	x		x			x		x	x		x	x		x		x	x	x
3. Direct dial into CS	x	x	x		x	x		x	x		x		x	x		x		x	x	x
4. Field sales visit			x	x			x	x								x		x		
5. Technical advice telephone call	x			x	x	x		x		x	x		x	x		x	x			x
6. Technical advice visit		x	x		x	x		x			x		x	x		x	x	x		
7. Customized product formulation		x	x				x	x		x	x		x	x		x	x			
8. Customized packaging		x			x	x	x	x			x		x	x		x	x	x		
9. Customized palletization					x	x	x	x			x		x	x		x				
10. Multi-language label	x	x	x		x	x	x										x	x		x
11. Co-branded label	x	x								x										
12. Temperature-controlled delivery	x		x		x	x	x	x		x	x		x	x		x	x	x	x	
13. Secure delivery/storage			x		x	x	x	x		x				x		x	x	x	x	
14. Priority delivery				x		x					x					x				
15. First delivery slot	x			x	x		x	x												x
16. Timed delivery slot			x	x		x				x	x		x	x				x		
17. Guaranteed delivery			x	x				x		x	x		x	x	x					
18. Automated delivery note			x	x	x	x	x	x		x			x					x		x
19. Order tracking			x	x	x	x	x	x		x										
20. Delivery tracking			x	x	x	x		x					x	x				x		
21. Overnight storage	x		x		x			x					x			x		x	x	x
22. Automated invoicing			x	x																
23. Self-invoicing					x	x	x			x			x			x		x	x	x
24. Consignment stock					x	x										x			x	x
25. Cross-docking					x															
26. Stockholding visibility	x	x						x		x	x					x	x	x	x	x
27. Online technical manuals			x		x	x	x	x		x	x		x			x	x	x		
28. Automatic re-ordering		x	x		x	x	x	x		x	x		x			x	x			x
29. Online delivery performance stats			x					x										x		
30. Local customer service centre			x					x		x	x	x				x		x	x	x

Figure 12.5 Map of service elements

Although a cluster analysis can identify patterns of service that may form the basis of service packages, these might not always represent the company's preferred service provision. For example, the second cluster identified above, which is using high service provision, might not be very profitable. Thus, the next step in service-based segmentation is to overlay customer profitability or lifetime value analysis.

Step 4: Overlay customer revenues and costs to serve

Step 4 gets to the heart of service-based segmentation by overlaying customer revenues and costs to serve on to the service packages. This enables the company to see whether the more profitable customers receive more services, or not.

In Figure 12.5, the customers along the horizontal axis were presented in descending order of revenues. However, once they have been re-clustered into segments, it is informative to see how much revenue and cost is associated with each cluster. This will provide some guidelines about which services are more essential than others. If there is a small cluster that is highly dependent on

> Calculating how much revenue and cost is associated with each cluster will enable informed decisions about whether to charge for some of these service elements, raise prices, or even discontinue a particular service.

high-cost services, the company can make some informed decisions about whether to charge for some of these service elements, raise its prices to this customer group, or even discontinue a particular service.[1]

The underlying philosophy of service-based segmentation is that the service package should be linked to the profitability of the customer or segment. The way in which relationships with customers are managed has a critical impact on how profitable they are. In other words, customers are not intrinsically profitable or unprofitable: it is the products and, particularly, the service that the company provides, which determines how profitable their customer relationships are; hence, the notion of managing customers as assets. The investment in a customer asset should be more than balanced by the returns from that asset.

> Customers are not intrinsically profitable or unprofitable: it is the products and, particularly, the service that the company provides, which determines how profitable their customer relationships are.

---

[1] Regulatory restrictions may prevent the adoption of some of these alternatives.

Step 5: Design service packages

The fifth step follows on from the analysis of the profitability of the clusters. Using the clusters of service patterns identified in Step 3, and taking into account the profitability of these clusters as identified in Step 4, the company should design service packages that are likely to appeal to customers while also being profitable. These service packages are likely to be based on the clusters of current service provision, but they may well not be identical. The company may decide that certain service elements are too expensive to provide to certain less-profitable customers; or it may use a segment map to identify opportunities for new service packages; the company may even increase the service levels to some customers.

> The company may decide that certain service elements are too expensive to provide to certain customers; or it may identify opportunities for new service packages; or increase the service levels to some customers.

Companies using service-based segmentation have differentiated service packages for each segment. This approach can be overlaid on to existing customer-based segments. So, if the company has an existing segmentation that is based on demographics, attitudes, or behaviours, this existing segmentation can be mapped against the service package clusters. For some companies, there will be a close match of existing segmentation and service-based segments; for many other companies, this exercise will reveal considerable anomalies. Many companies find that they suffer from 'service creep', where customers gradually receive more and more service over time, without any overview of whether the customer or segment is profitable or not. Service-based segmentation provides some clear structure and guidelines to the sales force and to the customer service team, so that they do not over-promise to customers and then put the organization in difficulties when it has to deliver.

Introducing defined service-based packages not only clarifies expectations in the customers' minds and gives the company more control over the customer equity in its customer portfolio through the prevention of 'service creep', but it also helps reduce complaints and arguments with customers. Particularly in business-to-business situations, customers in a particular industry sector tend to know one another, and they may compare notes about the service they are receiving from their suppliers. A clear service package structure removes allegations of unfairness and helps to manage expectations.

Step 6: Roll out to customers

The final stage of successful service-based segmentation is to roll it out to customers and then to manage it consistently. This can be problematic if customers are receiving higher service levels than their profitability really warrants, and so the adoption of a service package is going to reduce their effective service level. Implementation of the packages then becomes a matter of negotiation with the customer.

To implement the service-based package, the company needs to use the previous analysis to identify the most appropriate package for each customer, and then to migrate them on to this package. Although I use 'Gold', 'Silver', and 'Bronze' here, certain businesses may prefer not to give names to service packages that might suggest some customers are being treated less well than others (for example, 'Gold', 'Silver', and 'Bronze' is unlikely to appeal to 'Bronze' customers who are effectively being told that they are third-class citizens).

> Care is needed to avoid giving the service packages names that might suggest some customers are being treated less well than others.

However, the real value of the rollout is not simply to put customers on to new service packages; it is the way in which a capable sales or customer service team can negotiate with customers about their package. So, customers on a lower service level package ('Bronze') can still receive elements of the 'Silver' package, but they have to pay extra for it. In other cases, the sales force or customer service team will discuss with customers what levels of revenue or volume they would need from the customer to upgrade them to a 'Gold' package. In this way, service-based segmentation can open up negotiations with customers about the share of spend that the customer gives to the supplier. Table 12.2 summarizes the advantages and a possible disadvantage of service-based segmentation.

It is important when managing a customer portfolio using service-based segmentation that the supplier polices the system properly and prevents 'service creep', where the salesperson offers a bronze segment customer some elements of the silver or gold service for free, in order to win additional business. It is all too easy, in these circumstances, for the entire service-based segmentation system to become

Table 12.2 Advantages and disadvantage of service-based segmentation

Approach	Definition	Advantages	Disadvantages
Service-based	Based on a product/service package supplied to the customer. There are different product/service packages for each segment.	Closely linked to customer lifetime value, because the 'package' affects costs to serve. May be used in conjunction with other forms of segmentation.	May result in some customers having service levels downgraded, which could be problematic.

eroded over time by a series of 'special cases', so that eventually the firm is back to a series of individual deals with customers about service levels.

If it is based on careful analysis and implementation, service-based segmentation is a powerful tool for the profitable management of a customer portfolio.

Summary

The most widely-used methods of segmentation are based on customer attributes such as demographics, or the attitudes or behaviours of the customer.

Service-based segmentation is an alternative method of segmenting the customer base from the perspective of the company. Starting with the different service elements that the company provides, service-based segmentation creates packages of services that customers receive, based on their profitability as well as their needs. Additional services can be paid for separately, or customers can change to different service packages if they change the level or type of business they do with the supplier.

Service-based segmentation can be overlaid on to an existing segmentation using other methods.

The service package that companies provide to their customers has a tremendous impact on the profitability of those customers. Introducing service-based segmentation is one way in which companies can positively control and manage the value of their customer assets and therefore their customer equity.

When implementing service-based segmentation, companies need to consider the customers they want to acquire and those they want to retain. This important strategic decision is considered in the next chapter.

Note
Now use the worksheet on the following page to create a segment map

Worksheet: segment map

Dimension:

Dimension:

Where to find out more

McDonald, M. and Dunbar, I. (2004) *Market Segmentation: How to Do It, How to Profit from It*, Butterworth-Heinemann, Oxford. *Provides a detailed 'how to' guide to segmentation using a combination of demographics (who buys), behavioural (what, where, and when they buy), and attitudinal (why they buy).*

Section Three

The strategic decisions that maximize the value of your customers

Research has shown that there are some strategies that particularly impact the performance of the customer portfolio. These include the customers that the firm targets, how much it spends on retaining them, its pricing strategy and policies, and the way in which it creates and communicates value to customers. This section of the book focuses on three areas of marketing and sales strategy, exploring how managers can make the decisions that maximize the value of their customers. These three areas are:

- selective customer acquisition and retention;
- pricing;
- increasing customer equity through breakthrough value propositions.

Chapter 13 looks at active customer targeting through selective customer acquisition and retention. This includes demonstrating how to develop customer acquisition criteria and appropriate acquisition messages, how to predict and prevent customer defection, and if you need to, how to 'fire' a customer.

Pricing is one of the most important decisions that a company can make, because not only does it have a direct impact on the bottom line, but it also affects the customer's perceptions of quality. Chapter 14 reviews commonly-used pricing approaches for both new and existing products, but goes on to consider how you can predict and avoid cannibalization (customers switching from one of your products to another, rather than switching away from competitors). This chapter also looks at some innovative approaches to pricing, including total cost of ownership, total cost of relationship, and risk-based pricing. Finally, the practice of discounting is considered and the astonishing impact on the bottom line is demonstrated.

The final chapter of this section (and of the book) is Chapter 15, which looks at value propositions and how you construct a powerful message to the customer.

Two techniques are demonstrated. The first uses critical success factor analysis to show how a value proposition can be developed. The second uses a series of case studies to illustrate how some world-class companies think out of the box and almost integrate themselves into their customers' business, becoming indispensable as a result of their breakthrough value proposition. This chapter introduces the value chain analysis tool to demonstrate how a supplier might identify areas of potential weakness in its customers that it could address through a superior value proposition. The final challenge that this book offers is to ask you 'why should your customers buy from you (rather than from anyone else)?'. The VRIN tool is introduced and explained, and a method for using VRIN to answer the 'why us?' question is shown.

When you have read this section, you will be able to:

- set marketing/sales strategies for selective customer targeting;
- develop customer acquisition criteria;
- balance the costs and benefits of customer acquisition and customer retention and calculate customer payback;
- manage customer defection;
- understand the interplay between perceived price and perceived quality;
- set a pricing strategy and discount policy that is appropriate for your customer relationships;
- develop powerfully focused and effective value propositions that will make it difficult for your customers to leave;
- identify clearly the point of difference about your company and articulate why your customers should buy from you rather than from other suppliers.

Selective customer acquisition
13 and retention

What's in this chapter

- Why companies should not acquire certain customers
- How to define customer acquisition targets
- How to plan customer acquisition
- How to balance the costs and benefits of customer acquisition
- Conditions in which retention pays off
- How to tell if your customers are thinking of defecting, and what to do about it
- How to get rid of a customer

Key concepts discussed in this chapter

Conversion rates	The percentage of customers acquired compared to the number of customers approached in a particular campaign or period, or by channel.
Customer defection	Total loss of the customer to a competitor.
Customer payback period	The length of time, in months or years, until a customer generates profits equivalent to the cost of acquiring the person (business-to-consumer) or company (business-to-business).

Relationship quality	The quality of the relationship, usually as measured by both sides, on metrics such as satisfaction with the relationship, value generated, communication, etc. May generate differences of opinion that indicate areas for improvement, sometimes tackled collaboratively.

Key tools explained in this chapter

- Customer acquisition target: This not only provides the number of customers to be acquired, but also outlines what types of customers. Based on the firm's strategic objectives and likely customer lifetime value or customer equity.
- Customer profiling: Constructing a 'picture' of the key characteristics of a particular type of customer (usually, of an attractive customer) and then looking to acquire customers that match that profile. It is easier to profile existing customers than potential customers, because more is known about existing customers. However, it should be noted that the most attractive or valuable customers may not be found in the company's existing customer database.

Two-minute chapter summary

Not all customers are good customers. This important concept is sometimes overlooked in the excitement of selling a major deal. However, some customers may turn out to have negative lifetime value, or they may damage the company's brand or reputation or spread negative word of mouth.

Customer acquisition targets should be identified based on the objectives of the firm and using forecasts of likely customer lifetime value or customer equity. So, for example, if the firm has an objective to expand into other parts of Europe, it will tend to prioritize acquiring customers that are already doing business in that part of Europe so that it can learn about the potential new market and start to build its local credibility.

Word of mouth is a useful tool for targeted customer acquisition, because customers tend to mix with others of a similar profile. Thus, a profitable strategy is to profile the most valuable customers and then go out and find other customers with a similar profile.

Customer retention should also be selective. Generally, the more customers a company retains, the better off it will be. However, the firm must be able to retain its customers profitably. There is no point in spending so much on customer retention that the retained customer becomes unprofitable.

For this reason, companies need to make strategic decisions about the balance between customer acquisition and retention spending. The decision about balance will be affected by factors such as the cost of acquisition versus retention, the likely retention rates, and the customer equity generated by the retention activity.

Why companies should not acquire certain customers

The decision about which customers or segments to target is one of the fundamental decisions that a firm should make, if it is taking a strategic view of its marketing. Yet, far too many firms focus on making products or offering services using a 'fly paper' model in which they dangle their offers out into the market and wait to see what customers stick. A much better – and more efficient use of marketing and sales resources – is to think about which specific groups of customers the company wants to target. In some business-to-business situations, this may be as specific as identifying the individual organizations with which the firm wants to do business, and then targeting them one by one. It is said that IBM does this for the major corporations that it wants to deal with, even allocating a notional 'account manager' to a potential customer. Should the potential customer firm ever contact IBM, they would be directed to an account manager who already knows about their business.

It is not just customer acquisition that many firms fail to make strategic decisions about; at the other end of the relationship lifecycle, too many firms are not thinking clearly enough about which customers they want to retain and which, frankly, they should lose. This chapter will argue that not all customers are good customers, and that a sensible strategy to retain certain customers and allow others to leave should they choose to, can be a powerful tool in maximizing customer equity.

Selective customer acquisition

There is a widespread perception, particularly in business-to-business markets, that there is a power asymmetry in supplier/buyer relationships. It is perceived that buyers have far more power than suppliers, because they make the final decision whether to buy or not.

To a large extent, this is true. However, the asymmetry is not as great as it is often perceived to be. Smart firms increase their chances of attracting the customers they really want, through a strategic process of identifying and planning to acquire the most attractive customers or customer segments.

> The power asymmetry between suppliers and customers is not as great as it is often perceived to be.

This section shows you how to define which customers you want to acquire, and how to develop an acquisition plan that will improve your chances of success. Identifying the customers you want to target, and developing an acquisition plan for them, are both internal preparation and planning stages. A third stage is to develop a powerful value proposition that is likely to attract the customer or segment the firm is targeting: this is the subject of Chapter 15.

How to define customer acquisition targets

The kind of customers that a firm decides to target for acquisition will be informed by the kind of customers it finds attractive. This was covered in Chapter 10, where a process for prioritizing current customers based on their current attractiveness was discussed. Figure 10.5 (on page 214) illustrated this in terms of an 'attractiveness thermometer'.

Defining which customers to target for acquisition is a similar process, but it should not be confused with the prioritization of the existing customer base. There are a number of reasons why acquiring new customers and prioritizing existing customers are two separate activities:

- The current customer base may be less attractive than potential customers not yet acquired.
- There may be entire new segments or markets that are not yet represented in the current customer base.
- The firm may have longer-term strategic objectives that are not yet reflected in the current composition of the customer base, or that could not be achieved through the current customer base (e.g., rapid growth or expansion into new markets).
- The firm may not have taken a strategic approach to the acquisition of customers so far.
- There may be specific features or needs that a firm does *not* want in its customers.
- Customer targeting and acquisition is usually carried out by a different department than customer management (sales versus customer service or account management). In just the same way that managing a customer base for customer equity maximization means that marketing and customer service should prioritize customers, so too should the sales team receive specific guidance about the customers they target and acquire. Remember, 'not all customers are good customers'.

The starting point for defining customer acquisition targets should always be the strategic objectives of the firm.

The strategic objectives of the firm say what the firm is trying to achieve in the longer term.

These strategic objectives can be used to identify which customers or segments are the key targets. For example, if the firm has a strategic objective relating to growth, or to market share, larger customers and larger segments will be preferred. The high-level

> The strategic objectives of the business can be used to identify which customers or segments are key acquisition targets.

marketing objective that will deliver a strategic growth objective is market share, and therefore, the approach to targeting customers is broader. Extreme examples of this can be seen in the strategies adopted by mobile phone service providers during the 1990s, when market share gain was the principal objective. In these circumstances, the mobile phone companies did relatively little targeting of customers but simply aimed to maximize the number of new customers they could acquire. New customers were able to obtain good deals, phone handsets were heavily subsidized, and even low-usage customers were encouraged through pay-as-you-go schemes.

Later in the 1990s and into the 2000s, the mobile phone service providers changed their strategy. The previous approach had been highly successful in increasing ownership of mobile phones and expanding the market, but the focus on customer acquisition and the excellent deals offered to new customers resulted in very high levels of 'churn', in which customers regularly defected to other providers. This meant that the mobile phone companies were far from optimizing the return on their customer portfolio. To improve their returns, the companies started to become more selective in their targeting, and to offer longer-term contracts.

If the corporate objectives relate to profit maximization, as they often do in more mature markets, the appropriate strategy is to target customers that are likely to have high lifetime value. The way to do this is

> The appropriate strategy is to target customers with high lifetime value.

to identify the drivers of customer equity as described in Chapter 7 and then target customers who appear to have those characteristics. The decision process described in Chapter 7 is based on those profitability drivers.

There is an alternative method of defining customer acquisition targets that can be used where the company has a large number of customers, and this is to profile the most profitable customers or segments and then seek out more customers with that profile.

> **Note**
>
> Look up the strategic objectives of your company, if you don't already know them, and see what they indicate about what your customer acquisition policy should be.
>
> If there is no sales strategy or customer acquisition/retention strategy in place, this should now be done.

Using word of mouth to target customers

Word of mouth (also called advocacy or referrals) is an important way in which customers can be attracted to a company. Research has shown that word of mouth carries far greater credibility with potential customers than any of the marketing or sales efforts that the supplier can make. After all, who is the customer more likely to believe: the salesperson, who is paid to extol the virtues of the company's product and who probably receives commission on closing the deal; or the existing customer, who raves about the product or service from genuine experience and who is not being paid to sell it?

The value of word of mouth was discussed in Chapter 8, but the most important aspect for selective customer targeting is to remember that 'birds of a feather flock together'. In other words, customers tend to know people who have a similar profile to themselves. In the language of segmentation (Chapter 12), people make friends with others who share similar demographics, attitudes, and behaviours. So, people tend to make friends with other people of a similar age and income group, who share their values, and – because friends carry out activities together – tend to share similar behaviour patterns. This also holds true online, where people visit chat rooms that reflect their particular interests.

The same pattern of word of mouth being passed between similar customers is true in business-to-business markets, where buyers tend to know other buyers in their industry through trade fairs and will pass on recommendations to companies that are similar to their own or who have similar problems.

Although it is widely understood that people recommend to other customers that are similar to themselves, this essential fact is rarely used by companies to positively generate useful word of mouth. Many of the customer revenue and cost drivers (see Chapter 7) are related to the customer's income (or size in business-to-business markets), propensity to buy, and buying behaviours. Thus, a customer that a company acquires through word of mouth is likely to have a similar lifetime value to the customer who generated the word of mouth. The implication for the strategic management of customer acquisition is that the company should aim to generate recommendations from profitable customers.

Because customers are likely to recommend to potential customers with similar lifetime value, the company should positively aim to generate referrals from its most profitable customers or segments.

How to develop customer acquisition criteria

The purpose of customer acquisition criteria is to focus the efforts of the sales force or other sales channels on to the customers or segments that the company most wants to acquire. What is needed is a straightforward statement of customer acquisition criteria that will enable the targeting of sales offers on to the more attractive customers.

> The purpose of customer acquisition criteria is to focus the efforts of the sales force or other sales channels on to the customers or segments that the company most wants to acquire.

Customer acquisition criteria take the form of a small number of clear criteria about the desired characteristics of a target customer or segment. As discussed above, these criteria should be designed so as to deliver the strategic objectives of the organization. The criteria may also include attributes that the customer or segment should *not* have. Table 13.1 illustrates some customer acquisition criteria.

Table 13.1 Customer acquisition criteria for a business-to-business supplier

	Criterion	Score				
1	Size: Minimum revenues with us of $5m per annum within 3 years	1	2	3	4	5
2	Geography: US head office, but with interests in UK and/or Germany preferred	1	2	3	4	5
3	Brand profile: Preferably in top 3 in their market	1	2	3	4	5
4	Activities: Potential to buy from 2 or more of our product range	1	2	3	4	5
5	Requirements: Would *not* require servicing in Middle or Far East.	1	2	3	4	5

As the right-hand column of Table 13.1 illustrates, a simple scoring system can be used to apply the acquisition criteria and prioritize the customers that the sales force might contact.

For business-to-consumer situations, or where there are large numbers of customers, the customer database or CRM system can be used to profile the most attractive customers based on their customer equity or their overall contribution to the customer portfolio, as discussed in Chapter 10. Customers or segments that most closely approximate to this profile can be targeted. Figure 13.1 illustrates a comparison between an existing, very attractive, customer A and two potential customers B and C. Potential customer B is much closer in profile to A and would therefore be preferred as an acquisition target.

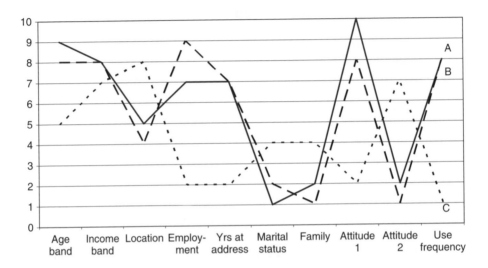

Figure 13.1 Identifying targets through profile comparison

This profiling can be implemented through both outbound and inbound channels. For outbound calling from a call centre, potential customers who have a profile like B's can be initially identified through commercial databases and then qualified by the outbound call centre operatives using questions designed to confirm the profile. For inbound calling or for website design, the call centre operatives or website can ask customers a few key questions that will determine their profile. This allows fast decisions to be made about whether to proceed with a potential customer or whether to disengage. The profiling approach is far more efficient and cost-effective than traditional 'broad brush' methods of customer acquisition.

Note

Consult with your IT or CRM team to see whether it is possible to profile attractive customers, and what tools they use to 'filter out' less attractive prospects.

How to plan customer acquisition

Once the target customers or segments have been identified, the next stage is to gather some essential facts about the customers so that the salesperson or call centre operator knows how to approach the customer and a value proposition can be developed (see Chapter 15).

The acquisition plan should answer some vital questions, as set out in Tables 13.2 and 13.3. Table 13.2 sets out the framework for an acquisition plan in a business-to-business context, where a major account or business segment is targeted. Table 13.3 sets out the equivalent framework for an acquisition plan in a business-to-consumer context.

Table 13.2 Questions that should be addressed by the acquisition plan (business-to-business)

Business-to-business	Where to get this information
What are the potential customer's strategic objectives?	Company report and accounts, especially the Chairman's statement; company website.
What are the key facts about this potential customer's marketplace and market position? What do its customers want?	STEEP analysis (see Chapter 6); market research reports; stockbroker reports.
What opportunities and threats does this potential customer face?	STEEP analysis (see Chapter 6).
What is this potential customer looking for, in a supplier?	Service level agreements or other supplier measurements that the potential customer uses; also, ask non-competing suppliers to this customer.
What competition would we encounter in supplying to this customer?	Porter's Five Forces analysis (see Chapter 6).
Who makes the decisions in this potential customer, and what is the process?	Difficult to establish, but ask the company itself for information and ask non-competing suppliers to this customer.
What is the buying style of this potential customer and its culture?	Difficult to establish, but ask the company itself for information and ask non-competing suppliers to this customer; read its public statements; interview former employees, if possible.

In a business-to-consumer situation, the likely targets will be a customer segment or a larger number of customers that have been profiled as discussed above. However, there are some parallels with the kinds of questions that are relevant to the business-to-business context.

Table 13.3 Questions that should be addressed by the acquisition plan (business-to-consumer)

Business-to-consumer	Where to get this information
What are these potential customers trying to achieve? What do they want/aspire to?	Market research reports; chat rooms; focus groups; publications and programmes targeting this group.
What are the key facts about this potential segment?	Market research reports; chat rooms; focus groups; publications and programmes targeting this group.
What issues do these potential customers face? What obstacles exist for them that would prevent them achieving their objectives?	Market research reports; chat rooms; focus groups; publications and programmes targeting this group.
What are these potential customers looking for in a supplier?	Market research reports; chat rooms; focus groups; also, ask non-competing suppliers to this customer.
What competition would we encounter in supplying to these customers?	Porter's Five Forces analysis (see Chapter 6).
Who makes the buying decision, and who influences it? Where do these customers get their information from?	Difficult to establish, but examine the way existing suppliers to this customer group target their advertising and promotions.
How and where do these potential customers like to buy?	Difficult to establish, but examine the way existing suppliers to this customer group target their advertising and promotions and examine the channels suggested in chat rooms.

Whether the targeted acquisition takes place in a business-to-business or business-to-consumer context, it is still important that the costs of acquisition do not outweigh the value that the company expects to secure from its relationship with this customer or segment.

How to balance the costs and benefits of customer acquisition

Returning to the theme of this chapter, which is that 'not all customers are good customers', it is worth noting that the costs of acquiring a customer can be greater than the expected profit. It is important to understand whether this is the case. Chapter 2 discussed the use of customer profitability analysis in calculating the payback period of a customer (in other words, the number of years that the customer would have to be retained before creating value for the company). Now, this issue will be reconsidered in the context of creating customer equity from the customer portfolio.

The strategic decision that needs to be made is the amount that the firm is prepared to invest in customer acquisition. If too little is spent on acquiring new customers, corporate profits will suffer in future years. However, if too much is spent on acquiring new customers, current year performance will be depressed because the costs of investing in customer acquisition are incurred in the current year whereas the benefits may not accrue until future years.

> The amount the firm is prepared to invest in customer acquisition is an important strategic decision: too high, and current profits suffer; too low, and future profits shrink.

Costs of customer acquisition

All customer acquisition activities should be considered in terms of how much value they create. However, as discussed in Chapter 2, it may take more than a year for a customer to create value net of acquisition costs, because the acquisition costs are so high. This problem is encountered in many business-to-business contexts, where formal tendering processes can cost millions of pounds. The same problem is found in business-to-consumer markets where complex products are sold, such as pension schemes. The acquisition costs for customers buying pension and life insurance products are typically very high, because a lot of time is spent in expensive face-to-face contact with the customer. The costs of sending a field salesperson out for several visits, plus the costs of the associated paperwork, need to be taken into account.

> All customer acquisition activities should be considered in terms of how much value they create.

In addition to the costs of acquiring that one customer, there are the costs associated with all the failed attempts to acquire customers in that segment or of that type. Thus, a basic approach to calculating the costs of customer acquisition would look simply at the specific costs of acquiring that customer. However, a more realistic approach that should be used in planning to optimize the returns from the customer portfolio is to consider conversion rates and customer payback.

Conversion rates and customer payback

The concept of conversion rates is associated with the notion of a pipeline of potential customers who have been contacted in some way but are not yet actual customers. Table 13.4 sets out two conversion rate calculations for a customer

Table 13.4 Calculating conversion rates

SEGMENT A: Call centre and field sales		Conversion rate
1.	No of outbound calls	100	
2.	Appointments set up	5	
3.	No of new customers secured	1	
			1/100 or 1%
4.	Cost of 100 calls	£1000	
5.	Cost of 5 appointments	£250	
6.	Per-customer paperwork and set-up costs	£40	
	Total costs	**£1290**	
	Costs per customer acquired	£1290/1 or **£1290**	
	SEGMENT B: Mailshot		
a.	No of letters mailed	30 000	
b.	No of enquiries generated	600	
c.	No of orders obtained	60	60/30 000 or 0.02%
d.	Cost of mailshot	£15 000	
e.	Cost of following up on enquiries	£600	
	Total costs	£15 600	
	Costs per customer acquired	£15 600/60 or **£260**	

acquisition campaign. The first campaign is aimed at Segment A and uses a combination of outbound call centre and field sales in the acquisition campaign. The second campaign is aimed at Segment B and uses a mailshot urging customers to call in to the company's call centre.

The figures in Table 13.4 are based on reasonably optimistic views of likely conversion rates and customer acquisition costs, which illustrate how expensive the process of customer acquisition can be. The cost of a campaign in Segment A is £1290 and in Segment B is £15 600. The conversion rate in the case of the Segment A campaign is 1% and for the Segment B campaign is 0.02%. On the face of it, this makes the Segment A campaign more successful although, in fact, the campaign in Segment B has attracted more customers at a much lower per-customer acquisition cost.

In addition to understanding the likely impact of these two campaigns on customer equity, managers need to think about customer payback periods. If customers in Segment A tend to generate annual profits of £240 and customers in Segment B tend to generate annual profits of £60, the payback periods are calculated as shown in Table 13.5.

Therefore, it takes more than five years before each customer in Segment A becomes profitable, and it takes over four years before a Segment B customer

Table 13.5 Customer payback calculation for segments A and B

	Segment A	Segment B
Customer acquisition cost	£1290	£260
Annual profit per typical customer in this segment	£240	£60
Monthly profit per customer	£240/12 = £20	£60/12 = £5
No of months before customer acquisition costs are covered	£1290/20 = 64.5	£260/5 = 52
No of years before customer becomes profitable	5.4	4.3

becomes profitable. If the company runs each campaign once a year, it will have run four campaigns in each segment and spent a total of £67 560 before it sees any return at all from its investment!

The calculations of customer payback in Table 13.5 assume that each of the customers acquired through these campaigns is retained long enough to become profitable. In the real world, this is not the case, and some of the customers acquired during the campaign would leave during the intervening four or five years before they became profitable. This would reduce the effective numbers of customers acquired and, therefore, increase the effective cost of acquisition of the remaining customers. This would mean that their payback period was lengthened.

Selective customer retention

Chapter 7 discussed the importance of customer retention in determining customer equity. Similarly, when making strategic decisions about how to maximize customer equity, managers need to take customer retention into account. However, customer retention in this context is not simply about customers deciding to leave. A customer's decision to leave is, after all, often influenced by their experiences with the supplier and the level of service the customer receives.

However, from the perspective that 'not every customer is a good customer', the retention issue should be considered as a strategic decision about which customers a company wants to retain. This translates into decisions about how much to invest in retaining a customer while not over-investing, which could lead to customer equity destruction.

> The customer retention issue should be considered as a strategic decision about which customers a company wants to retain to maximize customer equity.

Conditions in which customer retention pays off

For some years now, researchers have been showing that companies with higher customer retention tend to perform better, financially. This is true where i) the costs of customer acquisition are higher than the costs of retention; and ii) the customers that are retained have a positive customer lifetime value.

If the per-customer costs of customer acquisition are higher than the per-customer costs of customer retention, it pays the company to invest more in customer retention than in customer acquisition. To make decisions about the balance between customer acquisition and customer retention, companies need to understand the actual costs they incur, and also factor in the likely effect that changing the customer retention expenditure would have on the customer retention rate.

How to calculate the payoff to increasing customer service

The calculation of customer acquisition costs was explained earlier in this chapter. The costs of customer retention are effectively the costs to serve, and identifying these costs is explained in Chapter 3. Therefore, retention spending can include the development of loyalty schemes or offering improved service levels. Price discounts as part of a loyalty programme might be treated as increasing costs to serve or as reducing revenues, depending on the precise discount type (this point is discussed in Chapter 3).

When considering how to maximize customer equity, managers should carry out some simple calculations about the likely effect of increasing and decreasing service levels on the customer portfolio. An example of this kind of calculation is shown in Table 13.6.

Table 13.6 shows a notional calculation of the way that retention rates and customer equity might change, if spending on retention is altered. The first section of the table illustrates the current situation with two segments, A and B. Segment A has a high retention rate (85%) and a high customer lifetime value (£1300 per customer), but relatively few customers. Segment B has many more customers, although a lower retention rate and lower customer lifetime value. The table shows what would happen if costs to serve were doubled and what would happen if they were halved.

The table assumes that doubling the costs to serve (that is, increasing service levels to customers) will increase the retention rate. It increases only slightly in segment A, where there was already a high service level, and increases rather more in segment B. However, the increased costs to serve reduce the lifetime value of each customer. Overall, customer equity falls in both segments. Thus, increasing customer retention spending in either segment would be a poor strategic decision for this company.

In the second scenario, the company models the impact of reducing its spend on customer retention by reducing the costs to serve. The results are set out in the

Table 13.6 Calculating how much to spend on customer retention

	Segment A	Segment B
No of customers in segment	500	2000
Current retention rate	85%	70%
Customer lifetime value per customer	£1300	£650
Current p.a. cost to serve, per customer	£250	£80
Total current expenditure on costs to serve	£125 000	£160 000
Customer equity at end of period[1]	£552 500	£910 000
Effect of doubling costs to serve		
New retention rate	88%	75%
New lifetime value per customer[2]	£1050	£570
Customer equity at end of period	£462 000	£855 000
Effect of halving costs to serve		
New retention rate	80%	60%
New lifetime value per customer[3]	£1425	£690
Customer equity at end of period	£570 000	£828 000

[1] Based on number of customers retained multiplied by customer lifetime value.
[2] Customer lifetime value reduced because costs to serve increase.
[3] Customer lifetime value increased by half the costs to serve.

lower part of Table 13.6. This has the effect of increasing customer lifetime value, but reducing retention. The overall result for segment A is better than in the current situation. The customer equity for this segment increases from £552 500 to £570 000, suggesting that the segment might be over-serviced at the current spending level.

For segment B, however, the effect of reducing customer service levels by spending less on costs to serve is very different. Customer retention rates fall considerably, and customer equity is lower than in the current situation. So, it seems that the current expenditure on service to segment B customers is optimal at current levels.

It should be noted that the example given in Table 13.6 is simplified. For example, it assumes that customer lifetime value is not affected by the changes in customer service except by the increase or reduction in costs to serve. In reality, it might be the case that customers receiving better service might buy more, which would tend to offset the increase in service costs. Moreover, the effect on customer retention rates of increasing or reducing service levels may not be known for certain. However, the basic principle is that managers should try to calculate whether the current spend on customer retention is optimal and represents the best value for their retention investment.

The fundamental idea is that companies should not only have specific target customers in mind to acquire, but should also think about which customers they want to retain, and consider the optimal level of spending on customer retention.

How to tell if your customers are thinking of defecting

If a company is to take a strategic view about which customers to keep, it also needs to monitor the customers who might be thinking of leaving. Most managers believe that they receive little or no warning of a customer defection, but this need not be the case. The customers who may leave

> A company taking a strategic view about which customers to keep, also needs to monitor the customers who might be thinking of leaving.

can often – although not always – be identified, and there are positive measures that managers can take that alert them to a potential customer defection in time to do something about it. Chapter 11 discussed the risk of customer defection in detail: this section summarizes the sources of information about customers who might leave and suggests some positive actions that managers can take to monitor and manage the danger of defection.

Information about the possibility that customers may leave can be obtained from three sources:

- relationship quality metrics;
- major changes in customer circumstances;
- changed behaviour patterns.

Each of these important sources of information about potential customer defections will now be briefly considered.

Relationship quality metrics

Metrics that measure the quality of a relationship are increasingly used in business-to-business markets. The reason for this is that standard performance metrics, such as delivery performance, quality standards, etc., often seem to bear little relationship to customer retention. It is all too com-

> It is all too common for a supplier to deliver perfectly satisfactory performance based on traditional measures and yet find itself out on its ear at contract renewal time.

mon for a supplier to deliver perfectly satisfactory performance based on traditional measures and yet find itself out on its ear at contract renewal time. Even more frustrating is when suppliers feel sure that their products or services are better quality and/or cheaper than the products or services of the supplier who won the contract.

For this reason, suppliers in both business-to-business and business-to-consumer markets increasingly measure 'soft' relationship factors alongside 'hard' delivery and quality performance measures. There are a number of 'soft' measures of relationship quality. The precise circumstances of the relationship will determine which measures are selected.

Measures of relationship quality

- Customer satisfaction;
- share of spend;
- reliability and trust;
- communication;
- responsiveness and flexibility;
- value creation.

This is not a comprehensive list of relationship quality measures, but it does illustrate some of the factors that customers find important. For example, share of spend should be measured over time. If it starts to decline, this is a lead indicator of customer defection because it suggests that the customer is starting to switch its business to another supplier.

Measures such as reliability, trust, and communication are also important indicators of relationship quality. These can be jeopardized by personnel changes at either the supplier or the customer.

An ability to demonstrate their role in creating value gives a supplier an unassailable advantage in competitive situations. How this can be done is the subject of Chapters 14 and 15 on pricing and value propositions respectively.

Major changes in customer circumstances

Sometimes, customers are lost for reasons that have nothing to do with the performance of the supplier but simply because a change in the customer's circumstances means that the customer no longer needs the supplier's product or service, or is unable or unwilling to buy it. An example of this in business-to-consumer markets is mothers ceasing to buy nappies and baby products as their children grow up. In business-to-business markets, a common cause of sudden cessation of purchase is where a customer firm gets taken over. In a merger or acquisition situation, there is usually a review of suppliers of raw materials and of professional and business services, and the resultant shake-up usually benefits the supplier to the acquiring company. Meanwhile, the supplier to the acquired business can find itself without a customer.

Major changes in customer circumstances may not be preventable, but they should at least be monitored and should never come as a complete surprise to the supplier. Thinking about the end of a relationship lifecycle might suggest ideas for

> Thinking about the end of a relationship lifecycle might suggest ideas for new products or services that could extend the relationship duration.

new products or services that could extend the relationship (for example, the development of nappies and swimming pants for toddlers has extended the time for which children wear nappies). It might also suggest a re-think about the balance between customer acquisition and customer retention spending; if a number of customers are likely to be lost during the coming year, the firm will need to increase its spend on new customer acquisition to compensate for the loss of some existing customers.

> **Note**
>
> Talk to your Marketing/Customer Services/IT teams to see what capability the organization has to identify when customer circumstances change.

Changed behaviour patterns

One of the most powerful but silent indicators of an underlying problem with the relationship is where the customer changes his or her behaviour patterns for the worse. Thus, a customer who starts to complain more, or takes longer to pay, or disputes more invoices, or misses a direct debit, or pays off a lower proportion of the amount outstanding, may be giving off signals that relate to silent dissatisfaction or an intention to move.

Monitoring of changes in customer behaviour patterns to look for negative changes in behaviour is becoming much more common in business-to-business firms, particularly those where the customer has frequent transactions, such as banks, insurance companies, retailers, and mobile phone service providers. Companies like these are increasingly using predictive algorithms to identify 'at risk' customers. Depending on whether the customer belongs to a key target segment or not, offers can then be made to try and retain the customer and reverse the deterioration in the relationship.

Noticing changed patterns of behaviour is more difficult in other consumer and business-to-business markets, where there may be fewer interactions with the customer and less frequent transactions. However, installing a few simple systems to track changes in behaviour over time and to measure the relationship quality metrics discussed above, can act as a useful advance warning system. In the case of strategic or key accounts, companies may well choose to initiate a formal review of relationship quality every few years, in which both sides take part. These reviews can provide eye-opening information about the state of the relationship and point up areas for improvement, possibly with both sides working in collaboration.

> For key accounts, companies may review relationship quality every few years, with both sides taking part.

Note

Talk to your IT team to see whether your company can identify when customer behaviour patterns change.

What to do about a defecting customer

Customer defection is not inevitable, and there is much that a company can do to reduce the risks. Some of these ideas are outlined in this section.

> **How to reduce the risk of customer defection**
>
> - Self-report on performance;
> - measure relationship quality as well as 'hard' performance factors;
> - target possible defectors with a relationship recovery team;
> - bring in a different account manager to try and mend the relationship;
> - demonstrate lower overall costs;
> - develop breakthrough value propositions;
> - get closer to the customer;
> - develop a plan for the relationship;
> - if a customer defection is inevitable, leave the door open.

The first idea to reduce the risk of customer defection is for the supplier to measure their own performance and report it to the customer, as opposed to waiting for the customer to notice either good or bad performance for themselves. If the performance is good, it is worthwhile bringing this to the customer's notice; too often, a good performance simply means that the customer does not notice. Surprisingly, it is also better to bring a poor performance to the attention of the customer, apologize if necessary, and demonstrate a plan to improve matters, rather than just hoping that the customer will not notice that performance has been poor. Customers receiving more information will tend to judge the supplier's performance as better than when they are kept in the dark.

We discussed the measurement of relationship quality factors earlier in this chapter. Poor relationship quality, and/or changes in customer behaviour that may signal an impending defection, can be tackled directly by removing the relationship from the hands of the current account manager (who may be part of the problem) and

> Poor relationship quality can be tackled by removing the relationship from the hands of the current account manager (who may be part of the problem) and passing it over to a relationship recovery team.

passing it over to a relationship recovery team tasked to analyse the problem and develop a solution. Bringing in a new account manager can sometimes rectify matters.

One small business-to-business finance company used their managing director to do this: when a customer terminated a contract unexpectedly, the company invited representatives to have lunch with the MD. A frank discussion often ensued, which was of great value to the MD and also resulted in restoration of the relationship in about one-third of cases. Of course, a monitoring system that flags up potential problems is better than any amount of soft soap once the customer has decided to leave.

There are also very effective methods relating to lower costs or overall value creation that will be discussed in Chapters 14 and 15. The closer the relationship with the customer, the better the relationship and the earlier problems can be recognized. Developing plans for key accounts and for segments is an essential element of good practice in customer management (see the 'Where to find out more' section at the end of this chapter for more information about key account planning).

Finally, even if the customer defection becomes inevitable, this may not be the end of the relationship. Good practice in customer management is always to leave the door open so that the customer feels comfortable to return. This means that there must be positively no recriminations, some words of thanks recognizing the business that the customer has given the supplier in previous years, and some on-going but low-pressure contact in the future to keep the customer abreast of new developments at the supplier. This signals to the customer that they would be welcome if they were to choose to return.

How to get rid of a customer

The final topic considered in this chapter is the ultimate strategic decision in customer equity maximization, which is the decision to 'fire' a customer. Managers working their way through the analysis set out in the first and second sections of this book are bound to find instances in their current customer base of customers that they simply should not have. Reasons for getting rid of a customer may include negative customer lifetime value, zero or negative relational benefits, or simply a desire to move into other segments or markets. This section examines how to get rid of unwanted customers without damaging the company's reputation or market standing.

The first piece of advice for any organization contemplating sacking some of its customers is: DON'T. Wholesale sacking of unattractive customers might be very damaging to the supplier, both in terms of the impact it may have on the cost to serve other customers, and in the potentially negative impact on its market reputation. There are many strategies that can be implemented that might make an unattractive customer into a worthwhile one.

The first piece of advice for any organization contemplating sacking some of its customers is: DON'T. Many strategies can be implemented that change an unattractive customer into a worthwhile one.

The first step in understanding what these strategies are, is to analyse the revenue and cost drivers for these highly unattractive customers (see Chapter 7). This enables an understanding of what it is about these customers that is causing the low or negative customer lifetime value. This, in itself, may suggest strategies that can improve the situation.

Next, the relational value of these customers should be considered (see Chapter 8 for information on relational value). It is likely that there is no current relational value. It is even possible that the relational value of these customers is negative, because the customers themselves have a poor reputation in the marketplace or because they generate negative word of mouth. This second stage of the analysis may suggest strategies that managers can use to limit the damage of negative word of mouth.

The third stage of the analysis is to consider positive strategies to manage these less profitable customers. These strategies were discussed in greater detail in Chapter 9 but are recapitulated in the following box.

Strategies for dealing with unattractive/unprofitable customers

- Increase prices;
- price bundling;
- switch to cheaper channels;
- reduce delivery costs;
- pass customer to a distributor/refuse to deal direct;
- withdraw from the relationship.

It is far, far better to persuade less attractive customers to change their behaviour so that they become more attractive to retain, than it is to fire them. For this reason, price increases or price bundling are great strategies if the regulatory environment allows for this. The introduction

> It is far, far better to persuade customers to change their behaviour so that they become more attractive to retain, than it is to 'fire' them.

of service-based segmentation, discussed in Chapter 12, offers an opportunity to develop service packages or 'bundles' that can be offered to less attractive customers. If the previous goods or services have been withdrawn so these customers are unable to buy them, they may decide to take up the new package (thus increasing their attractiveness through higher revenues), or they may decide to leave, thereby solving the problem.

Generally, companies can implement price increases faster than they can reduce costs to serve, which is the other way in which unattractive customers can be made attractive. Cost reduction strategies will be determined by the cost drivers that are making these customers so unattractive in the first place, but could include reducing or stopping visits by field salespeople, moving these customers to desk based or Internet based account management, imposing minimum order quantities, requiring them to collect products, switching them to direct debit payments or requiring payment in advance, closing down local offices that disproportionately service unattractive customers, or any of a whole host of other measures aimed at reducing their costs to serve.

Of course, just as with price increases or price bundling, a proportion of these unattractive customers may elect to leave for another supplier. If this happens, it is important that the supplier holds firm: after all, if the point of the exercise is to make customers attractive or lose them, there is no point making concessions.

The strategies of increasing prices and/or reducing service levels are, at least in part, passive strategies to get rid of customers. In other words, the offer to the customer is being unilaterally adjusted by the supplier with the understanding that some or all of the unattractive customers may choose to leave as a result. This leaves the final strategy to get rid of unattractive customers, which is to positively withdraw service from them. As discussed in Chapter 9, this needs careful handling. It might involve transferring some customers to third party suppliers, such as distributors, wholesalers, or resellers. If this is done carefully and marketed positively, it may be possible actually to increase the service to unattractive customers (because they are now in the care of local distributors) while removing them from the supplier's books.

The ultimate strategy is to withdraw service from the customer and simply to refuse to supply them at all. This is a dangerous and extreme strategy and should only be attempted if the customer remains profoundly unattractive even where all the other strategies have been implemented. This situation might arise where the customer's reputation is so bad that the supplier no longer wishes to be associated with them. So, if a customer has been engaged in criminal, disreputable, or unethical activity, ongoing association with them might be very damaging to the supplier's brand regardless of any profit the firm might generate from the relationship. In these circumstances, a rapid – and possibly very public – disengagement might be in order.

> The ultimate strategy is to refuse to supply customers. This is an extreme strategy that should only be attempted if the customer remains profoundly unattractive.

Another disengagement situation may arise where a company decides to withdraw from a particular market or service. This again needs careful handling, because decisions like these can cause customer distress and generate negative publicity. The advice of a good marketing or public relations agency can be useful when a firm chooses to withdraw from customer relationships.

Summary

Not all customers are good customers. Some customers turn out to have negative customer lifetime value; or they may have negative relational value because they have a bad market reputation themselves or because they spread negative word of mouth. For this reason, companies seeking to maximize customer equity should have strategies specifying the customers they want to acquire and the customers they want to retain.

Two key strategies that are involved in attracting and retaining customers are pricing and the creation of powerful value propositions. These two topics are the subject of the final two chapters of this book.

> **Note**
>
> If your company does not yet have a profile of its most attractive customers/customer targets, use the worksheet on the following pages to begin building the profile. It would be interesting to involve sales and marketing colleagues at this point, to see whether your views coincide.

Worksheet: customer profiling

Demographic factors:

Income/revenue

Size

Age/lifecycle stage

Profile/status, etc

Other: ....

Behavioural factors:

Types of product purchased

Channel/purchasing behaviour

Decision process

Other: ....

Attitudinal factors:

Attitude towards supplier

Ethical/CSR stance

Other: ....

Where to find out more

Ryals, L.J. and McDonald, M. (2008) *Key Account Plans: Powerful Plans for Profitable Customer Management*, Butterworth-Heinemann, Oxford. *A step-by-step guide to creating a comprehensive plan for the company's most powerful customers. Aimed at practising key account managers in business-to-business markets.*

McDonald, M. (2007) *Marketing Plans*, Butterworth-Heinemann, Oxford. *A best-selling book describing how to create strategic marketing plans segment by segment.*

The role of pricing in creating or destroying value

What's in this chapter

- How companies destroy value through poor pricing decisions
- Traditional approaches to new product or service pricing
- How to predict cannibalization
- Relationship and value-in-use pricing
- Total cost of ownership (TCO) and total cost of relationship (TCR)
- Risk-based pricing
- How to work out how much discount to give

Key concepts discussed in this chapter

Cannibalization	When a company launches a new product or service, the degree to which it attracts its own customers (who switch) rather than new customers.
Cost-plus	Pricing by calculating the costs to manufacture a product or deliver a service and then adding a margin on to the top.
Competitor pricing	Pricing relative to the competition. Tends to lead to 'me too' price changes.
Downward-sloping demand curve	Concept from economics, which says that higher prices result in lower sales volumes and progressively lower prices are associated with progressively higher sales volumes.

Economies of scale	The degree to which the per-item costs of production are lower when volumes are higher.
Learning curve effects	Also known as the 'Experience Curve' effect. The more times that people carry out an operation, the better (and faster) they tend to do it. Reduces the per-unit cost of production.
Penetration pricing	Setting the price for a new product relatively low in order to stimulate demand. Used where economies of scale and learning curve effects are strong.
Reducing skim	Beginning with a skimming price for a new product and reducing the price in steps over time so as to capture as many sales as possible. Assumes a downward-sloping demand curve.
Relationship pricing	Pricing with respect to the customer's overall relationship with the firm, rather than an individual transaction.
Risk-based pricing	Where the risk of a purchase is shared between the supplier and customer; also associated with relationship pricing.
Skimming pricing	Setting the price for a new product relatively high in order to yield higher per-unit profits. Used where economies of scale and learning curve effects are low, e.g., in customized products or luxury goods.
Target pricing	Pricing a new product according to a volume target, and therefore assuming in advance that the launch will be successful. The target price is likely to be lower than the penetration price, because it assumes considerable economies of scale.
Total cost of ownership	TCO. Transactional plus lifecycle cost. For example, the TCO of a car is the purchase price plus insurance, fuel, servicing, etc., minus the residual value.
Total cost of relationship	TCR. TCO plus the cost to the customer of managing the relationship with a supplier.

Key tools explained in this chapter

- Cannibalization radar chart: Charts the appeal of existing and new offers against the Critical Success Factors (CSFs) of a target segment for the new product. Where there is considerable overlap, high cannibalization should be expected. Where there is little overlap, low cannibalization should occur. The radar chart should also give some indication of the attractiveness of the product to the target segment.

- Features/needs/benefits: An approach to selling a new product that links particular features of the product to the customers' needs and particularly to the benefits they will get. Useful as a preliminary guide to value-in-use.
- Diffusion of Innovation: Describes how innovations 'diffuse' through a market, from Innovators and Early Adopters through to Laggards. Suggests pricing and sales messages at each stage.
- Discount payoff calculator: Demonstrates how to calculate whether giving a discount is likely to have a positive or negative overall effect on firm profitability, and how much additional sales volume is needed to 'break even' on the discount.

Two-minute chapter summary

In practice, most businesses price goods and services according to how much they cost to make and deliver, rather than according to the value that customers think they are getting. Pricing for ongoing products or services might be based on cost-plus, where the 'plus' is the profit margin. The size of the profit margin is likely to be affected by the prices of competitors, where these are known, and so most pricing methods involve some form of competitive pricing.

For new products or services, the pricing could either be skimming or penetration. Skimming involves setting a higher initial price but accepting that volumes will therefore be lower; skimming pricing might be adopted where there is low competition, and/or low economies of scale or learning curve effects. Penetration involves setting a lower initial price, which is appropriate where there are economies of scale, learning curve effects, high competition, or where it would be useful to establish an installed base.

Adopting either skimming or penetration means that some value will be lost. In skimming pricing, value is lost because the downward-sloping demand curve indicates there are people who would buy the product if the price were lower. In penetration pricing, value is lost because there are some people who would have paid more for the product. Thus, an approach called 'reducing skim' may be used, where the price of the product is reduced stepwise over a period of time. The reducing skim method is widely used for technology products.

A completely different approach to pricing is based on value-in-use. Here, the price reflects the value the customer perceives he or she gets from the product or service. This may be considerably higher than the cost-plus approach. Moreover, price affects perception of quality.

Where the focus is on the profitable management of customers, value-in-use pricing is preferable but there is an alternative approach that looks at the overall relationship that the customer has with the company and prices accordingly.

Relationship pricing is a powerful tool for managing customer lifetime value. It is also very difficult for competitors to imitate. Relationship pricing rewards customers progressively for their relationship with the supplier, and so it is a very different approach from 'first time buyer' incentives that reward customers for switching. Relationship pricing is a disincentive to switching behaviour. To implement relationship pricing, companies need to have a good understanding of the lifetime value of their customers; otherwise, they have no basis on which they can make relationship pricing offers.

Another aspect of relationship pricing is to price according to the total cost of ownership (TCO) or total cost of relationship (TCR). TCO takes into account the servicing and maintenance costs of a product or service over its economic lifetime; thus, buying a more expensive product might be a better overall decision when the lifetime costs are considered. TCR looks at TCO but also considers the customer's costs of managing a relationship with a supplier; TCR pricing can justify a decision to use a supplier with higher TCO, if there are fewer delivery failures, complaints, etc. TCR, in particular, is associated with close business-to-business relationships.

Still in a business-to-business context, some companies have been experimenting with risk-based pricing. Risk-based pricing not only incorporates relationship pricing, but also involves some degree of risk sharing between both sides. Thus, a supplier may loan a customer some or all of the purchase price, or supply goods or services in exchange for a share in the customer's business.

Thus, there are a number of different strategic approaches to pricing that a company can take. Even the best strategic pricing plan, however, can be undone by a lax approach to tactical price discounting. Price discounting should only take place where the effects on customer lifetime value are understood.

How companies destroy value through poor pricing decisions

If there is one way in which companies persistently destroy value, it is through ill-thought-out or poorly-applied pricing. Far too many firms expend enormous amounts of effort on creating powerful value propositions for customers and then 'give them away' at inappropriately low prices, so that all the value created passes into the hands of the customer. Pricing in business-to-consumer markets is difficult enough, but it is even more difficult in business-to-business markets where there may be little information about the prices charged by competitors and where transactions may be far less frequent. Where there are long-term contractual relationships in place, a poor pricing decision can be crippling to the business, which may be locked into the delivery of a product or service at zero profit or even at a loss.

This chapter examines the theory and practice of pricing from a relationship management standpoint. Generally, the theory and practice of pricing has lagged behind the developments in customer asset management, so that managers have become more capable at developing and managing a customer portfolio while pricing was still done in an old-fashioned way. However, there are now signs of change in the way that companies price their products or services. New approaches to pricing are emerging based on the customer relationship rather than on pricing products or services for individual transactions.

To ensure that companies are not destroying value through poor pricing decisions, they need to adopt an appropriate pricing strategy and also have an appropriate policy towards tactical pricing, particularly discounting. This chapter begins with a look at traditional pricing processes, and then moves on to consider newer ways of thinking about pricing. In the final section, the practice of discounting is put under the microscope, revealing how overly generous discounting approaches can undermine a firm's profitability and its image.

Traditional approaches to new product or service pricing

When a new product or service is launched, managers are faced with a decision about how to price it. This is a particularly taxing decision if the product or service is new to the world; where the product is a 'me too' product, there are existing competitor products whose prices can be taken into consideration.

The core decision in pricing for new products has always been thought of as a strategic decision between higher initial product pricing ('skimming') and a lower initial price ('penetration'). A skimming strategy sets the price of the new product high, in the expectation that fewer units will be sold but at a very high margin over cost. Penetration pricing sets prices

> The core decision in pricing for new products has always been thought of as a strategic decision between higher initial product pricing ('skimming') and a lower initial price ('penetration').

low so that more units will be sold, relying on economies of scale to reduce costs sufficiently so that the company makes a profit on each product sale. Skimming pricing makes sense where there are few economies of scale (such as in specialist consulting firms or labour-intensive production of luxury goods) or where it is difficult for competitors to compete directly (such as patented products). Penetration pricing is thought of as a better option where there are potentially valuable economies of scale, so that it makes sense to price lower and obtain higher volumes, or where there is value in establishing your product or service as the industry benchmark or as the platform on to which you will sell additional products or services (Table 14.1).

Figure 14.1 illustrates skimming versus penetration options. Setting a skimming price will result in fewer unit sales. Setting a lower penetration price will lead to higher sales. Both these conclusions assume a downward-sloping demand curve.

Table 14.1 Skimming versus penetration pricing

High-price skimming where	Lower-price penetration where
Economies of scale are low	Economies of scale are high
Competitors would find it difficult to enter, or the product is protected by patents	Barriers to entry to competitors are low, or the product or service would be straightforward to copy
Offer is highly differentiated and first to the market	Firm has low differentiation or is later to the market
Learning curve effects are low, so there is little benefit to 'learning by doing'	Learning curve effects are strong, so the more often a product is produced or a service is performed, the more efficient it becomes
Company brand is strong and positively valued in the new situation	Company brand is weak or little-known
	There is a benefit to establishing a 'platform' or installed base of users of the new product or service, so that additional products or services can be sold on in the future

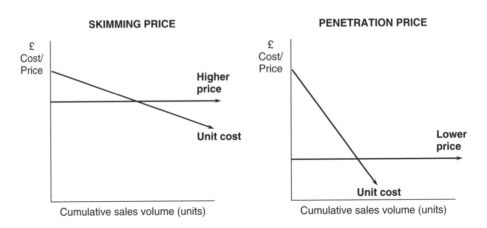

Figure 14.1 Skimming and penetration pricing and the effect on costs

The downward-sloping demand curve implies that higher prices will lead to lower unit sales because higher prices are less attractive to customers and fewer customers can afford to pay them. Lower prices are more affordable and are associated with a higher volume of sales.

Either strategy, however, leaves a large area of potential value untapped. Setting a skimming price leaves untapped people or firms who would buy if the price were lower. Setting a penetration price gives

> Setting prices too low can be a damaging strategy: many customers may have been prepared to pay much more.

away value because some people would have been prepared to pay more. Setting prices too low can be a damaging strategy in customer portfolio management: it can lead to widespread sales to customers who would have paid more, and sometimes much more.

To capture this lost value many companies use the combination pricing strategy known as 'reducing skim' illustrated in Figure 14.2, where the skimming price is gradually reduced over time towards the penetration price.

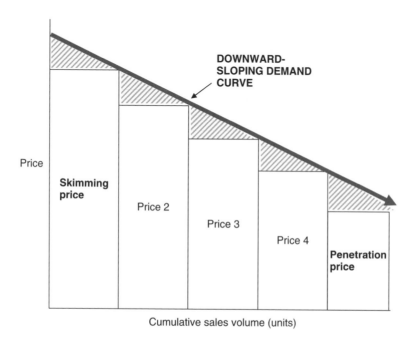

Figure 14.2   Reducing skim pricing for new products

With reducing skim pricing, the area of lost value is reduced to the small shaded areas shown in Figure 14.2. Reduced skim is a widely-used strategy over time, and is often seen in high-technology products such as wide-screen TVs, digital cameras, etc.

There are two drawbacks with reducing skim pricing. One is that, if customers discover that the reducing skim method is being used, many of them will defer their purchases until the price comes down. This is an entirely rational response by customers – why should they pay more than they have to? – but may lead the supplier to conclude, erroneously, that customers are highly price-sensitive. This in turn may lead to the company using price cuts and discounting as pricing mechanisms where it is not really necessary. This sets up a vicious spiral, where customers expect to be able to secure discounts and special prices and become unwilling to buy without a discount. Hey presto, the market has just become price-sensitive!

The second drawback with the reducing skim method is what happens where the firm does not supply the customer direct but uses wholesale or retail channels, value-added resellers, or managing agents. In these situations, there can be stock in the supply chain at higher prices. Care needs to be taken to handle the relationship with the channel appropriately, if the supplier is planning a series of price reductions over time as part of the reducing skim strategy.

> **Note**
>
> Think about the last two or three product launches. What pricing strategy did your company employ – skimming, penetration, or reducing skim? Was this an appropriate strategy given the market circumstances?

Customer portfolio considerations and new product/service pricing

Skimming and penetration pricing start from the viewpoint of the product or service, not from the customer perspective. When managing a customer portfolio, there are substantive considerations that should be taken into account. In a nutshell, these are:

- Will this new offer cannibalize existing products or services we sell to customers?
- How do we selectively acquire the customers we want, through this new offer?
- How should the price be set?

How to predict cannibalization

Cannibalization is where a new product or service simply replaces existing customer purchases, rather than attracting additional share from the competition. Cannibalization results in little or no impact on customer lifetime value. Launching a new product or service can be a costly business, and if all it does is to cannibalize existing sales, it could result in higher costs. These may or may not be offset by a higher price for the new offer.

In some cases, of course, cannibalization may be the purpose of introducing the new offer. It may be the case that the supplier actively wants customers to switch over, in which case the focus will be on migrating customers to the new product or service without losing them (increasing customer churn). Mostly, however, the intention with a new offer is to win business from the competition.

The key to understanding the likely impact of a new product introduction is to evaluate the extent to which it meets the customers' need differentially, compared to the existing product or service they already buy. To do this, managers can use the Critical Success Factor (CSF) analysis described in Chapter 10. Using a market research technique called conjoint analysis, the existing offer can be presented to customers together with new and potential offers. If the results are mapped as in Figure 14.3, the likelihood of cannibalization can be evaluated.

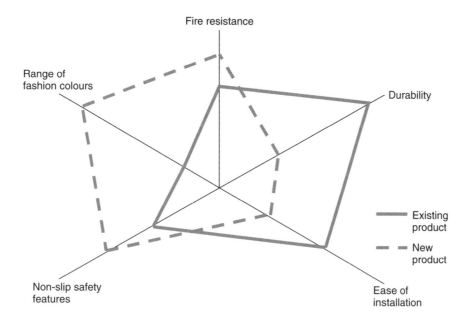

Figure 14.3   Cannibalization radar chart for retail design segment

Figure 14.3 shows a CSF cannibalization radar chart for a building products company. The company wants to understand the likely cannibalization of an existing industrial flooring product by its new product. A key target segment is retail designers. The map shows the CSFs for the new product, together with the degree to which the new product meets these needs. Customers say they need a product that has a more fashionable, brighter-coloured finish and is easy to install. Durability is less important, because the product is likely to be replaced regularly, but fire and safety considerations are extremely important. The existing product, which is a more complex and durable product but with fewer colour options, does not compete strongly with the new offer.

The radar chart can be re-drawn to show the overlap between the new offer and competing offers; here, a high degree of overlap is a good sign, because a new offer that delivers the customers' CSFs better than the competition is likely to win market share from them.

Note

Has your company – or a competitor – ever managed
to cannibalize itself? Think about why this happened,
using the radar chart technique.

How do we selectively acquire the customers we want, through this new offer?

Chapter 13 argued the case for selective customer acquisition as a vital element of a profitable customer portfolio management strategy. The pricing and marketing of new products and services is a key tool in successfully maximizing the value of customers.

The first step is to ensure that any new product or service is likely to appeal to the target customer group. This sounds a very obvious point, but all too many product launches fail thanks to poor market research. A proven selling technique is to focus on what benefits the customers would receive, and/or how the product addresses their need. Inexperienced salespeople often try to sell product features, rather than addressing customers' needs and selling them the benefits (Table 14.2).

Table 14.2 Sell benefits, not features

Product feature	Customer need	Benefits
Reduced fat	To lose weight	'Can aid in weight loss if used as part of a calorie-controlled diet'

The second step of successful and selective customer acquisition is to find out how to access the customers to be targeted, so they hear about the new offer. This is covered in Chapter 13 in the discussion of planning for customer acquisition.

The third step is to make the offer attractive to the customer, through a combination of pricing and other methods. To see how this might work, managers need to understand the following value equation:

Value to customer = Benefits customer gets minus sacrifices customer makes

Value is created by the features of the core product itself, plus the service 'wrapper' that the firm puts around that core product. Where physical product is concerned, the service wrapper might be fast delivery, technical advice, delivery tracking, etc. Where the core product is a service such as

> Value is created by the features of the core product itself, plus the service 'wrapper' that the firm puts around that core product.

business advice, the wrapper might be key account management, fast response to queries, self-reporting on performance, etc.

The sacrifices that customers make include the price that they pay, but may also be affected by their perception of risk. This is particularly the case where new products are concerned, or where the customer is contemplating switching to a new supplier. In either case, the customer has to take some risks. The product might not perform as well as claimed, or delivery might be slower than expected, or it might take time to learn how to use the product, or there might be psychological reasons why the customer is reluctant to buy the new product. One example of the latter is the old saying that 'you never get fired for buying IBM'; in other words, a tried and trusted existing supplier can be preferred because it is a known name, whereas a new supplier represents an unknown quantity and, hence, a risk.

From the customer's point of view risk can, to some extent, be reduced by reducing the price. This reduces the sacrifice that the customer has to make in order to acquire the product. However, there are limits to this approach. First, it is costly for the supplier (see the section 'Deciding on price discounts' later in this chapter). Second, too much price discounting will undermine the customer's perception of the supplier's quality and also of their trustworthiness. If the price can be reduced, this suggests that it is not worth as much as the supplier initially claimed; it also suggests that the supplier was trying to overcharge the customer with its original price. As a general rule, the customer will take the price that is being asked as an indicator of the quality of what is being offered.

> Too much price discounting will undermine the customer's perception of the supplier's quality and trustworthiness. It suggests that the supplier was trying to overcharge the customer with its original price.

> As a general rule, the customer will take the price that is being asked as an indicator of the quality of what is being offered.

Thus, the way that the offer is made to the customer can be at least as important as the price, if not more so. Pricing can be used in conjunction with other sales methods to launch a new product successfully.

This concept can be illustrated through the widely-known tool called the Diffusion of Innovation (Figure 14.4).

The Diffusion of Innovation suggests that, in every market, there are some customers who react positively to new products or services, and other customers who are more conservative and are slower to adopt new trends. The process of diffusion therefore moves through the market in stages, as shown in Figure 14.4. This diffusion effect has been demonstrated in a range of different marketplaces.

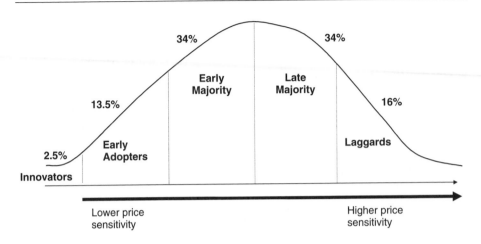

Figure 14.4 The Diffusion of Innovation

In his widely-quoted book, *Crossing the Chasm*, Geoffrey A. Moore discusses the diffusion of technology products, where the effect seems to be particularly noticeable. One of the interesting points he makes relates to pricing and how to sell to different types of customer at different points along the diffusion of innovation curve.

To the left of the curve, there is a very small group of innovators. Innovators may account for only 2.5% of the market, making them too small a group to target separately. Innovators have a very high propensity to buy new products or services, just because they are new, and are risk-takers in the sense that they will even buy products that are not yet reliable or are in the beta-test stage. Some innovators may be prepared to pay a very high price to be ahead of the crowd, although others may be price-sensitive.

Because innovators are such a small group, marketers and sales teams usually prefer to concentrate on the early adopters (13.5% of the market). The early adopters are trendsetters and they like new, unusual products or services. They also have a role

> Early adopters like new, unusual products or services. As opinion-formers, they are a key target market.

as opinion-formers, and so they are a key target market. They will often pay high prices for new products or services, and to be ahead of the crowd. Thus, the offer to early adopters is based on the newness and exclusivity of the product, often linking this to how it will support the brand or image (professional or personal) of the buyer.

The early majority account for over a third of the market and they are important to win over, if a new product or service is to be successful. The offer to the early majority might have to be a somewhat lower price (if the reducing skim process is being followed) but is also about keeping up with the opinion-formers. Therefore, endorsements may be sought from early adopters to entice the early majority to buy.

The late majority is another very substantial part of the market but tends to be more risk-averse and also more price-sensitive. If these customers are risk-averse, the supplier can reduce the perceived risk of buying a newish product or service through case studies and research, pointing to its widespread adoption in the market. The late majority need to be persuaded that they are 'behind the curve' and need to catch up, or that it is time to upgrade. Sometimes, to persuade the late majority to buy, the sales team may have to reduce the price.

Finally, there are the laggards. Although laggards represent 16% of the market, they are not an attractive target because they tend to be slow in deciding to buy and are also rather price-sensitive. Salespeople should be discouraged from trying to sell to laggards, because the way to their hearts is often through a deep discount.

In summary, the Diffusion of Innovation curve provides a further rationale for the use of a reducing skim product pricing strategy. This curve suggests that new products or services diffuse through the population in a pattern that follows willingness to adopt new products and innovative solutions. Early adopters are highly motivated to try new things and are relatively price-insensitive. This influential group are attracted by promotional campaigns stressing the newness of a product or service and prepared to pay higher prices (they have lower price sensitivity), although most customers will prefer to wait a little longer before committing themselves to purchase and may be attracted by lower prices (higher price sensitivity).

> **Note**
>
> Does your sales team know about, and use, the Diffusion of Innovation technique? If not, why not?

How should the price be set?

Traditionally, pricing decisions have been product-based; that is, companies have generally set prices for their products or services based on their costs of manufacturing the product or providing the service (cost-plus pricing), or relative to what competitors were charging (competitor pricing). Broadly, this meant that prices for the same product or service would be the same to all customers and adjustments to those prices (in the form of discounts or rebates) would tend to follow volume purchases of that specific product or service.

Research has suggested that the majority of pricing decisions for on-going products and services are based on some combination of cost-plus and competitor pricing. In other words, most companies calculate the cost of manufacture or delivery and then add on a profit percentage. The percentage they add on is influenced by what the competition might charge. Successful buyers know this, and will attempt to play their suppliers off against one another to reduce the price. The result is that suppliers suffer lower profit margins and, if they are not very careful in calculating their costs, may even end up supplying goods or services at a loss.

Some suppliers take a different, longer-term perspective. Based on the notion of the downward-sloping demand curve and the knowledge that they can lower their production costs considerably if they can achieve higher volumes[1], they set a price that may be *lower* than the current costs of production but should result in rapid acquisition of market share and economies of scale. This strategy, known as 'target pricing', can be successful in driving out competitors but does require considerable nerve and financial strength. If it goes wrong, it may well ruin the business.

However, there is a more general question that some companies have asked themselves, which is why price should have any set relationship with cost of manufacture. Why not price my product or service according to the customers' willingness to pay? This is an important consideration in service businesses, where the absence of a tangible product will lead customers to associate price with quality. So, for a hairdresser or management consultant, setting a low price might simply suggest to customers that the service is not particularly good. Another reason for firms to divorce price from cost is that service businesses are time-based and this makes them capacity-constrained. There are only so many hours in the day, and there is often a shortage of skilled people. So, the only way to increase profits is to increase prices.

> Why not price my product or service according to the customers' willingness to pay?

These kinds of thought processes have led to an increasing interest in customer-based pricing, where prices are influenced by the customers' overall relationship with the supplier, including their purchases of other goods and services. This change has a lot to do with the emergence of relationship marketing. Relationship marketing has as its emphasis the lifetime relationship that customers have with a company. Researchers in relationship marketing have demonstrated that loyal, retained customers can be considerably more profitable than new customers, in part because the cost of acquiring new customers (advertising, selling, etc.) is so high.

Relationship pricing

Rather than use methods such as the Diffusion of Innovation and reducing skim, adjusting prices over time to attract new groups of customers, it may be more effective for a firm to price according to the relationship it has with the customer. This approach of course depends on the absence of regulatory constraints on differential pricing. Three aspects of relationship pricing will be considered in this section: value-in-use pricing, pure relationship pricing, and risk-based pricing.

---

[1] Higher volumes will result in economies of scale and learning/experience curve effects, as discussed in Table 14.1.

Value-in-use pricing

Value-in-use pricing aims to identify the value that the customer obtains through use of the product or service, and to price accordingly. The value that customers get in use is, however, difficult to measure and tends to differ from customer to customer (or from segment to segment).

> Value-in-use pricing aims to identify the value that the customer obtains through use of the product or service, and to price accordingly.

Value-in-use pricing has become of greater interest to organizations over the past few years with the emergence of new research techniques that can help answer the question of how much customers would be prepared to pay. Wider use is being made of techniques such as conjoint analysis, which asks customers to 'trade off' product attributes. The degree to which customers are prepared to trade off one feature against another indicates their strength of preference. Other techniques include ethnographic (observation-based) research and semiotics (speech/text analysis) that reveal how customers use a product or how they describe it. The Repertory Grid technique asks customers to compare and contrast several products and helps elicit the underlying constructs that may affect choice.

These kinds of techniques may uncover not only the needs that customers know they have, but also may reveal hidden needs that explain why customers sometimes seem ready to pay unexpected prices (or why they sometimes will not pay prices that the supplier thinks are perfectly reasonable). They may also identify features of the product or service that customers do *not* value, allowing the supplier to tailor products or services more closely to customer requirements without necessarily increasing costs.

Value-in-use pricing is still, however, largely a transactional approach, focused on an individual sale rather than on a lifetime relationship with the customer. The growing importance of customer portfolio and customer asset management has led to a fresh approach to pricing. As evidence has emerged of the link between customer profitability and shareholder value, companies have begun to recognize that maximizing their price on an individual transaction might damage their long-term relationship with the customer. Thus, a shift from transactional to relationship pricing is occurring.

From transactional to relationship pricing

Traditional pricing is based on an underlying assumption that the provision of products or services is what drives profits. This is a largely transactional approach in which the price is more or less the same to each customer and each transaction with the customer is, by and large, treated as a separate event. Relationship pricing takes a rather different view. In relationship pricing, the company's relationship with the customer is viewed as the main driver of profits. Rather than pricing based on individual transactions, relationship pricing takes into account the entire portfolio of products or services purchased by that customer. Many different aspects of pricing (such as discounts, rebates, payment holidays, special offers on additional purchases) may be used. So, in a relationship pricing scheme, a customer buying a third or fourth product may be offered a rebate against the first or second product they bought.

A major advantage of relationship pricing is that it rewards customers for loyalty and for increasing the share of spend they place with a company. This is in stark contrast to product-based price discounting strategies, which encourage frequent switching and discriminate against loyalty.

> A major advantage of relationship pricing is that it rewards customers for loyalty and for increasing the share of spend they place with a company.

Relationship pricing helps initiate a virtuous circle. Because customers are rewarded for buying more products from a company they increase their share of spend with that company. Research has repeatedly shown that, the wider the range of products or services a customer buys, the more likely they are to remain loyal to that supplier. This is at least in part because it is more hassle to change suppliers of more than one product; it is also because a multiple-product supplier is more important to the buyer and a relationship is more likely to form.

Relationship pricing strategies also offer better protection against competition. As discussed above, there is an inertial effect that keeps customers with a multiple-product supplier for longer. In addition, the relationship pricing strategy is difficult for competitors to emulate unless they have an identical or better relationship with the customer. This is because the special offer, discount, etc. is not offered on the current purchase, but against previous purchases.

It is important to note that, to do relationship pricing successfully, companies need information systems that enable them to view the whole picture of their relationship with customers. Sometimes, the internal organization of the supplier firm makes this difficult. If a customer is supplied from several locations, it may be difficult to see the overall picture. Still worse, there may be an internal reluctance to share customer information because each business unit thinks it 'owns' the customer relationship.

Relationship pricing is an interesting technique where firms have customers buying a range of different products and where the frequency of transactions is reasonably high. Thus, it is a useful technique in retail financial services, for example. It is less useful in large-scale

> Relationship pricing is an interesting technique where customers hold a range of products and where the frequency of transactions is reasonably high.

business-to-business purchases such as defence, power plant, or large-scale software systems, where the customer might only place one order every decade.

In larger-scale purchases, price is less likely to be the main decider. Instead, the customer will probably be more concerned about total cost of ownership (TCO) and risk.

Total cost of ownership (TCO)

In many purchasing situations, there will be a distinction between the cost of the purchase itself (the 'transaction cost') and the cost of the consumables etc. that a product will require over its lifetime ('lifecycle cost'). Thus, a car or lorry has an initial purchase cost but will also require insurance, fuel, lubricants, servicing and spares, etc. over its life. The same is true of some services, such as software systems or databases that require periodic upgrades, deduplication, etc.

It is not uncommon for lifecycle costs to exceed the initial transaction cost. This is especially clear with products such as desktop printers, where the cost of purchase is very low but the cost of printer cartridges is high (up to 25% of the initial transaction cost). So, if a printer has a life of two years and needs four cartridges per year, the lifecycle costs will be twice as high as the initial transaction cost.

Understanding lifecycle costs opens up an opportunity for suppliers to manage negotiations over initial prices through discussion of the total cost of ownership (TCO). The total cost of ownership is the initial transaction cost, plus lifecycle costs, minus any residual value that the asset has at the end of its life (if the printer or car can be re-sold).

TCO = (Initial transaction cost + lifecycle costs) − residual value

A well-made quality product may have a much higher transaction cost, but a lower TCO because it requires less servicing and repair, and because it does not need replacing as frequently – it has a longer life. In this situation, it would be unnecessary to match a competitor's lower transaction price, because the TCO of the competitor's product is higher. TCO discussions are often preferable to straightforward pricing discussions that focus unduly on the initial transaction cost; in fact, both parties could benefit from a discussion about TCO. TCO-based negotiations will tend to favour the higher quality suppliers. They are less relevant where the product is a disposable one, because the life is so short that the transaction cost and the TCO are virtually identical. TCO has little relevance to one-off service episodes such as haircuts or plane flights, although the introduction of loyalty schemes such as air miles can reduce the total cost for the customer of doing business with a single airline.

Where both sides are contemplating a longer-term relationship, and where the supplier has a service level that is better than its competition, it may be worth negotiating not just on TCO but on the total cost of the relationship.

Total cost of relationship (TCR)

The total cost of the relationship is the TCO plus the cost to the customer of managing the relationship, from placing orders to sorting out complaints.

> TCR = (Initial transaction cost + lifecycle costs + lifetime relationship
>
> management costs) − residual value
>
> or
>
> TCR = TCO + lifetime relationship management costs

Calculating the TCR would involve estimating how much time and cost the customer would incur in placing orders (for initial product and for consumables), arranging servicing and maintenance, planned and unplanned downtime, processing paperwork, sorting out problems, and generally managing the relationship (time spent in meetings with the supplier, gathering and reviewing performance data, etc.).

The TCR approach favours more efficient suppliers, especially those that have better processes and better project management skills and a better tracking system that can identify time costs. The customer's costs of managing the relationship can be

> Effectively, with TCR, the supplier is reducing or transferring some of the customer's risk to itself.

surprisingly high, especially in complex projects where there are time and/or cost overruns. Effectively, by negotiating on TCR, the supplier is offering to reduce the customer's risk. If penalty clauses are involved, the supplier is actually transferring some of the customer's risk to itself. The issue of risk transfer or sharing is discussed in more detail in the next section on risk-based pricing.

TCR is likely to be of interest to more sophisticated buyers who are more aware of the costs of supplier management. It can be difficult to persuade a customer, particularly a new customer, that the supplier is more efficient than its competitors, and so evidence in the form of previous performance, other customer endorsements, or penalty payments/guarantees, may be needed. It is a pricing approach that could be of great interest to time-critical customers. If the TCR approach offers the customer the chance to streamline their own processes and thereby reduce their own costs, it could even be of interest to some low-cost customers. Generally, TCR would be implemented in closer relationships where there was an intent to work together over a period of time and to improve process efficiency.

As already discussed, TCR results in an implicit risk transfer from the customer to the supplier. The stage beyond TCR is risk-based pricing. Risk-based pricing *explicitly* transfers risk, or shares risk, between two collaborating supply chain partners.

Risk-based pricing

Risk-based pricing is a more unusual approach to pricing that is used almost exclusively in long-term partnering-type relationships. The idea of risk-based pricing is that risk as well as returns are explicitly transferred between the partners. This makes it different from TCR, where the supplier is shouldering some of the customer's risk unilaterally.

From the customer's point of view, the risks in a relationship with the supplier may include late delivery, poor performance, and excessive amounts of management time. There is also a risk that the product or service is not needed as much as had been thought, so that an expensive asset

> The customer's risks in a supplier relationship may include late delivery, poor performance, and excessive amounts of management time.

is underutilized. From the supplier's point of view, the main risks in its relationship with the customer are that the customer stops buying (short relationship lifetime followed by customer defection or migration, discussed in Chapter 11), or that the customer is late in paying or defaults altogether, plus the time involved in managing the relationship and sorting out problems.

Risk-based pricing may result in some unusual pricing strategies. One example is risk sharing, where a supplier may lend a customer the money to buy its products, or may lease products to its customers. Here, the supplier runs the risk that the customer will default on the payments. Because the customer takes immediate delivery of the products without having to pay up front, some of its financial risk is shared with the supplier. An even closer risk-sharing approach involves companies taking an equity stake in a customer business in exchange for supplying a business critical system that the customer could not afford to purchase for cash. This strategy is sometimes used by suppliers where the customer is a small start-up business that is cash-poor but has a promising future. The supplier takes on additional financial risk, but has the possibility of a large future return if the customer company performs well and the shares increase in value.

Other risk reduction strategies may include longer-term contracts so that the supplier can offer lower prices but is assured of sufficient business to make the relationship profitable; or variable pricing to reflect the risk of the customer.

Companies using risk-based pricing may work with the customer to try to reduce the risk. One obvious candidate for risk reduction is the amount of management time needed for the relationship, which is an issue for both sides. In addition, the supplier is taking on increased financial risk, so it may seek to mitigate this risk by working with the customer on improving market sensing or on strengthening the customer's own internal processes. Either or both of these actions would help to improve the customer's chances of success and, hence, the likelihood that the supplier's investment will eventually pay off. Instances of this can be found in business-to-business insurance, where the insurer provides risk mitigation consultancy to some of its customers. Although the customer may need less insurance if its risks were better managed, the overall financial risk to the insurer is reduced.

Deciding on price discounts

A discount is a price reduction agreed with a customer before the purchase is signed off. It may be given in exchange for some concession on the part of the customer, such as an agreement to buy in quantity, to pay early, or to pay in cash. This contrasts with a rebate, which is usually a retrospective arrangement related to the quantity that the customer buys.

The big question about discounting is not 'how much discount should we give' but 'why do it at all'. The performance of procurement people is often measured on how much they can get a supplier to reduce its list price or initial quote. Salespeople

> The big question about discounting is not 'how much discount should we give' but 'why do it at all'.

often collude in this process, because giving a discount is an easier and quicker way of winning an order than negotiating. In some industries this process results in a situation where the list price is a complete fiction. In one case, a supplier of automotive components told us that discounts of 80–90% off the list price were routine in his market. If so, why have a list price at all?

There is an intriguing asymmetry in the way that salespeople manage the discounting process. If salespeople win an order, this is always because of their superior selling skills. If they lose an order, it is never because they negotiated or sold badly. Instead, the loss of the order is blamed on the company failing to allow the salesperson to give sufficient discount!

Not surprisingly, sales managers are often under pressure from their salespeople to allow the latter to give discounts. To decide what to do about this, sales managers need to consider their overall pricing strategy. As discussed earlier in this chapter, there is a relationship between price and perceived quality, and reducing the price may affect that perception. There may also be an issue about whether the customer considers the supplier to be untrustworthy ('if they can afford to offer it cheaper, the initial price must have been a rip-off'). Finally, there is the consideration that, if the customer manages to secure a discount on one occasion, he or she is sure to keep on asking for a discount on all future occasions.

That said, discounting is a feature of business life. If a discount is to be given, the sales manager needs to answer the following two questions:

- How much discount should I give?
- What will my company get, in return?

How to work out how much discount to give

Figure 14.5 illustrates a fairly typical cost and margin structure for a manufacturing company. If this company is going to give a price discount to a major customer, the sales manager should calculate what happens to total profits when a discount is given and then work out how much additional volume the company would need to sell, in order to get the same total profit.

The manufacturing company shown in Figure 14.5 sells 1000 units at €10 each. The profit margin is 10%, and this means that it makes €1 profit per unit and total profits are €1000. Its cost of manufacture is €9.

If the company gives all its customers a 2% discount, the selling price per unit falls to €9.80 but, if all other things remain equal, the cost of manufacture stays at €9 per unit. Therefore, the profit per unit falls from €1 to €0.80. In other words, a 2% discount has caused a 20% fall in the profit margin.

To make the same €1000 total profit as before, the company needs to sell 1250 (€1000/€0.8) units. So, a 2% discount means that the company has to sell 25% more units just to maintain its previous level of total profit. If it gives a 5% discount, it will need to sell 2000 (€1000/€0.5) units, or double its previous sales, just to stand still. If it gives a 10% discount, it will wipe out all its profits. The discount payoff calculator shown in Table 14.3 shows how these figures were derived.

This example is only a rough calculation because there might be some economies of scale and learning curve effects that would reduce the cost of manufacture as volumes rose, so that the company would not need to sell quite as many additional units. However, it is a useful calculation for the salespeople to understand. The bottom line is that even a very modest discount will need to result in very substantial volume increases to make it worthwhile.

> The bottom line is that even a very modest discount will need to result in very substantial volume increases to make it worthwhile.

These kinds of calculations, which reflect some fairly typical cost and profit situations for Western companies, explain research findings showing that companies that allow their salespeople to give discounts generally perform less well than those that do not allow their salespeople to give discounts, and that pricing managers tend to set prices too low (see the 'Where to find out more' section at the end of this chapter).

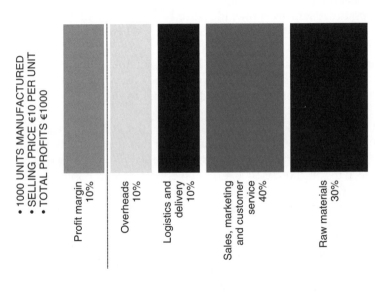

- 1000 UNITS MANUFACTURED
- SELLING PRICE €10 PER UNIT
- TOTAL PROFITS €1000

Profit margin
10%

Overheads
10%

Logistics and
delivery
10%

Sales, marketing
and customer
service
40%

Raw materials
30%

Figure 14.5 Overview of cost, profit margin, and sales

Table 14.3 Discount payoff calculator

		How calculated	Without discount	2% discount
A	No of units sold	As given	1000	1000
B	Selling price	As given	10	9.80
C	Costs of manufacture	$3 + 4 + 1 + 1 = 9$	9	9
D	Profit per unit	B − C	1.0	0.80
E	Profit margin	D/B	10%	8.2%
F	Total profits made	A × D	1000	800
G	**Units sold to make initial profit**	**F/D**	**1000**	**1250**

Another way of thinking about this is to consider the costs shown in Figure 14.5 and calculate what happens when sales rise by 10%, when raw material prices fall by 10%, and when prices rise by 10%. Assuming no other changes, the impact on total profits would be:

- Sales rise by 10%, total profits rise by 10%.
- Raw material prices fall by 10%, total profits rise by 30%.
- Prices rise by 10%, total profits rise by 100%.

Getting a positive return on a discount

If giving a discount becomes inevitable, the cardinal rule is always to ensure that as little as possible is given away and as much as possible is secured in return.

This is where the customer lifetime value calculation (Chapter 6) comes into its own. If a large customer is asking for a discount, the account manager should be calculating the additional volume that would be needed to maintain the customer lifetime value at the same level, and trying to build that into the contract[2].

Other things that could be negotiated in return for a discount might include a longer relationship lifetime or faster payments. Either or both of these can be factored into the customer lifetime value calculation and both of them would increase the

> In return for a discount, greater volumes, a longer relationship lifetime, or faster payments might be negotiated.

lifetime value of that customer. Note that accelerated payment terms would increase the value of the customer to the firm, although the simplified method of calculating

---

[2] Be careful about how this is communicated to the customer, if you do not want them to know how much profit you are making out of the relationship.

the discount rate shown in Chapter 6 might have to be modified to take account of the earlier receipt of the cash.

Sometimes, large customers request – or demand – an annual price reduction. This is quite a serious matter, because volumes need to rise year-on-year to compensate. To see what the impact would be, the account manager needs to factor the annual price reduction and associated volumes into the customer revenues going forward.

The customer lifetime value calculation can be used to show what the returns would be on a discount. If the discount is thought of as an investment in the relationship, and the effect on overall customer lifetime value is calculated, the relationship between the cost of the discount and the impact on customer lifetime value is the return on the discount. If the return on giving a discount is negative, the account manager or director has to make a strategic decision whether to refuse it or not. Deciding whether to say 'no' to a customer is tricky and will depend on the financial value of the customer, their possible relational value (Chapter 8), and how easy it would be for the customer to find an alternative supplier (the inverse of the risk of defection, which was discussed in Chapter 11).

There is also a decision to be made here about how open the supplier wants to be with the customer about the customer's profitability to them. Some suppliers have moved to open book arrangements with their customers in which they agree a reasonable figure for the profit that the supplier gets from the relationship. This is only ever done in close, long-term supplier/buyer relationships. It has the benefit that the customer gets transparency and knows that it is not being overcharged; the supplier gets some protection from unreasonable demands for price reductions or additional services on the part of the customer. Interestingly, the customer will also benefit from continuity of supply and the knowledge that the supplier will survive. Customers that have negotiated too strongly and driven their suppliers away or, in extreme cases, into bankruptcy, find that this behaviour often comes back to bite them. Replacement suppliers of comparable quality or reliability are not always easy to find, and cheaper suppliers in distant locations can stretch the supply chain and reduce the customer's ability to respond to changing market conditions. Some suppliers will even factor this in to their calculation of the total cost of relationship and point out to customers that finding a replacement source can be a costly exercise.

Summary

Traditional product-based pricing may not meet the needs of firms that are developing strategies for customer asset management, where the emphasis is on maximizing the value of that customer relationship throughout its lifetime. Companies wanting

> A customer discount should be thought of as an investment in the relationship, and should yield a positive net return.

to develop a relationship orientation should reevaluate their pricing strategies and consider moving to a relationship or risk-based pricing approach. Where discounts have to be given, the impact of these on customer lifetime value should be calculated. A customer discount should be thought of as an investment in the relationship that should yield a positive net return; if not, consideration should be given to refusing it.

Pricing discussions are some of the most difficult and fraught elements of customer asset management. Far better is the situation where the price is considered as a relatively small part of the overall negotiation, because the value that the supplier adds to the customer is so substantial that the former becomes an important or even integral part of the latter's business. In the final chapter, the notion of 'breakthrough' value propositions is discussed. Breakthrough value propositions are developed where the supplier creates an offering so powerful that it effectively inserts itself into the customer's value chain. In these relationships, negotiations about price take second place to discussions about quality, service, and value creation.

Note

Now review your company's discounting policy and see whether it makes economic sense. Use the worksheet on the following page to see whether discounting pays off, for your company.

Worksheet: calculating the impact of a discount

Calculation:

A	Total profits without discount	
B	No of units under discussion	
C	Proposed discount (%)	
D	Profit per unit before discount	A/B
E	Profit per unit after discount	(A − C)/B
F	Total profits after discount	B×E
G	No of units that would need to be sold to make initial profit	A/E

Where to find out more

Moore, G.A. (1999) *Crossing the Chasm: Marketing and Selling Technology Products to Mainstream Customers*, second edition, Capstone, Oxford. *Readable management classic discussing the application of the diffusion of innovation to selling technology products.*

Urbany, J.E. (2001) 'Are your prices too low?', *Harvard Business Review*, 79(9), pp. 26-27. *A short but intriguing thought piece arguing that there are psychological and historical reasons why managers set prices too low.*

15 Increasing customer equity using value propositions

What's in this chapter

- How to develop value propositions that will keep your customers loyal
- Essential information for developing value propositions
- Developing – and delivering – breakthrough value propositions
- Maintaining a competitive edge using VRIN
- Benefiting from collaboration[1]

Key concepts discussed in this chapter

Collaboration	Informal partnership between two companies. May be limited to a specific project or may be a wider collaboration. Usually involves some form of information exchange and a degree of openness.
Value chain	Series of end-to-end processes in the firm that create or support value.
Value proposition	A tailored offer to a customer or to a customer segment. The value proposition examines whether the customer is likely to buy from the supplier on this occasion. Value propositions may be developed using customer CSFs or value chain analysis.

[1] I am indebted to Neil Rackham for his detailed advice and the supporting materials that he provided for this chapter.

Key tools explained in this chapter

- Value proposition: Sets out the value that the supplier is offering to a particular customer or segment, defined as benefits minus costs and risks. The value proposition takes the customer's viewpoint as central. Therefore, a key question that the firm should ask is, 'is this value proposition compelling for this customer or segment?'. Not only must the value proposition clarify the benefits to the customer, but also those benefits must be ones that are sufficiently compelling that the customer will be prepared to pay for them. Understanding how attractive the value proposition actually is to the target customer or segment is an invaluable step in deciding whether to pursue an opportunity or not. Value propositions may be developed from an analysis of the customer's CSFs and the supplier's relative strengths. Careful analysis of the CSFs is needed, in order to identify points of competitive differentiation. They may also be developed by analysing the customer's value chain (this is particularly relevant in business-to-business markets).
- Value chains: Analyses the way in which companies transform raw materials and add value to them. Core value-adding processes such as manufacturing, marketing, and selling are shown along the lower part of the value chain, and support processes such as procurement and HR are shown along the upper part of the chain. Close analysis of the chain may reveal areas of customer strength or weakness, and the supplier can then tailor its offer accordingly by creating a specific value proposition.
- VRIN: Method of thinking about competitive edge through the mnemonic VRIN: Valuable; Rare; Imperfectly Imitable; and Non-substitutable. This approach was first set out by Barney in 1991 (see 'Where to find out more' at the end of this chapter). The better the product or service performs against each of the VRIN factors, the greater the competitive edge and the more difficult it is for the customer to find comparable alternative suppliers.

Two-minute chapter summary

This final chapter tackles the important topic of value propositions, the specific offers that companies make in order to try and attract and keep customers. For the profitable management of customers, these offers should be linked to the value of the customer (as discussed in Chapter 12). However, a really good value proposition has the potential to create extraordinary value for both sides. Where customers feel they are getting unusual value they are more likely to be loyal and more likely to become advocates.

Usually, a company will have several value propositions. These are unlikely to differ hugely from one another, but they will be slightly tailored to specific customers or segments.

The starting point for developing value propositions is to develop a good understanding of the needs of the target customer or segment using a Critical Success Factor (CSF) analysis (as described in Chapter 10). By examining the supplier's relative performance on the factors that are really critical in the customer's buying decision, opportunities can be identified that will create more value for customers.

For companies that want to develop a closer relationship with their customers, and have a capacity for flexibility and innovation, there is an opportunity to develop breakthrough value propositions. These are about identifying completely new ways to create value for customers. To develop breakthrough value propositions the supplier needs to insert itself into the customer's value chain. The value chain is a set of processes that take place that create value or support the creation of value.

Even after the value proposition has been developed, there remains the problem of maintaining the competitive edge. Here, a useful tool is VRIN, which stands for Valuable; Rare; Imperfectly Imitable; and Non-substitutable. Using the VRIN checklist regularly will help keep the value proposition up-to-date.

The final aspect of creating value for customers is to do so collaboratively with the customers themselves. Considerable evidence has mounted up in business-to-business research to show that both sides benefit from collaboration, and that the benefits are generally more equally shared than one might expect. Collaborative partnerships are associated with close, long-term relationships and can deliver major value creation to both suppliers and buyers.

How to develop and use profitable value propositions

Suppliers in almost all 21st century markets have many competitors and markets are more open than ever before. Therefore, it is more important than ever that suppliers understand why their customers choose them (or not) and that they offer attractive value propositions that enable them both to retain their customers *and* to realize the customer equity in the relationship.

Value propositions are a method for deciding the offers that companies make to their customers. Customers then weigh up these value offers and compare them to the price that the supplier is asking (pricing is discussed in Chapter 14). This enables the customer to make judgements about how expensive or not the offer is. It is important to recognize that 'expensive' or 'good value' is never an absolute judgement – it is a judgement that is made relative to the value that is offered by the firm, competing offers, and the price being asked by the firm and by its competitors. Customers may also take risk into account, asking themselves what the chances are that the supplier will actually deliver the promised value. So, another way to think of a customer reaction that a product or service is 'too expensive' is to recognize that the customer also means 'not enough value being offered for the price' or 'too risky'.

In summary, customers make decisions about whether to buy or not depending on the balance between benefits and impact, less costs and risks (Figure 15.1).

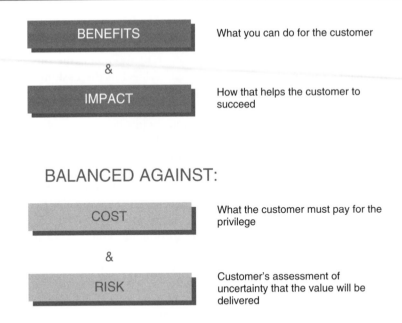

| BENEFITS | What you can do for the customer |

&

| IMPACT | How that helps the customer to succeed |

BALANCED AGAINST:

| COST | What the customer must pay for the privilege |

&

| RISK | Customer's assessment of uncertainty that the value will be delivered |

Figure 15.1 Components of a value proposition (based on discussions with Neil Rackham and on lectures he gave at Cranfield during 2008)

The value offered (in the customer's eyes) comprises the benefits that the customer could receive and the impact (the degree to which the benefit is useful to the customer). Many companies fail to understand that there is a difference between the benefit that the customer *could* get, and the impact on them. Even if the benefits offered by a product or service exceed the price, this is not a guarantee that the customer will buy. The customer may simply not need the product (in which case the impact is low or zero); or they may not be able to afford to buy; or they may consider a purchase of that product from that supplier to be too risky.

The components of a value proposition shown in Figure 15.1 highlight an important function of the value proposition, which is that it helps a supplier decide which opportunities to pursue, and which are unlikely to succeed. This makes it useful for salespeople as an opportunity selection tool. The first section of this chapter uses a CSF analysis of the value proposition to show how it can be used to select opportunities.

The second section of this chapter looks at value propositions as a competitive differentiation tool. Building on the CSF analysis from the previous section, this section considers how to establish and maintain a competitive differential using VRIN.

In addition to its role as an opportunity selection and as a differentiation tool, the value proposition can and should be used by the supplier to understand whether it will make money from the relationship. This is the value proposition as a financial evaluation tool. The value proposition can be used to help set prices, and should be used to understand costs of delivery. The third section of this chapter discusses how to convert value to the customer into value for the firm, using the notion of value exchange.

The final two sections examine value propositions as a breakthrough tool, opening the door to closer collaborative relationships. Breakthrough value propositions are developed through a superior understanding of customer needs using value chain analysis. Breakthrough value propositions can create a whole new layer of customer equity by attracting and retaining customers.

> **Four uses of value propositions**
>
> - Opportunity selection tool;
> - competitive differentiation tool;
> - financial evaluation of value propositions;
> - breakthrough value propositions.

Value propositions as an opportunity selection tool

Selling, particularly personal selling through a sales team, is expensive. Much sales force effort is squandered in the pursuit of hopeless opportunities. Salespeople are relentlessly optimistic about their chances of closing a deal, even in a 'no hope' situation. Since it costs the supplier money – sometimes, a great deal of money – to chase opportunities, the sales team must learn to chase only those opportunities where there is a reasonable prospect of success, and to pull out if it is clear that they are not going to win.

The starting point for the development of any value proposition is to understand the customer's requirements using a Critical Success Factor analysis (see Chapter 10). CSFs are the critical factors that customers take into account when making a decision which product or service to purchase. These CSFs may differ by segment (or by customer, in key account management situations). This means that value propositions can and should differ between different customers and segments, and indeed may be tailored to one specific opportunity, although they should still reflect the core values and capabilities of the supplier. There is no point in developing a value proposition that has zero credibility for customers!

> Value propositions can be different for different customers or segments.

The CSFs come into play when customers have to make choices between competing offerings. Before that point, and in order for an offering to be considered at all, it has to meet some essential criteria. These essential criteria are also known as the 'hygiene factors'. Hygiene factors might include basic quality, safety and reliability features, ballpark price, apparent ability to deliver, credible supplier name, etc. If the hygiene factors are all in place and are credible in the customer's eyes, that may lead to the company being considered as a possible supplier although it will *not* lead to the supplier automatically getting the order. However, if any of the hygiene factors are *not* there, then the business will probably be lost. Thus, for example, if the product does not meet basic safety standards, it is unlikely to be considered seriously, no matter how cheap it is. The first round of the supplier selection criteria may be designed to find out whether or not the competing offerings all meet these criteria, and to eliminate any that do not. After that, the decision to buy is based on the value-adding elements of the competing offers.

A common mistake made by companies is to over-emphasize the hygiene factors, thinking that attributes such as product quality or technical competence serve to distinguish them from the competition in the eyes of the customer. All too often, this is simply not the case.

> A common sales mistake is over-emphasizing the hygiene factors, thinking that they will differentiate the supplier from the competition.

The real quality of a product may not become evident until months, if not years, after purchase; the real quality of a service is not usually tested until something goes wrong, as in the case of an insurance or legal claim. It is often surprisingly difficult for customers to tell the difference between competing product or service offers. This is not a message that companies or their sales forces actually want to hear, but it is often the case. Relying on the hygiene factors alone to win you the business is therefore a dangerous and complacent approach to customer management.

> It is often surprisingly difficult for customers to tell the difference between competing product or service offers. This is not a message that companies or their sales forces actually want to hear.

The practical result of this selection based on CSFs rather than hygiene factors is that final decisions may sometimes be made based on what seem, to the supplier, to be rather curious factors. Thus, in both business-to-business and business-to-consumer markets, there are examples of customers selecting products based on their packaging, or service providers based on the way in which they presented their offering, rather than based on some intrinsic feature of the product or service.

This is why the firm needs a very clear idea of what is really *critical* in shaping a customer's purchasing decision (the CSFs), and what is simply assumed or taken as standard (the hygiene factors). To understand these differences, firms may need:

- a dialogue with their customers;
- market research;
- hidden needs analysis (customers don't always know what they want, or what may be useful to them).

Using value propositions to select opportunities

The starting point for developing value propositions is to identify the CSFs and the supplier's performance relative to the competition, *from the customer's point of view*.

The information in Table 15.1 was originally shown in Table 10.3 in Chapter 10; here, it will be used to show how this supplier could develop a value proposition for this customer. This example is based on a business-to-business segment. The segment could be characterized as 'high dependency' or 'worriers', because the two most important factors for this segment are the availability of technical support and the quality of installation advice and training. The supplier's technical prowess is less important to these customers.

Table 15.1 Critical Success Factors

Segment:.........X.........		Relative performance					
Critical Success Factors	Importance weighting to customer (%)	Supplier		Competitor 1		Competitor 2	
		Score	WxS	Score	WxS	Score	WxS
24/7 availability of technical support	30	6	1.8	6	1.8	6	1.8
Quality of installation advice and training	25	7	1.75	5	1.25	6	1.50
Technological differentiation of product	20	5	1.0	6	1.2	2	0.4
Product scalability	15	6	0.9	5	0.75	5	0.75
Corporate brand	10	8	0.8	7	0.7	3	0.3
	100		6.25		5.70		4.75

Table 15.1 shows that the supplier has a narrow bottom-line lead over the competition in this segment, scoring 6.25 compared to 5.70 for the nearest competitor. However, the supplier's position is rather more precarious than this might suggest, since the technical support score is the same across all suppliers and the quality of its installation advice and training is only slightly higher than the competition. A standard value proposition focusing on technology and advice has a marginal chance of success, and this would need to be weighed against the cost of bidding for this sale.

Another way to interpret the CSF analysis is that this segment is concerned about the reliable functioning of this product. This in turn implies that the product is essential to some aspect of the customer's business. If the customer's underlying worry is failure of the product, the value proposition that this supplier could develop might include guarantees, case studies emphasizing the product's ease of use and reliability, and possibly some end-of-life management. This more creative approach deals with the risk issues that these customers may have (see Figure 15.1); in this context, reducing the apparent risk through guarantees and case studies may be more valuable to the customer than any amount of brochures extolling the technical virtues of the product. This, in turn, may enable the supplier to command a higher price.

Perceived value and the buying experience

In both business-to-consumer and business-to-business markets, the core product is not the only element to create value. In fact, in many customer encounters, it is the *experience* of buying (rather than the specific attributes of what is actually bought) that has the biggest impact on the perception of value. Careful research will be needed to identify the CSFs that include the customer experience. A really successful customer experience is one that makes customers feel really good about their purchase, and about themselves for having bought it.

> In many customer encounters, it is the experience of buying (rather than what is bought) that has the biggest impact on value perception.

Note

Go back to Chapter 10 and complete a CSF analysis for one customer or segment if you have not already done so. Then compare this to your company's current value proposition for this customer/segment. Do they fit?

A successful and fast-growing business that has created a striking value proposition by analysing its customers' needs and experiences is Bravissimo (www.bravissimo.com).

Bravo for Bravissimo

Until a very few years ago, most lingerie retailers stocked bras in relatively small cup sizes: A to D. Larger cup sizes might have to be ordered specially and the bras were often ugly and functional, rather than pretty and feminine. One consequence of this was that many British women wore an incorrect bra size, too small in the cup and too large (in compensation) around the body. These bras did not provide the necessary support, which could lead to back problems, and the whole process of buying larger sizes was embarrassing and frustrating. Recognizing this, Sarah Tremellen founded Bravissimo, a mail order catalogue for larger cup bra sizes D to K. A wide range of pretty bras from many manufacturers are offered, and women can choose them at home and try them on in privacy, returning any that they do not like. To reduce the returns that this policy might lead to, Bravissimo offers advice on how to fit one's bra size and positively encourages customers to fit themselves so that they order the correct size in the first place. The customer services team provides excellent service (exclusively by women) and the bras are packed into attractive tissue-lined boxes for delivery. Thus, the product and the service surround are both excellent.

However, part of the added value that Bravissimo offers its customers relates to the more intangible elements of the customer experience. It presents a very positive image of larger bra sizes ('a celebration of your curves'). Endorsements from customers are included in the catalogue, and these endorsements are about how these women feel about themselves, rather than about the products or the Bravissimo service. Moreover, each edition of the catalogue includes a letter from the founder. This approach, and the catalogue notes on the various products, promote an ethos of belonging to a club.

Since its inception in 1995, Bravissimo has opened 18 shops and has expanded its range into swimwear, nightwear, shirts and tops, jackets, and dresses. The business now has more than half a million customers and a multi-million pound turnover.

Bravissimo is interesting in its own right as a highly successful small business with a strong value proposition and high levels of customer advocacy. It is also interesting, however, for the effect that it has had on the traditional lingerie retailers; they have learned that there is a substantial market in more elegant bras in larger cup sizes and are responding by creating new ranges and extending the range of sizes they offer.

Source: Reproduced by permission of Bravissimo Ltd

The process of developing value propositions is a vital one for businesses. Most companies start from the position of not understanding even the basics about why their customers buy, and so carrying out the CSF analysis and using it to create

> Most companies start from the position of not understanding even the basics about why their customers buy.

value propositions that are aimed at specific segments, customers, or opportunities is a good starting point. Provided the CSF analysis is correctly carried out, and the competitor evaluation is honestly done from the customer's point of view, the value proposition can help weed out the 'no hope' situations, leaving the sales force free to pursue the real opportunities.

Value propositions as a competitive differentiation tool

The CSF analysis does not just provide a way of evaluating opportunities; it also offers an indication of competitive differentiation at a point in time. It is more difficult to maintain this differentiation over a number of years. Chocobel[2] is an unusual example of a supplier that has managed to sustain its competitive differential with its main customer for almost two decades.

Chocobel is a specialist manufacturer of moulded chocolate such as hollow chocolate animals and other novelty shapes. Although Chocobel is a small company with a total turnover of less than €50 million, it has managed to build a substantial relationship with one of Europe's largest confectionary manufacturing companies. In fact, in many ways Chocobel's far larger customer is dependent on its supplier to design, produce, and package many of its principle seasonal products.

Case study: Chocobel chocolate shapes

The Chocobel story illustrates some interesting points about the strengths and weaknesses of its major customer. The big confectionery company that accounts for a high proportion of Chocobel's turnover has enormous financial strength and buying power. It uses these to source the packaging, not only for its own products but also those of Chocobel. The customer's packaging supplier delivers packaging for customer-branded products to Chocobel's factories. The customer also has powerful brands and excellent marketing and sales capabilities that Chocobel could never emulate.

---

[2] Not the real company name, which has been disguised for reasons of commercial confidentiality.

However, the customer also has considerable weaknesses. One of the main weaknesses concerns technological developments and R&D. Despite – or, perhaps, because of – its size, the customer is not particularly innovative, either in terms of its production methods or in its packaging. Spotting this weakness, Chocobel has begun to act almost as an outsourced R&D department for its customer, producing extraordinarily complex chocolate shapes through innovative chocolate moulding technology. It has also had to develop new technology to package these complex and fragile products. Chocobel has become so advanced in its capabilities that the customer and its packaging supplier have to struggle to keep up with it.

Chocobel complements its customer in another way. The customer has great operational strengths in long and efficient production runs of standard products. By contrast, Chocobel has a far more flexible manufacturing operation. This enables it to respond quickly to changes in customer tastes or to variations in demand, and this in turn has led to considerably lower stock holding levels and therefore reduced costs for the customer.

The Chocobel relationship with its main customer is tremendously important and financially valuable to both parties, and not surprisingly it has lasted for many years. Chocobel is a smart, savvy, and enterprising supplier with a good understanding of its customer. It is now offering its customers a still closer relationship that includes joint planning and information sharing about end markets and the supply chain.

Maintaining a competitive edge using VRIN

The problem with value propositions is that your competitive edge is always being eroded by competitors. Therefore, the firm needs to keep monitoring its value proposition and the reaction of customers, ensuring that it stays ahead of the competition.

In 1991, Barney proposed a useful technique for thinking about how to maintain a competitive edge. This technique is called VRIN (Table 15.2). VRIN is a checklist of questions that relate to what makes the firm's offering unique. It stands for: Valuable; Rare; Imperfectly Imitable; and Non-substitutable.

If a value proposition is Valuable, it provides value to the customer or a cost advantage to the supplier, or both. The shared benefits of collaboration between suppliers and their customers are discussed later in this chapter.

Rarity is also important if the firm wants to sustain its competitive edge. Rarity means that it is not easy for competitors (or, indeed, customers) to acquire this value proposition elsewhere. If Rarity depends on product or service features, the

Table 15.2 VRIN and the value proposition

	Stands for	Defined as	Chocobel example
V	Valuable	Creates customer value or gives the firm a cost advantage	Flexible manufacturing that reduces stockholding costs for the customer
R	Rare	Customers cannot buy it in sufficient quantity on the open market	Innovative approach to manufacturing and packaging
I	Imperfectly imitable	Competitors cannot easily imitate this	Innovative approach to manufacturing and packaging
N	Non-substitutable	There is no other easy way to do this; unlikely that other offerings will come into the market that compete strongly	Move towards closer relationships that involve joint planning and information sharing

firm will need to apply patents or trade marks and defend them vigorously. Rarity might come from the customer experience and corporate ethos, as in the Bravissimo example earlier in this chapter. Or, it might come from the innovative culture and flexible response of suppliers like Chocobel.

Rarity is linked to Imperfectly imitable, which means that competitors cannot easily copy the offering. The Bravissimo example illustrates this point: department stores and lingerie retailers may now offer a better range of larger bra sizes, but they cannot readily imitate the friendly, reassuring, and positive customer experience that Bravissimo offers.

Non-substitutability means that there are no real alternatives in the foreseeable future. At first reading, it sounds unlikely that a firm could really develop a value proposition so extraordinary that it would distance it from the competition. However, non-substitutability means that there are no offerings that the *customer would consider to be a substitute*. There are a number of examples of companies that have attained this status and whose customers will pay a premium and are fiercely loyal to their suppliers. Some examples include Coca-Cola, Nike, First Direct, John Lewis, and Amazon in business-to-consumer markets. In business-to-business, Rolls-Royce collaborated with Boeing on the development of the 787 Dreamliner, producing a number of innovations that Boeing would be hard-pressed to substitute. These include an innovative and fuel-saving air conditioning system, and improved engine status information that can be transmitted directly from Rolls-Royce to the airline pilot during flight should there be any issue with the performance of the engine.

The final column of Table 15.2 applies the VRIN idea to Chocobel, illustrating how unusual the Chocobel value proposition is and how it is unlikely that a competing supplier could 'poach' Chocobel's customer. The VRIN test is a simple but powerful tool that firms should apply regularly to test the power of their value propositions. A

> The VRIN test is a simple but powerful tool that firms should apply regularly to test the power of their value propositions; the more VRIN, the greater the competitive edge.

value proposition does not need to perform on all of the VRIN factors, but the more VRIN there is in the value proposition, the greater the competitive edge.

> **Note**
>
> Apply the VRIN analysis to your own company, using the worksheet at the end of the chapter. Is it difficult to identify what is unique about you? Why? Plus, if you can't say what's different about you, why would you expect your customers to see it?

Financial evaluation of value propositions

Keeping ahead of the competition is all very well but may be very expensive. If customers are to be managed profitably, it is essential that the company understands the costs of its value proposition and is able to trade the costs off against the likely price that it can command from customers. To understand the cost of delivering a value proposition look back at the cost calculation information in Chapter 3.

When considering what customers might be prepared to pay for a particular value proposition, sophisticated companies try to calculate what that value proposition is worth to the customer. The value proposition may offer tangible financial benefits to customers, either by increasing the customer's revenues (this is particularly relevant in business-to-business markets) or in reducing the customer's costs, or both. There may also be intangible benefits to the customer, perhaps related to risk reduction or to positive psychological effects such as association with a powerful brand. Figure 15.2 sets out a pro-forma for analysing the tangible and intangible value to customers of a value proposition.

Figure 15.2 sets out a detailed set of offerings that this company, which supplies automotive components to vehicle manufacturers, could offer to its major Original Equipment Manufacturer (OEM) customers. The value elements are listed according to whether they relate to the pre-transaction stage, or after the transaction. There are also two further columns, relating to advice and consultancy or strategic services.

	Pre-transaction	During and post-transaction	Advice, training, or consultancy	Strategic services
Increases customer's revenues	Help with downstream marketing		User training	
Decreases customer's costs	Help with specification Prototyping	Carry out installation for customer, test, and check	On-site engineer seconded to customer	Vendor-managed inventory
Intangible benefits to customer	Help selling the concept higher up the organization – 'engaging the boss'	24/7 service hotline		

Figure 15.2　Putting a value on a VP

The possible value offerings are shown according to whether they would increase the customer's revenues, reduce its costs, or provide psychological benefits (to the buyer).

The next stage, once this initial map of possible offerings has been identified, is to place a financial value on the potential increase in revenues and/or reduction in costs, for that customer. This has to be done customer by customer, by the account manager, because the value may differ for each customer. A specific example from Figure 15.2 is the value of strategic services (vendor-managed inventory, or VMI). This service has tangible financial benefits to the customer if it can save on inventory losses and damage, on warehousing and picking costs, etc. A general rule for the total cost of inventory holding is that it is 25% of the value of that inventory per year. Thus, for a customer previously holding stock worth $1 million, this service is worth up to $250 000 per year. For a customer holding $50 000 of stock, it is worth only $12 500 per year.

The third stage is to compare the financial value of each service offering to the customer, with the cost to the supplier company of providing that service. The results of this calculation are shown in Table 15.3.

In this case, the direct financial value to the two customers is the reduction in their stockholding costs of $250 000 and $12 500 respectively. However, as Table 15.3 shows, there may be other benefits to a customer in having a supplier manage its inventory for it, including savings in management time and a reduction in risk, and this is listed as the managerial or psychological value. Putting a financial value on this is difficult, although it can be thought of as the difference between the direct financial value of the service and the incremental amount that the customer would be prepared to pay for it. Sometimes, of course, this difference is a negative

Table 15.3 Cost/benefit analysis of a value proposition

Service offering: VMI	Customer A ($)	Customer B ($)
Direct financial value to customer	250 000	12 500
Managerial/psychological value to customer*	50 000	12 500
Total value to customer	300 000	25 000
Cost of providing this service	150 000	30 000
Net financial impact for supplier	150 000	(5000)

* See explanation in text

number, signalling either that the customer disagrees with the supplier about the financial value it would obtain, or that there is actually a psychological *cost* to the customer, perhaps because of a perception that risk might *increase* through outsourcing inventory management.

Once the total value to the customer has been estimated, the supplier should always consider the incremental costs of providing the service and compare these to the value the customer gets. In the case of Customer A, the costs of providing the service are considerably lower than the value to the customer, and so the supplier can price this offering anywhere between $150 000 and $300 000, have a good chance of winning the business, and still make money. For Customer B, however, the supplier would have to price the service at more than $30 000 to make any money out of it and it is unlikely to get the business at that price; therefore, it should not offer the service to Customer B unless there are other good financial or relationship reasons for doing so.

The discipline of having to think about the financial consequences for both the customer and the supplier is an essential process in developing value propositions for profitable customer management. Some value propositions, however, go beyond creating additional revenues or reducing costs in the customer's current business. These 'breakthrough' value propositions are the subject of the next section.

Breakthrough value propositions

Breakthrough value propositions are not only about addressing the customer's current hopes and fears, but also about identifying new areas of value for the customer. To do this, the sophisticated supplier must be able to uncover hidden needs by inserting itself into the customer's value chain (Figure 15.3).

The primary value chain runs along the lower half of the figure: companies buy in raw materials and hire people; they use these materials and people to produce and deliver goods and services; they market and sell these; and they provide follow-up service.

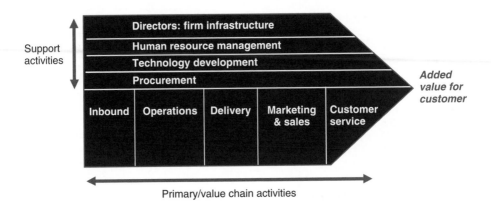

Figure 15.3 Value chain as developed by Michael Porter

At the top of Figure 15.3, there are the support activities that every company needs. These include the leadership of the business; human resources; research and development; and procurement.

Analysing customer strengths and weaknesses using the value chain

Porter's value chain can be used to develop powerful value propositions for the customer by analysing places where the supplier can add value. Both parts of the value chain can be analysed for the customer's business, and this may give ideas about where the supplier can offer additional services that would be of great value to the customer.

The first step in this process is to use the value chain to identify the customer's strengths (Table 15.4) and weaknesses (Table 15.5) at each point along the chain.[3] Tables 15.6 and 15.7 later in the chapter illustrate how these principles can be applied to analysing an actual company.

The first column of Table 15.4 shows each element of the value chain, including both primary and support activities. The second column asks for an analysis of the customer's strengths against each element. This will require in-depth knowledge and analysis of the customer. Not all this information will be readily to hand and some of it may even be unknown to the customer, and so completing the second column does require some judgement on the part of the supplier.

---

[3] I am indebted to my colleagues Professor Malcolm McDonald, Dr Sue Holt, and Alan Smart, for suggesting many of the ideas in this section.

Table 15.4 Analysing customer strengths using the value chain

Value chain element	Customer's strengths	Competitive situation	Implications for customer
Primary elements			
Inbound			
Operations			
Delivery			
Marketing and sales			
Customer service			
Support activities			
Direction/infrastructure			
Human Resources (HR)			
Technology development and Research and Development (R&D)			
Procurement			

The third column prompts for an evaluation of the competitive situation. This is a reminder that a customer only has relative strengths, not absolute strengths. A strength is only a strength if the supplier is better at it than the competition. The 'competitive situation' column is an invitation to take a good, hard look at the customer's apparent strengths and decide whether they are actually strengths relative to the competition. This could be indicated by plus/minus signs, or a rating on a scale of 1 to 5 (where 1 indicates much weaker than the competition and 5 indicates much stronger than the competition), or simply by indicating High/Medium/Low.

> A strength is only a strength if the supplier is better at it than the competition.

In the final column, implications for the customer should be noted. These can be positive or negative implications. Therefore, a huge strength for a customer such as having a large installed base within its market might have the implication for the customer that it is locked in to this technology and slow to innovate. This could, in turn, present an opportunity for a supplier.

The process for completing Table 15.5 is analogous to Table 15.4, except that the second table asks for an analysis of the customer's value chain weaknesses. This is even more important than the strengths analysis, because analysing areas in which the customer has weaknesses is even more likely to turn up opportunities for the supplier to develop breakthrough value propositions (see the next sections). Again, a weakness is only a weakness if the customer is weaker than the competition.

Having completed the analysis of a customer's strengths and weaknesses using the value chain, the next step is to consider how this analysis could be used to develop breakthrough value propositions.

Table 15.5 Analysing customer weaknesses using the value chain

Value chain element	Customer's weaknesses	Competitive situation	Implications for customer
Primary elements			
Inbound			
Operations			
Delivery			
Marketing and sales			
Customer service			
Support activities			
Direction/infrastructure			
Human Resources (HR)			
Technology development and R&D			
Procurement			

Using the value chain to develop breakthrough ideas

Tables 15.6 and 15.7 summarize the analysis of the customer's relative strengths and weaknesses for each element of the value chain and suggests how the supplier might address them. The first column of each table lists the value chain element: primary activities (Table 15.6) and support activities (Table 15.7). The second column summarizes the customer's real strengths and weaknesses, relative to the competition, and indicates some of the implications for the customer. This second column summarizes Tables 15.4 and 15.5 into a single column.

The real 'meat' of Tables 15.6 and 15.7 comes in the final columns, which set out the supplier's ability to help. It is worth filling this out in a creative thinking or brainstorming session, setting down all kinds of ideas at this point. In the end, not all of these will result in the development of breakthrough value propositions, but some of the more offbeat observations or ideas could just throw up a world-beating idea.

Tables 15.6 and 15.7 illustrate how a supplier could use the value chain analysis on a customer to identify places where the supplier could provide added value in creative and unusual ways. Some of the areas in which the supplier could help the customer might have nothing to do with the supplier's day-to-day business. So, in Table 15.6, there are suggestions relating to shared distribution sites and providing website support. In Table 15.7, there are ideas about joint planning and joint procurement. None of these relate to the products or services that the supplier actually supplies to the customer, but all of them are ideas that could be worked up into hugely attractive value propositions for the customer.

Table 15.6 Primary value chain activities

Primary value chain activity	Customer's capability	Supplier's ability to help
Inbound	Good inbound logistics and paperwork but high raw materials stocks	Inventory management; automated paperwork
Operations	New machinery but some processing problems	Offer benchmarking against our processes
Delivery	Accurate order processing but customer's delivery company sometimes lets them down	Link our inbound delivery to their outbound, for greater transport efficiency? Offer to share a distribution centre?
Marketing and sales	Effective sales force and literature, though website is not easy to use and sometimes sales are lost	Offer to support their website?
Customer service	High service quality and coverage; good call centre	None – but we could learn from them

Table 15.7 Support activities

Support activities	Customer's capability	Supplier's ability to help
Direction/infrastructure	Good strategic planning	Offer to plan jointly; share market information and plans via dedicated extranet
HR	Good recruitment and people retention	Offer internships/placements
Technology development and R&D	Fair to good	We have better e-commerce capability that we could share
Procurement	Planning move to e-auctions to reduce procurement costs	By procuring jointly, we could help them reduce their procurement costs and perhaps reduce the impact on us of the planned e-auctions

---

> **Note**
>
> Carry out the analysis in Tables 15.6 and 15.7 for a major customer. Look for creative ideas about how you could help them. You may even like to get the customer involved in the analysis. Remember, customers like talking about their business. Plus, you are asking them for information, not making a conventional sales call! Don't forget to consider the financial costs and value of any breakthrough value proposition before offering it to the customer.

Developing breakthrough ideas into value propositions

The precise value proposition that comes out of the breakthrough ideas will depend on the supplier's ability and willingness to 'think out of the box' and on the customer's (or segment's) susceptibility to the ideas and concepts presented to it, plus its ability and willingness to pay more for this kind of value offer. New value propositions can have – or can *appear* to have – considerably higher risks to customers, so it is worth considering how these risks can be mitigated and the role that price will play in signalling facts about the supplier to the customer (see Chapter 14 for a fuller discussion of both these issues).

Delivering the kinds of breakthrough value propositions that are under consideration here requires the supplier not only to think creatively about what it could offer, but also to engage its whole business in delivering the offer. This means that the supplier's business must be internally integrated. Thus, the marketing and sales departments may create and/or market the proposition, but the operations and logistics functions of the supplier will probably be the ones to deliver it.

> Delivering breakthrough value propositions requires the supplier to engage its whole business.

A compelling case study of a supplier developing a breakthrough value proposition for its customers is provided by Muylle *et al.* (2007) in their study of the relationship between Daikin Europe and Europal (see 'Where to find out more ' at the end of this chapter).

Daikin Europe is a global leader in industrial air conditioning systems (www.diakineurope.com) and Europal is a medium-sized family company supplying packaging, crating, and logistics services to Daikin (www.europal-group.com). This example illustrates how the supplier needs to manage its own internal processes, as well as those of its customers, if it is to deliver on a breakthrough promise.

Case study: Daikin Europe and Europal

Air conditioning manufacturer Daikin Europe had signalled to its Supplier Conference in 2000 that it was looking for novel solutions to supply and packaging logistics. The Europal CEO responded by visiting the customer's premises so that he could develop a really deep understanding of its operations. This analysis revealed that Daikin's own customers wanted flexible delivery of different products, short lead times, and low inventories. Then Europal worked out what Daikin's real packaging costs were, based on Total Cost of Ownership (TCO)[4]. The TCO approach enabled Europal to understand not only Daikin's materials costs for packaging, but also costs of waste, interim storage, shuttle costs, etc.

Armed with this thorough analysis and understanding, Europal proposed a novel concept to Daikin, which it called its 'warehouse on wheels'. The concept was a supply chain centre physically located close to Daikin, plus a 'warehouse on wheels' located immediately outside Daikin's factory doors and containing all the packaging materials that Daikin would need for the next two hours.

To implement Europal's suggestion, some changes in process between the two companies were needed. Europal gained access to Daikin's production plans, so that it could calculate how much packaging materials Daikin would need over the coming days and weeks. On the production line, Daikin employees began scanning barcodes each time a product was finished so that this information could be transmitted to Europal. There were also regular planning and control meetings.

The results of the project were sensational. Delivery reliability went up from 93% to (consistently) 99.8% in four years. In 2005, Daikin reported that its collaboration with Europal had enabled it to free up 3000m^2 of warehouse space and €500 000 of assets, as well as offering it full transparency of its packaging costs.

Daikin is not the only firm to benefit from this extraordinary partnership. Thanks to its track record with Daikin, Europal has acquired a series of major corporations as customers. Europal has also instituted a highly efficient information sharing and delivery system with its own major supplier, Prowell, and now has an international network of supply chain partners.

The Europal case illustrates how a comparatively small supplier can create an overwhelming competitive advantage for itself, and can develop a long-term relationship with a much bigger and more powerful customer. Europal is planning to improve the efficiency of its service to Daikin still further, including beginning to manage some

---

[4] To find out more about Total Cost of Ownership, see Chapter 14.

of Daikin's other suppliers for them, and will implement advanced e-procurement processes between the two companies.

In addition, there is a definite 'halo effect' with other customers, building Europal's market share. It has also applied these skills to the management of its own supplier relationships.

This is an illustration of the fact that companies with breakthrough value propositions should not stand still – continuous innovation and improvement is necessary to maintain a competitive edge.

> Continuous innovation and improvement is necessary to maintain a competitive edge.

Benefiting from collaboration

Where suppliers have created breakthrough value propositions, they have often benefited from close and long-term relationships with their customers and high levels of recommendation. Examples of this phenomenon in business-to-consumer markets include First Direct and Dyson. Both these companies created breakthrough value propositions – First Direct in banking services and Dyson in vacuum cleaners – and research has shown them to enjoy high levels of customer advocacy. Amazon, Ebay, and Apple have all developed powerful value propositions and associated market success.

In business-to-business markets, much research has been carried out in recent years exploring the financial value of collaborative relationships with supply chain partners (buyer-supplier collaboration/key account management). This research

> Business-to-business research consistently shows that both companies benefit from collaboration.

consistently shows that both sides benefit from collaboration. In other words, even where a very small supplier is engaged in a relationship with a very large customer, both sides benefit. In theory, the big, powerful customer might try to appropriate all the benefits of collaboration to itself. In practice, this does not seem to happen, perhaps because small suppliers with powerful value propositions have more power than might at first appear. Thus, in the case of Chocobel reported earlier in this chapter, it has an extremely valuable capability – innovation – that its customer could not readily replace if its relationship with Chocobel ended.

As one might expect, research shows that there are substantial benefits for customers in collaborating with suppliers. These benefits include:

- improved supplier performance;
- continuity of supply;
- cooperation/flexibility;
- tailored products/service/delivery;

- faster response from supplier;
- improved levels of customer satisfaction with supplier's service;
- lower costs.

The lower costs are often associated with lower inventory levels, reduced storage space, and asset reallocation where physical stock is concerned. There may be lower total costs of ownership overall. In service-based businesses, customers may experience lower costs because there is reduced need for checking or rework, and lower admin costs or other process efficiencies.

On the supplier side, suppliers benefit from collaboration through:

- higher revenues;
- higher growth rates;
- lower costs;
- higher profitability;
- reduced risk.

Higher revenues and growth rates are linked with an increase in the share of customer spend that is typically experienced by suppliers who successfully collaborate with their customers. Process efficiencies and, sometimes, lower finished good stock, lead to lower costs. Lower costs yet higher revenues in turn result in higher profitability. Reduced risk is interesting, because the increase in share of customer spend means that more of the supplier's business is coming from fewer customers (and greater dependency on a smaller customer base is normally considered to be higher risk). However, the possibility for longer relationship duration in collaborative relationships, coupled with more efficient processes and the degree of integration and transparency in the relationship, mean that the break-up of the relationship would be traumatic for both sides and the risk of losing the customer can be greatly reduced (see Chapter 11 for an examination of managing risk in customer relationships).

Summary

The purpose of the value proposition is to make it absolutely clear to the supplier why a customer would buy from it, and to help the supplier figure out how much to charge. This is true whether the purchase takes place in a business-to-consumer or business-to-business situation. Value propositions should identify what is special or unique about the firm, and should link this to the needs, preferences, and expectations of the customer.

> Value propositions should identify what is special or unique about the firm and link this to the needs, preferences, and expectations of the customer.

In developing a value proposition, a good place to start is with CSFs, the really critical factors that lead a customer to select one supplier over another. The CSFs might relate to product or service uniqueness, or they might be about ethos, culture, the customer experience, or some unique and valuable capability of the supplying firm. Careful research may be needed to establish what the CSFs are, remembering that customers themselves may not consciously be aware of why they prefer one supplier to another.

Value propositions can be tailored to appeal to different customer segments or groups of customers. Of course, this needs to be done with care and needs to be credible, and so it is unlikely that radically different value propositions would be developed and put out into the marketplace. Therefore, a company would not project itself as 'ethical and fair trade' to one segment but as 'cheap and cheerful' to another segment. It is unlikely that these would be credible as co-existing value claims.

This chapter has also shown that the most powerful form of value propositions is breakthrough value propositions. These are value propositions that challenge the prevailing orthodoxy, the way that things are normally done, and bring extraordinary

> The most powerful form of value propositions is breakthrough value propositions that challenge the prevailing orthodoxy.

levels of value to customers. The starting point for breakthrough value propositions is an in-depth analysis of the customer's value chain and strengths and weaknesses. This analysis is then used to develop solutions that are hard for others to replicate.

Finally, the chapter concludes with a brief description of how collaborative relationships can benefit both sides in business. This brings us back to one of the main themes of this book, which is that there has been a fundamental shift from transactional to relationship-based views of customer management. Collaborative relationships are often long-duration relationships and ones in which there is close involvement between the two parties. This close involvement leads to high learning, mutual disclosure, and transparency, and thereby to mutual commitment. The financial results have been recorded in a number of studies: collaborative relationships pay off, for both parties. However, suppliers need to manage their relationships with customers in a positive and constructive way to ensure that they maximize the value they obtain from the relationship. Customers are smart, and they are not saints – they will always be looking for a better deal and will very often try to negotiate a better price. The techniques shown in this book will help managers to negotiate the best possible outcomes for their companies, based on a clear understanding of the financial and relational value of customers and on the position of the customer in the portfolio.

Note

Now use the worksheets on the following pages to analyse the value chain and to identify your VRIN factors.

Worksheet: value chain analysis

Value chain element	Customer's strengths/ weaknesses	Implications for customer	What we could do to help
Primary:			
Inbound			
Operations			
Delivery			
Marketing and sales			
Customer service			
Support activities:			
Direction/infrastructure			
Human Resources (HR)			
Technology development and Research and Development (R&D)			
Procurement			

Worksheet: VRIN

Stands for:		Defined as:	Our VRIN:
V	Valuable	Creates customer value or gives the firm a cost advantage	
R	Rare	Not easy to buy it on the open market	
I	Imperfectly imitable	Competitors cannot easily imitate this	
N	Non-substitutable	No easy other way to do this; strongly competitive offerings unlikely	

Where to find out more

Muylle, S., Roodhooft, F. and de Vlieger, A-K (2007) 'Value creation through total cost of ownership in the extended supply chain'. Case study, Vlerick Leuven Gent Management School, Ghent, Belgium. European Case Clearing House no. 607-001-1. *Interesting case study describing the Europal/Daikin relationship.*

Anderson, J.C., Narus, J.A. and van Rossum, W. (2006) 'Customer value propositions in Business Markets'. *Harvard Business Review*, **84**(3), pp. 90–99. *Readable article about value propositions and selling in business-to-business situations.*

Barney, J. (1991) 'Firm resources and sustained competitive advantage', *Journal of Management*, **17**(1), pp. 99–120. *Describes the VRIN approach.*

Some of the material in this chapter, including Figure 15.1, is based on discussions with Neil Rackham and on lectures he gave at Cranfield during 2008. These are not publicly available, but some of the foundation ideas are explored in his books, in particular: Rackham, N. and de Vincentis, J. (1999) *Rethinking the Sales Force*, McGraw-Hill, USA.

Bibliography

Chapter 1

Christopher, M., Payne, A. and Ballantyne, D. (2002) *Relationship Marketing*, second edition, Butterworth-Heinemann, Oxford.

Ryals, L.J. (2005) 'Making CRM work: The measurement and profitable management of customer relationships', *Journal of Marketing*, **69**(4), pp. 252-261.

Chapter 2

Cooper, R. and Kaplan, R. (1991) 'Profit priorities from activity-based costing', *Harvard Business Review*, May–June, **69**(3), pp. 130-135.

Dunn, S. (2007) 'Romance is dead with First Direct', *Independent on Sunday*, 11th February 2007, p. 23.

Kaplan, R. and Cooper, R. (1997) *Cost and Effect: Using Integrated Cost Systems to Drive Profitability and Performance*, Harvard Business School Press, Boston, MA.

Chapter 3

Wilson, C. (1996) *Profitable Customers: How to Identify, Develop and Retain Them*, Kogan Page, London.

Chapter 4

Van Raaij, E.M., Vernooij, M.J.A. and van Triest, S. (2003) 'The implementation of customer profitability analysis: A case study', *Industrial Marketing Management*, **32**(7), pp. 573-583.

Chapter 5

Ryals, L.J. (2005) 'Making customer relationship management work: The measurement and profitable management of customer relationships', *Journal of Marketing*, **69**(4), pp. 252-261.

Chapter 6

Berger, P.D. and Nasr, N.I. (1998) 'Customer lifetime value: Marketing models and applications', *Journal of Interactive Marketing*, **12**(1), pp. 17-30.

Calciu, M. and Salerno, F. (2002), 'Customer value modelling: Synthesis and extension proposals', *Journal of Targeting, Measurement and Analysis for Marketing*, **11**(2), pp. 124-147.

Chapter 7

Blattberg, R.C., Getz, G. and Thomas, J.S. (2001) *Customer Equity: Building and Managing Relationships as Valuable Assets*, Harvard Business School Press, Cambridge, MA.

Gupta, S. and Lehmann, D.R. (2006) 'Customer lifetime value and firm valuation', *Journal of Relationship Marketing*, **5** (2/3), pp. 87–110.

Chapter 8

Stahl, H.K., Matzler, K. and Hinterhuber, H.H. (2003) 'Linking customer lifetime value with shareholder value', *Industrial Marketing Management*, **32**(4), pp. 267–279.

Womack, J.P., Jones, D.T. and Roos, D. (1990) *The Machine that Changed the World*, Rawson Associates, New York.

Chapter 9

Berger, P.D. and Bechwati, N.N. (2001) 'The allocation of promotion budget to maximise customer equity', *Omega*, **29**(1), pp. 49–61.

Bowman, D. and Narayandas, D. (2004) 'Linking customer management effort to customer profitability in business markets', *Journal of Marketing Research*, **41**(4), pp. 433–447.

Rust, R.T., Lemon, K.N. and Zeithaml, V.A. (2001) 'Where should the next marketing dollar go?', *Marketing Management*, **10**(3), pp. 24–28.

Chapter 10

Reichheld, F.F. (2003) 'The one number you need to grow', *Harvard Business Review*, **81**(12), pp. 46–54.

Rogers, B. (2007) *Rethinking Sales Management*, John Wiley & Sons, Ltd, Chichester.

Ryals, L.J. and McDonald, M. (2008) *Key Account Plans: The Practitioners' Guide to Profitable Planning*, Butterworth-Heinemann, Oxford.

Chapter 11

Ryals, L.J., Dias, S. and Berger, M. (2007) 'Optimising marketing spend: Return maximisation and risk minimisation in the marketing portfolio', *Journal of Marketing Management*, **23** (9), pp. 991–1012.

Ryals, L.J. and Knox, S. (2007) 'Measuring and managing customer relationship risk in business markets', *Industrial Marketing Management*, **36**(6), pp. 823–833.

Chapter 12

McDonald, M. and Dunbar, I. (2004) *Market Segmentation: How to Do It, How to Profit from It*, Butterworth-Heinemann, Oxford.

Chapter 13

McDonald, M. (2007) *Marketing Plans*, Butterworth-Heinemann, Oxford.

Ryals, L.J. and McDonald, M. (2008) *Key Account Plans: Powerful Plans for Profitable Customer Management*, Butterworth-Heinemann, Oxford.

Chapter 14

Moore, G.A. (1999) *Crossing the Chasm: Marketing and Selling Technology Products to Mainstream Customers*, second edition, Capstone, Oxford.

Urbany, J.E. (2001) 'Are your prices too low?', *Harvard Business Review*, **79**(9), pp. 26–27.

Chapter 15

Anderson, J.C., Narus, J.A. and van Rossum, W. (2006) 'Customer value propositions in business markets', *Harvard Business Review*, **84**(3), pp. 90–99.

Barney, J. (1991) 'Firm resources and sustained competitive advantage', *Journal of Management*, **17**(1), pp. 99–120.

Muller, S., Roodhooft, F. and de Vlieger, A-K (2007) 'Value creation through total cost of ownership in the extended supply chain'. Case study, Vlerick Leuven Gent Management School, Ghent, Belgium. European Case Clearing House no. 607-001-1.

Rackham, N. and de Vincentis, J. (1999) *Rethinking the Sales Force*, McGraw-Hill, USA.

Index